unDers

movies

unɒer

LOUIS D. GIANNETTI
Case Western Reserve University

standing movies

PRENTICE-HALL INC., ENGLEWOOD CLIFFS, NEW JERSEY

UNDERSTANDING MOVIES by Louis D. Giannetti

C–13–936146–4
P–13–936138–3

Library of Congress Catalog Card Number: 73–159277

Printed in the United States of America

Current Printing (last number):

10 9 8

PRENTICE-HALL INTERNATIONAL, INC., London
PRENTICE-HALL OF AUSTRALIA, PTY. LTD., Sydney
PRENTICE-HALL OF CANADA, LTD., Toronto
PRENTICE-HALL OF INDIA PRIVATE LIMITED, New Delhi
PRENTICE-HALL OF JAPAN, INC., Tokyo

In Memoriam
LYNN R. JONES

O, how thy worth with manners may I sing,
When thou art all the better part of me?
What can mine own praise to mine own self bring?
And what is't but mine own when I praise thee?
Even for this let us divided live,
And our dear love lose name of single one,
That by this separation I may give
That due to thee, which thou deserv'st alone.
O Absence! what a torment wouldst thou prove,
Were it not thy sour leisure gave sweet leave
To entertain the time with thoughts of love,
Which time and thoughts so sweetly doth deceive,
And that thou teachest how to make one twain,
By praising him here who doth hence remain.
                                    WILLIAM SHAKESPEARE

CONTENTS

editing, 79

3

sound, 103

4

ILLUSTRATIONS FROM FILMS

PREFACE

The motion-picture medium has an extraordinary range of expression. It has in common with the plastic arts the fact that it is a visual composition projected on a two-dimensional surface; with dance, that it can deal in the arrangement of movement; with theatre, that it can create a dramatic intensity of events; with music, that it can compose in the rhythms and phrases of time and can be attended by song and instrument; with poetry, that it can juxtapose images; with literature generally, that it can encompass in its sound track the abstractions available only to language.

MAYA DEREN

As Miss Deren's observation suggests, analyzing a good movie is no easy task. Because films can express many ideas and emotions simultaneously, the viewer is sometimes overwhelmed by the sheer density of meanings he is bombarded with. The following chapters may be of use in helping the moviegoer understand some of these complex elements. Each chapter isolates the basic techniques film directors have used in conveying meanings. Naturally, the chapters do not pretend to be exhaustive: they are essentially starting points.

The organization develops from the most specific and narrow aspects of a film ("Picture") to the most abstract and comprehensive ("Theory"). But the seven chapters are not tightly interdependent. A reader coming from a background of the theatre might prefer to begin with Chapter 5, "Drama." Similarly, the more literary-oriented reader might prefer to begin with the subsection on language in Chapter 4, "Sound," and then move on to Chapter 6, "Literature." Inevitably, such looseness of organization involves a certain amount of overlapping, but I have tried to keep this to a minimum. Technical terms are defined when they first appear in the text, but for those who read the chapters out of sequence, the glossary at the end of the book should provide adequate temporary clarifications. Glossed terms appear in **boldface** the first time they are mentioned in each chapter.

I have tried to avoid the dogmatizing, the sentimental reminiscing, and particularly the profusion of examples which flaw so much of the writing on film. In most instances, I offer only one example, if I feel that it might truly clarify a general principle. This deliberate austerity involves a certain amount of simplification, but I believe that the advantages gained outweigh the shortcomings. For those readers who wish to pursue the implications of a chapter further, a short **xiii** bibliography of useful articles and books is provided at the end of each chapter.

A number of people have helped me in the writing of this book: Jim Monaco, who served considerably beyond the call of duty; my students at Emory University, who kept me honest; and my friend and colleague, Floyd C. Watkins, of Emory University, who kept me clear and coherent. I am also grateful to Gerald Barrett, of the University of Delaware, William Bell, of the College of DuPage, Jack Ellis, of Northwestern University, Jameson Goldner, of San Francisco State University, and Arthur Knight, of UCLA, for their comments and suggestions.

Color stills, from Michelangelo Antonioni's *Red Desert*, are courtesy of Ottorino Moresco of Rizzoli Film, s. p. a., of Rome. I wish to thank Walter Dauler, Branch Manager of Audio-Brandon Films, for his helpful assistance and generosity in supplying the film, Jim Monaco, who selected the frames, and Harvey Zucker, who made the prints.

The introductory epigraphs and brief quotations in the text are taken from the following sources: Maya Deren, "Cinematography: The Creative Use of Reality," in *The Visual Arts Today*, edited by Gyorgy Kepes (Middletown Conn.: Wesleyan University Press, 1960); Marcel Carné, from *The French Cinema*, by Roy Armes (New York: A. S. Barnes & Co., 1966); Richard Dyer MacCann, "Introduction," *Film: A Montage of Theories* (New York: E. P. Dutton, & Co., Inc., 1966), Copyright © 1966 by Richard Dyer MacCann, reprinted with permission; V. I. Pudovkin, *Film Technique* (London: Vision, 1954); "The Pusher," by Steppenwolf, Columbia Pictures and Dunhill (ABC Records); André Bazin, *What Is Cinema?* (Berkeley: University of California Press, 1967); Michelangelo Antonioni, "Two Statements," in *Film Makers on Film Making*, edited by Harry M. Geduld (Bloomington: Indiana University Press, 1969); Alexandre Astruc, from *The New Wave*, edited by Peter Graham (London: Secker & Warburg, 1968, and New York: Doubleday & Co.); Akira Kurosawa, from *The Movies as Medium*, edited by Lewis Jacobs (New York: Farrar, Straus and Giroux, 1970); Jean Cocteau, from *Jean Cocteau*, by René Gilson (New York: Crown Publishers, Inc., 1969); Pauline Kael, *I Lost it at the Movies* (New York: Bantam Books, 1966); John Grierson, *Grierson on Documentary*, edited by Forsyth Hardy (New York: Harcourt, Brace and Co., 1947). The audio-visual score (Figure 61) is reprinted from *The Film Sense* by Sergei Eisenstein, translated and edited by Jay Leyda, © 1942 by Harcourt Brace Jovanovich, Inc. and reproduced with their permission.

LOUIS GIANNETTI

Cleveland, Ohio

understanding movies

PICTURE

One must compose images as the old masters
did their canvases, with the same preoccupation
with effect and expression.

MARCEL CARNÉ

The basic characteristics of "motion pictures"—as the phrase implies —are images and movement. Film is both a temporal and spatial art form. As such, it shares some of the qualities of music and literature (experienced in time), the pictorial arts (experienced in space), and the theatre, which is both temporal and spatial, though in a different sense than film. Movies, then, are mixed media, though unlike drama, films are fundamentally visual. There are some great films that are not particularly dramatic, but there are none that are not visually excellent. The film director is ultimately judged on the quality of his images: like a painter or photographer, he must express ideas and emotions through the arrangement of lights, colors, shapes, and textures on a two-dimensional surface.

MEDIA: FORM AND CONTENT

Meaning in film is expressed in the picture itself. The image is no mere *illustration* of an idea, for this implies a separation of form and content. In the hands of a sophisticated critic, the terms "form" and "content" can be useful concepts. Used naively, these terms can prevent a moviegoer from evaluating a film intelligently. The writer Archibald McLeish once said that "a poem should not *mean*, but *be*." Similarly, the media theorist Marshall McLuhan has stated that "the medium is the message." Both men were warning against the tendency to separate form from content, as though they are not actually the same thing. As McLuhan has pointed out, the "content" of one medium is always another medium. Thus, a painting (image) depicting **3**

a man eating fruit (taste) involves at least two different media: each
medium communicates information—"content"—in a different way.
A description of the painting employs yet another medium (words),
which communicates information in yet another manner. In each
case, the information is determined by the medium.

In literature, the naive separation of form and content is sometimes called "the heresy of paraphrase." For example, the "content"
of *Hamlet* can be found in a college outline, yet no one would seriously suggest that the play and the outline are the same "except in
form." The differences in other media are even more obvious. What
is the "content" of a taste? Or a sound? A mathematical formula?
All of these communicate information, each in a different way. To
paraphrase any of this information—in words, for example—is inevitably to change the content as well as the form. An argument could
be made that the "form" of *Oedipus Rex* and many hack mystery
plays are the same; similarly, the "content" of a Raphael madonna
and a cheap holy card can also be said to be the same. In literature
and painting—which have older critical traditions than cinema—only
the most insensitive critics would make such observations without
going on to subtler (and more basic) issues. Unfortunately, most
film criticism is almost exclusively devoted to discussions of "content." Very few critics come to grips with the basic elements of film
—images and movement. A parallel situation in literature would be
an extended critique of *Hamlet* based only on a reading of a college
outline of the play, or a discussion of Mozart's *Magic Flute* based
only on a consideration of its "plot."

One reason why the overwhelming bulk of movie criticism is bad
or misleading is that most critics never go beyond the "content" of
a film. Such criticism might just as easily be about a novel or a play
(though seldom a painting). Shallow commentaries of this sort do
not tell us specifically why and how a movie succeeds (or fails)—
they merely give us a general notion of what a film is "about."
Herman G. Weinberg, in his excellent study, *Josef von Sternberg*
(Dutton, 1967), puts this matter most succinctly, when he states:

> The way a story is told is part of that story. You can tell the same story
> badly or well; you can also tell it well enough or magnificently. It
> depends on who is telling the story. That is perhaps why form is, in the
> last analysis, . . . of more decisive importance than content, though
> under ideal conditions the latter dictates the style of the former.

No intelligent critic of literature or painting would value a work
because of its "thematic importance." To do so would put one in the
dubious position of preferring a post-office mural to a portrait of an
ancient hag by Rembrandt, or of preferring a mediocre epic novel
like *Gone With the Wind* to a "domestic love story" like *Pride and
Prejudice*. As obvious as this may seem, in the area of film criticism,
such superficial judgments are being made all the time—by otherwise **4**

cultivated and intelligent people. A film by Alfred Hitchcock is dismissed as a "mere thriller," despite the fact that *Hamlet*—on this level of criticism—could be similarly dismissed. A discussion of Hitchcock's *Psycho* without an appreciation of its subtle and complex images is just as irresponsible as a discussion of *King Lear* without an appreciation of its language. On the other hand, critics often praise a didactic potboiler like Stanley Kramer's *Ship of Fools* because of its "important" theme, yet visually it is a dull and uninspired movie.

"Form" and "content" are best used as relative terms, useful for temporarily isolating specific aspects of art for the purposes of closer examination. Such an unnatural isolation is, in a sense, artificial, yet frequently this technique yields more detailed insights into the work of art as a whole. In criticism, one can even consider "pure" forms, such as colors, shapes, or sounds. But psychologists have discovered that even nonrepresentational forms suggest ideas, emotions, sensations—that is, information.

PSYCHOLOGY OF VISUAL PERCEPTION

"Meanings" can be embodied in purely formal artistic devices. In his book, *Art and Visual Perception*, Rudolf Arnheim demonstrates how the visual artist is sensitive to these "form-meanings," either consciously or instinctively. The desire of all artists and viewers is to want to see a balanced composition, a harmonious equilibrium of formal elements. This desire for balance is analogous to man's balancing on his feet, and indeed, to most man-made objects which are balanced on the surface of the earth. Instinctively, man assumes that balance is the norm in most human enterprises.

The human eye automatically attempts to harmonize the major formal elements of a composition into a unified whole. Apparently the eye can detect as many as seven or eight separate elements of a composition at a time; when there are more, visual confusion is the result. The eye also groups various elements into ordered patterns. For example, even in a complex design, the eye will "connect" similar shapes, colors, textures, etc. The very repetition of a shape, color, or texture can suggest the repetition of an experience (Fig. 1). These connections form a kind of visual "rhythm," forcing the eye to leap over the surface of the design in order to perceive the overall balance. John Huston's film, *Reflections in a Golden Eye*, exploited this psychological phenomenon in its use of color. Virtually all the images were muted to a bland sepia, suggesting the monotony of army camp life. The only other color permitted to escape was red, or monochromatic variations of red, which generally suggested sexual passion. **5**

FIGURE 1. *The Heiress*
Directed by William Wyler.

The use of deep-focus photography is common in Wyler's work, particularly
in his adaptations of plays. The lighting of such scenes is complicated,
for all distance ranges must be clearly yet unobtrusively illuminated.
In deep-focus long shots, the *mise-en-scène* must also be more complex, for
the audience is encouraged to examine the interrelationships between the
various depth planes of the composition. The repetition of the circular
shape in this shot suggests the repetition of an experience.

FIGURE 2. *Strike Up the Band*
Directed by Busby Berkeley.

Totally symmetrical compositions like this are rare in film. The axis point of
the composition is at the exact center: all sides of the image are equally
weighted from this axis point.

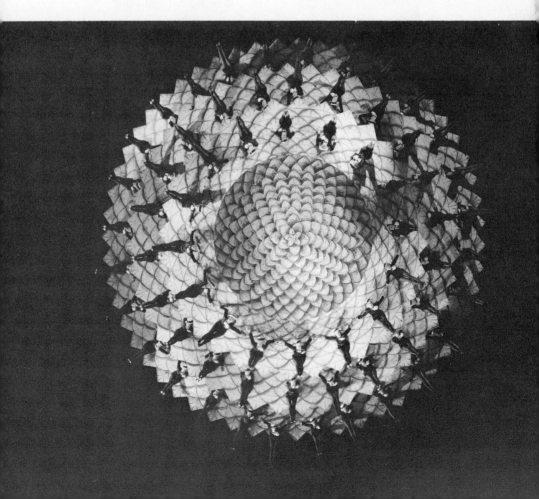

Thus, if any variation of red appeared on the surface of the screen, the viewer instinctively grouped the pattern of colors, and formed appropriate symbolic and thematic "connections" as well.

In a totally symmetrical design—almost never found in movies—the visual "weight" is distributed evenly, with the center of the composition as the axis point (Fig. 2). Since the overwhelming majority of compositions are not symmetrical, however, the weight of one element is often counterpoised with another different element. A shape, for example, counteracts the weight of a color. Psychologists and art theorists have also discovered that certain portions of most compositions are "intrinsically" weighted. The German art historian Wölfflin, for example, discovered that we tend to "read" pictures from left to right, a habit derived perhaps, from reading. In order to be balanced, a picture must therefore be more heavily weighted on the left, to counteract the intrinsic heaviness of the right (Fig. 3). Overweighting on the left can be obvious (Fig. 4), or it can be accomplished more subtly, by having a person look towards the left, for example (Fig. 5).

FIGURE 3. *Tristana*
Directed by Luis Buñuel.

Since the eye tends to travel from left to right, many directors weight the left side of their compositions to counterbalance the intrinsic heaviness of the right.

FIGURE 4. *Sunnyside*
Directed by Charles Chaplin.

An obvious example of excess weight on the left, here used for comic
purposes. Even the cactus plants are bent in this direction.
Part of the comic incongruity of the shot is due to the tension between the
weighted left and the eye's natural tendency to move toward the right,
along the lines of the two girls' extended legs—
the most extreme angle of the triangular composition.

Similarly, bright colors are weightier than darks. In an evenly
divided composition of black and white, for example, the white appears larger than the black. Bright colors also tend to come forward,
while darks tend to recede (Fig. 6). The upper part of a composition
is heavier than the lower. For this reason, skyscrapers, columns,
and obelisques taper upward, or they would appear top-heavy. A
landscape is seldom divided horizontally at the midpoint for this
very reason: the sky would appear to oppress the earth (Fig. 7).
Certain film directors like Sergei Eisenstein and John Ford create
some of their most disquieting effects with precisely this technique:
they let the sky dominate through its intrinsic heaviness, and the
terrain and its inhabitants seem overwhelmed (Fig. 8).

9

FIGURE 5. *La Dolce Vita*
Directed by Federico Fellini.

The intrinsic heaviness of the right can be counterbalanced by having the
characters face left. By placing the figures between the two door panels,
the sides of the image are subtly neutralized, thus producing an
essentially vertical composition.

FIGURE 6. *The Seventh Seal*
Directed by Ingmar Bergman.

In most black and white images, lights tend to come forward,
while darks tend to recede. The harshly contrasting lighting of this shot
produces a "torn-up" surface, a sense of violence and disfigurement which
is psychologically appropriate to the dramatic context.

FIGURE 7. *Shame*
Directed by Ingmar Bergman.

Because of the intrinsic heaviness of the upper portions of the screen,
the horizon line in most natural scenes is generally well
above the midpoint of the composition.

FIGURE 8. *L'Avventura*
Directed by Michelangelo Antonioni.

When the horizon line is below the center of a composition, the director
generally wants to suggest a sense of dominance or envelopment.
Here the sky seems to swallow the figures,
oppressing them in a sea of whiteness.

Isolated objects tend to be heavier than those in a cluster. Sometimes one object can balance a whole group of other "equal" objects, merely by virtue of its isolation (Fig. 9). In many films, the protagonist is shown apart from a hostile group, yet the two seem somehow equally matched despite the arithmetical differences. This effect is conveyed through the psychological "weight" of the hero in isolation.

Psychological experiments have revealed that certain lines suggest directional movements. Though verticals and horizontals tend to be visually "at rest," if any movement is perceived, horizontal lines tend to move from left to right (Fig. 10), and vertical lines from bottom to top (Fig. 11). Diagonal or oblique lines tend to be naturally more dynamic, or "in transition," and also tend to move upward (Fig. 12). Triangular or wedge shapes tend to be perceived as being in movement, usually in the direction of the most extreme angle (Fig. 13).

FIGURE 9. *Wild Strawberries*
Directed by Ingmar Bergman.

When a single figure is isolated from a group,
he can balance the weight of the group by virtue of his isolation.
The dominant contrast in this image is the sharply defined edge of the
curtain, dividing the brightly lit group from the dark-enshrouded single figure.

FIGURE 10. *Eclipse*
Directed by Michelangelo Antonioni.

Horizontal lines tend to suggest stasis, or lack of movement. In this shot,
motion is kept to a minimum, though the eye tends to travel toward the right,
where the girl's silhouette brings the movement to a gentle stop.

FIGURE 11. *Alphaville*
Directed by Jean-Luc Godard.

The formal elements of this shot all conspire to suggest an upward sense of
movement. The vertical lines, which slant slightly toward the center,
the neutralizing masking of the shutter and window,
and the triangular shape of the girl's forearms guide the viewer's eyes
toward the top of the composition.
The lighting from above (reflected in the window)
suggests a kind of spirituality which is reinforced by the
upward-directed eyes and the girl's serene and contemplative expression.

FIGURE 12. *Birth of a Nation*
Directed by D. W. Griffith.

Diagonal or oblique lines tend to move upward and suggest disharmony and confusion. Movement in oblique directions often seems wild and out of control.

FIGURE 13. *Birth of a Nation*
Directed by D. W. Griffith.

Triangular or wedge shapes seem to move in the direction of the most extreme angle, in this case toward the wounded soldier and his rescuer. Much of Griffith's film was inspired by the Civil War photography of Matthew Brady.

These psychological phenomena are important to the visual artist, especially the film-maker, for often the subject matter or dramatic context is not conducive to certain effects. For example, if a director wishes to show a character's inward agitation within a calm context, he can convey this quality through the dynamic use of line: an image composed of tense diagonal lines can suggest the character's inner conflict, despite the apparent lack of drama in the given context (Fig. 14). Indeed, some of the most subtle cinematic effects are achieved precisely through the contrast of "meanings" between an image and its dramatic context (Fig. 15).

FIGURE 14. *The 400 Blows*
Directed by François Truffaut.

Often the context of a scene does not permit a director to express emotions dramatically. Here, the boy's anxiety and tenseness are expressed in purely visual terms. His inward agitation is conveyed by the diagonal lines of the fence. His sense of entrapment is suggested by the tight framing (sides, top, and bottom), the shallow focus (rear), and the obstruction of the fence itself (foreground).

15

FIGURE 15. *The Third Man*
Directed by Carol Reed.

By tilting the camera somewhat to its side, the natural horizontal and
vertical lines of a scene can be converted into diagonals,
thus producing a sense of imbalance, of impending disaster.
(Note the figure—Orson Welles—at the top of the ruin.)

THE FRAME

Unlike the painter or the still photographer, the film director does not
conceive of his framed composition as self-sufficient. Since film is a
temporal as well as spatial art, each **frame** is necessarily an artifi-
cially frozen image, never intended to be wrenched from its temporal
context. For critical purposes, it is sometimes necessary to analyze
a still frame in isolation, but the viewer must always keep the dramatic and temporal contexts in mind. For the film artist, "balance"
is necessarily a temporal as well as a spatial matter. **16**

Another aspect of the movie frame is its dimensions. Unlike the painter or still photographer, the film director does not fit the frame to the composition, but the compositions to the single-sized frame, whose horizontal and vertical ratios remain constant. Movie screens come in a wide variety of ratios, especially since the introduction of CinemaScope, but the majority of conventionally shaped screens are approximately 4 by 3. Most wide screens are roughly 5 by 3 (Fig. 16). The screen dimensions, then, are imposed from without, and are not organically governed by the composition. This is not to say that all movie images are therefore "inorganic," for like a sonneteer, the good film director is able to work within given formal confines. The constant size of the movie frame is especially difficult to overcome in vertical compositions: a sense of height must be conveyed in spite of the dominantly horizontal shape of the screen.

One method of overcoming this problem is masking. In *Intolerance*, for example, D. W. Griffith blocked out portions of his images through the use of black masks. To emphasize the steep fall of a

FIGURE 16. *Zabriskie Point*
Directed by Michelangelo Antonioni.

The horizontal dominance of movie screens was intensified by the introduction of CinemaScope. Some directors timidly ignored the edges of their compositions, while the more gifted exploited the new screen size by making their *mise-en-scène* more complex. Here, Antonioni stresses the differences in life style between the two characters by placing them at the extreme edges of the composition. Psychologically, the distance between them also suggests the restraint and suspicion that each character feels for the other.

soldier from a wall, the sides of the image were masked out. To PICTURE
stress the vast horizon of a location, Griffith masked out the lower
third of the image—in effect, he created a CinemaScope screen.
Many kinds of masks are used in this film, including diagonal, circular, and oval shapes. Oddly enough, this technique was not picked
up by many subsequent directors, perhaps because it tends to call
attention to itself. Most directors after Griffith tended to prefer more
natural types of masks. By placing a tall object between two "screen-
ing" devices (in a doorway for example, or between two trees), the
lateral portions of the composition are in a sense neutralized, and
the resultant visual effect is vertical (Figs. 5, 11).

As an esthetic device, the frame performs in several ways. The
sensitive director is just as concerned with what is left out of the
frame as with what is included. The frame selects and delimits the
subject, it edits out all irrelevancies, and presents us with only a

FIGURE 17. *On the Waterfront*
Directed by Elia Kazan.

When movement is in a downward direction, a sense of tension and
opposition is often suggested, for the eye tends to move upward over a
composition. In this shot, this sense of entrapment is reinforced by the
enclosing walls on both sides.

"piece" of reality (Fig. 41). As such, it is the basis of composition, representing the order that art carves out of the chaos of reality. The frame is thus essentially an isolating device, a technique that permits the director to confer special attention on what might otherwise be overlooked in a wider context. In **close-ups** particularly, the enclosing frame can pinpoint the most minute details.

The frame is also a confining device, and can suggest a sense of restriction and entrapment (Fig. 14, 17, 47). The darkness of the theatre—outside the frame—is sometimes used to suggest oblivion, the fearful unknown, mysteriousness (Fig. 9). In one scene of D. W. Griffith's *Birth of a Nation*, for example, the villain forces his amorous attentions on an unwilling heroine. One particularly effective shot shows the heroine cringing at the extreme lower right side of the composition, while the villain, kissing the hem of her dress, presses closer and closer, almost forcing her out of frame, into the "darkness." In many films about people who want to remain anonymous, or those who are suicidal, the darkness outside the frame is also used metaphorically. By placing a character at the fringes of the frame—out of the limelight—a director can suggest the character's desire for privacy, for death.

Some directors use the frame voyeuristically. Thus, in many of the films of Alfred Hitchcock, for example, the frame is likened to a window through which the audience may satisfy its desire to probe into the intimate details of the characters' lives. (One famous Hitchcock film, *Rear Window*, employs this peeping technique literally.) Other directors use the frame in a less snooping manner. In Jean Renoir's *The Golden Coach*, for example, the frame suggests the proscenium arch of the threatre, and appropriately so, for the controlling metaphor of the film centers on the idea of life as a stage.

DOMINANT CONTRAST

Most movie images are structured around one **dominant contrast**, which in turn is complemented by a series of **subsidiary contrasts.** Through the dominant contrast, the visual artist is able to guide the viewer's eye to virtually any area of the image surface. This is accomplished by stressing some formal element which contrasts noticeably with the other elements of the image. In black and white movies, the dominant contrast is generally achieved through a juxtaposition of lights and darks. For example, if the director wishes the viewer to look first at an actor's hand, rather than his face, the lighting of the hand would probably be harsher than the face, which would be lit in a more subdued manner. In color films, the dominant is often achieved by having one color stand out from the others. Virtually any formal element can be used as a dominant contrast: a shape, a line, a texture, and so on.

19

FIGURE 18. *The Pawnbroker*
Directed by Sidney Lumet.

The dominant contrast of this shot would ordinarily be the police car,
since it constitutes the area of greatest contrast.
In this shot, however, the "intrinsic interest" of the wounded boy
(hidden by the crowd) is the dominant, for in certain contexts, dramatic
elements take precedence over purely visual ones.

After the viewer takes in the dominant contrast, his eye then scans
the subsidiary contrasts, which the artist has structured as variations
of the dominant. In a totally symmetrical picture, the dominant contrast is the exact center of the composition: from this axis point,
each portion of the design is equally weighted. When the dominant
is off center, the picture seems off balance at first. But since the axis
shifts with the dominant, and all sides of the axis are equally weighted,
the composition is actually still in balance, though in a more subtle
manner. Since cinematic images have both dramatic and temporal
contexts, the dominant contrast is often movement itself, and what
some estheticians call **"intrinsic interest."**

"Intrinsic interest" simply means that the audience, through the
dramatic context of a story, knows that an object is more important
than it would otherwise appear. Thus, despite the fact that a toy **20**

might occupy only a small portion of the surface of an image, if we PICTURE
know that the toy is *dramatically* important, it will assume dominance
in the picture, despite its visual unimportance, for in a given context,
dramatic meanings tend to take precedence over visual ones. In
The Pawnbroker, for example, Sidney Lumet wants to show the relative indifference of city dwellers to a murder that has just taken
place. The young boy's body lies bleeding on the sidewalk, while
people pass by, or stare impassively. In a number of the shots, the
boy's body is not even visible to the viewer, but because of its
"intrinsic interest," it forms the dominant contrast of these images
(Fig. 18).

Even a third-rate director can guide the viewer's eye through the
use of movement, for motion is almost always an automatic dominant
contrast. For this reason, many uninspired film directors simply
ignore the potential richness of their images, and rely solely on movement as a means of capturing the viewer's attention. On the other
hand, a great director will vary his dominant contrasts, sometimes
emphasizing movement, other times using movement as a subsidiary
contrast only. In general, the importance of motion varies with the
distance between subject and camera. Movement tends to be less
effective when the subject is far away, more effective when the subject is close.

THE SHOTS

The amount of picture included within the frame is the basis for the
different cinematic **shots**. In practice, shot designations vary considerably: a **"medium shot"** may represent two quite different distances to two different directors. Furthermore, the longer the shot,
the less precise are the designations. In general, however, shots
tend to be determined on the basis of how much of the human figure
is in view. The more area covered by a shot, the less detailed it is.
The less area covered, the more disorienting is the image in terms
of its spatial context. **Realist** directors—those who wish to preserve
the spatial continuity of a scene—tend to favor the longer shots, for
they preserve the relationships between people and their contexts.
Expressionist directors, on the other hand, tend to favor the closer
shots, which fragment real space into a series of detailed pieces of
the whole. In actual practice, it is a matter of emphasis: the terms
"realistic" and "expressionistic" are relative, for no director can
totally dispense with either long or close shots.

The **extreme long shot** is taken from a great distance, sometimes
as far as a quarter of a mile away: it is almost always an exterior
shot, and shows much of the locale. Extreme long shots serve, too,
as spatial frames of reference for the closer shots, and for this reason, are sometimes called **"establishing shots."** If people are in-

FIGURE 19. *Intolerance*
Directed by D. W. Griffith.

Extreme long shots are almost always exterior shots, showing a vast portion
of the locale. They are particularly useful in epic films, in which the
dramatic values are often sweeping and larger than life.
The human figure tends to be dwarfed into insignificance in extreme long shot,
for the locale dominates. Except for mass movements,
motion tends to be minimal at these ranges.

cluded in extreme long shots they usually appear as mere specks, and seldom constitute the dominant contrast of the image (Fig. 19). The most effective use of these shots is often found in **epic films**, where locale plays an important role: westerns, war films, historical movies. Not surprisingly, the greatest masters of the extreme long shot are those directors associated with the epic genre: D. W. Griffith, Sergei Eisenstein, John Ford, and Akira Kurosawa.

The **long shot** is the favored shot of most realist directors, since it shows the human body in full, and also includes a considerable portion of the locale. Long-shot ranges approximately correspond to the distance between the audience and stage in the legitimate theatre. For this reason, Orson Welles and William Wyler, both of whom have adapted plays into films, tend to favor long shots (Fig. 1). Charles Chaplin and Robert Flaherty use long shots because they preserve the spatial interrelationships between people and things (Fig. 20).

FIGURE 20. *The Gold Rush*
Directed by Charles Chaplin.

The long shot tends to be the preferred range of most realist directors, for it preserves the important interrelationships between man and his environment. Chaplin's films use mostly long shots in order to endistance the audience from the characters. "Long shot for comedy, close-up for tragedy" is not an arbitrary dictum of Chaplin's, for he realized that the audience tends to identify with a character in close-up, whereas the viewer is more objective when a character is kept at a distance.

The **medium shot** contains a figure from the knees or waist up. PICTURE A functional shot, it is useful for shooting exposition scenes, for carrying movement, for transitions between close-ups and long shots, and for **reestablishing** after a long or close shot. There are several variations of the medium shot. The **two-shot** contains two figures, from the waist up (Fig. 21). The **three-shot** contains three figures; beyond three, the shot tends to become a long shot, unless the other figures are in the background (Fig. 22). The **over-the-shoulder shot** usually contains two figures, one with part of his back to the camera, the other facing the camera. This shot is useful as a variation of the standard two-shot, and as a way of emphasizing one person's dominance over another.

FIGURE 21. *Blonde Venus*
Directed by Josef von Sternberg.

Despite the absurd plots and shallow dialogue of most of his films, the lush surfaces of von Sternberg's images are still much admired for their richness and complexity—a magnificent triumph of technique over subject matter. **24**

FIGURE 22. *Alexander Nevsky*
Directed by Sergei Eisenstein.

Costumes can suggest symbolic ideas and values. Here the helmets of
Nevsky and his soldiers suggest Russian Church spires,
the chain mail recalls the fishing nets used by the peasant
fishermen earlier in the film.

FIGURE 23. *Shame*
Directed by Ingmar Bergman.

The close-up permits the viewer to perceive the subtlest nuances of the
human face. Gunnar Björnstrand, shown here, is one of Bergman's most
brilliant actors, and has appeared in a number of his best films.

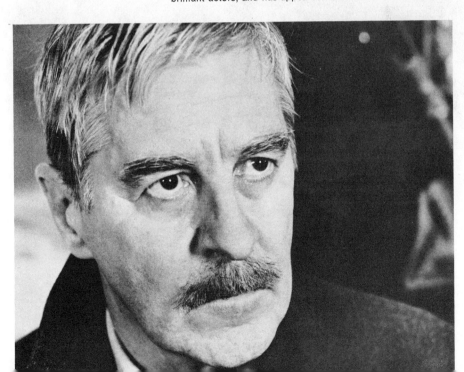

The **close-up** shows very little if any locale, and concentrates on a relatively small object—the human face, for example (Fig. 23). Since the close-up magnifies the size of an object hundreds of times, it tends to elevate the importance of things, often suggesting a symbolic significance. In Hitchcock's *Notorious*, for example, the heroine suddenly realizes that she is gradually being poisoned by her evening coffee. Suddenly, a close-up of the coffee cup appears on the screen—a huge distortion of its real size. The image of the delicate demitasse captures not only the heroine's sudden realization, but also the veneer of elegance that protects her corrupt poisoners from being detected. In short, the image becomes a symbol for the particular life style of "respectable" Nazis at the end of World War II. The **extreme close-up** is a variation of this shot. Thus, instead of a face, the extreme close-up might show only a person's eyes, for example, or his mouth (Fig. 24).

FIGURE 24. *Eclipse*
Directed by Michelangelo Antonioni.

The extreme close-up can zero in on a minute area,
expanding the size of an object thousands of times on the screen.
In this wide-screen shot, even the reflection in the man's eyeglasses can
be distinguished. Movement at this range tends to seem cataclysmic:
Imagine the screen area affected if the man were to blink his eyes.

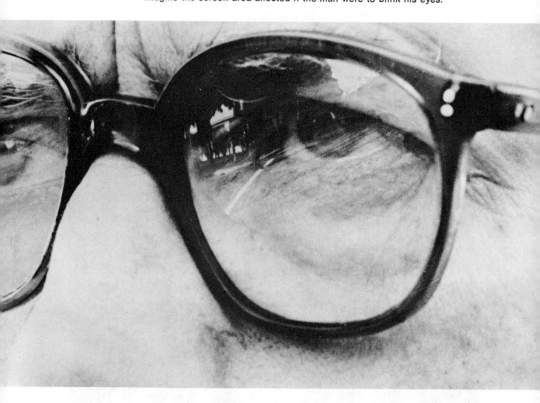

FIGURE 25. *The Silence*
Directed by Ingmar Bergman.

Deep-focus shots are actually a variety of shots combined in one set-up and
photographed in depth. The *mise-en-scène* in deep-focus shots is
generally more complex than in shallow focus, for all spatial
distances must be harmonized and coordinated simultaneously.
Here, the action takes place on three spatial planes:
the woman facing the camera in the foreground,
the boy in the midground, and the woman in the background.

The **deep-focus shot** is actually a variation of the long shot, consisting of a number of focal distances, and photographed in depth.
Sometimes called a "wide-angle shot," this technique captures objects at close, medium, and long distances simultaneously (Fig. 25).
The shot is especially useful for preserving spatial continuity. The
objects in a deep-focus shot are carefully arranged in a succession
of spatial planes: this *mise-en-scène* guides the viewer's eye, generally from close ranges to medium to long. A famous scene from
Citizen Kane employs the deep-focus shot effectively. Kane's wife
has unsuccessfully attempted suicide, and is resting in bed. At the
bottom of the screen, in close-up range, stands the bottle of poison;
in the middle of the screen, in medium range, lies Mrs. Kane in bed;
in the upper portion of the screen, in long range, Kane enters through
a door. The shot also suggests a kind of cause–effect relationship:
(1) the poison was taken by (2) Mrs. Kane because of (3) Kane's inhumanity.

27

The physical angle from which an object is viewed often forms the dominant contrast of an image, particularly if the angle is extreme. Angles can be likened to a writer's adjectives: they often reflect the author's attitude towards his subject. If the angle is slight, it can serve as a kind of subtle emotional coloring; if the angle is extreme, it can represent the major meaning of an image. The form–content dichotomy is particularly meaningless in this context. A picture of a man photographed from a **high angle** actually suggests opposite meanings from an image of the very same man photographed from a **low angle** (Fig. 26). In a sense, the content is the same in both cases. In terms of the information we derive from the images, however, it is clear that the form *is* the content, the content the form.

Directors in the realistic tradition tend to avoid extreme angles. Most of their scenes are photographed from eye level, roughly five to six feet off the ground—approximately the way in which an actual observer might ideally view a scene. Usually, these directors attempt to capture the clearest view of an object. Eye-level shots are seldom intrinsically dramatic, since they tend to be the norm. Virtually all directors use some eye-level shots, particularly in routine expository scenes. Even realist directors use a variety of different angles, however, especially in **point-of-view shots**—when the camera records what (and how) a character sees. Thus an image of a man looking from a ladder might be followed by a high-angle point-of-view shot, showing both the subject and the manner of the man's observation.

Expressionist directors are not always concerned with the clearest image of an object, but with the image that best captures an object's essence. Extreme angles almost always involve distortions. Yet many directors feel that by distorting the surface realism of an object, a greater reality is achieved—an inner psychological reality. Both realist and expressionist directors know that the viewer tends to identify with the camera's lens. The realist wishes to make the audience forget that there is a camera at all; the expressionist is constantly calling attention to it. The realist's use of angles is guided by physical probability; the expressionist's by psychological and dramatic appropriateness.

FIGURE 26. *Photos by Barry Perlus*

The angle from which a subject is photographed determines much of its meaning. Here the same subject is captured from eye level (a), and from high and low angles (b and c). Although the content is nominally the same, each shot suggests different meanings. Eye-level shots put us on an equal footing with the subject, implying a sense of parity. High angles tend to reduce a subject to insignificance, suggesting vulnerability; we are superior to the subject. Low angles, on the other hand, increase a subject's importance, creating a sense of dominance over the viewer. **28**

(a)

(b)

(c)

High-angle shots involve the viewer's looking down on a subject. The camera is placed above a scene—on a **crane**, or some natural high promontory. Psychologically, this angle tends to give the audience a kind of Godlike omnipotence. Somewhat akin to the omniscient point of view in literature, high angles give the viewer a bird's eye view of things; he feels he is in control of all the relevant variables of a scene (Fig. 19). In terms of the object photographed, high angles reduce the height of objects. Movement is slowed down: this angle tends to be ineffective for conveying a sense of speed, useful for suggesting tediousness. The importance of setting or environment is increased: the locale often seems to swallow people. John Ford's high-angle long shots are particularly effective in conveying this sensation. High angles reduce the importance of a subject. A man seems harmless and insignificant photographed from above (Fig. 26). This angle is also effective for conveying a character's sense of self-contempt.

Low-angle shots have the opposite effect. They increase height, and thus are useful for suggesting verticality. More practically, they can increase a short actor's height. Motion is speeded up in low angle: in scenes of violence especially, this angle best captures the sense of confusion. The battle scenes of Kurosawa's *Seven Samurai* are magnificently effective, in part, because many of them are photographed from low positions. Environment is usually minimized in low

FIGURE 27. *Citizen Kane*
Directed by Orson Welles.

The portentous low angles in *Citizen Kane* added much to the rich characterization of the protagonist. The problems of lighting such shots were complex, for the ominous ceilings which were included in most of the low-angle shots precluded the possibility of lighting the sets from above.

FIGURE 28. *The Seventh Seal*
Directed by Ingmar Bergman.

Low-angle shots tend to magnify the importance of the subject,
sometimes creating a sense of awe and fear in the audience.
The viewer is made to feel insecure, for a man photographed at low angle
seems to tower above us threateningly. The tree to the left,
in soft focus, suggests the brush strokes of a painter rather than the
recording of a camera. Indeed, the entire image suggests the abstract patterns
of lights and darks of a nonrepresentational painting.

angle, and often the sky or a ceiling is the only background. There
are exceptions, however. In *Citizen Kane*, for example, the overhead
ceiling is a constant reminder of how Kane is "confined" by his own
possessions, especially his mansion. Lighting for interior low-angle
shots cannot be from above (its usual position), since the lights
would appear in the picture. In this case, they are placed in front, on
the sides, or behind (Fig. 27). Psychologically, low angles heighten
the importance of the subject. The figure looms threateningly over
the spectator, who is made to feel insecure. A man photographed
from below inspires fear, awe, and respect (Fig. 28). For this reason,
low angles are often used in propaganda films, or scenes depicting
heroism.

An **oblique angle** involves a lateral tilt of the camera. When the
image is projected, the horizon is tilted. A man photographed at an
oblique angle will appear as though he were about to fall to one side.
Psychologically, oblique angles suggest tension, transition, and movement: the natural horizontals and verticals are forced into diagonals
(Fig. 15). Oblique angles are not often used, for they tend to disorient
a viewer. In scenes of violence and confusion, however, they can be
effective in capturing precisely this sense of violent disorientation.
Oblique angles are sometimes used for point-of-view shots, to suggest the imbalance of a drunk, for example.

Lights and darks often form the dominant contrast of a film image, particularly one in black and white. Lighting in films is seldom static, for with even the slightest movement of the camera or the subject photographed, the lighting shifts. Movies take so long to complete in part because of the enormous complexities involved in lighting each new shot. The lighting technician must account for every shift of movement within the scene. Each different shape, color, and texture reflects or absorbs differing amounts of light. If an image is photographed in depth, an even greater complication is involved, for the lighting must also be in depth. Gregg Toland, the cinematographer who pioneered many in-depth techniques, was largely responsible for the brilliant lighting effects in *Citizen Kane.* Unlike the still photographer, then, the cinematographer must account for shifting temporal and spatial variables in his lighting. Furthermore, the filmmaker does not have at his disposal many of the darkroom techniques of a still photographer: variable paper, dodging, airbrushing, choice of development, enlarger filters, etc. In a color film, the subtle effects of lights and darks are often obscured, for color tends to obliterate shadings and flatten images. Color is also a distracting element, and often takes over as the dominant contrast where lights and darks might dominate the same image in black and white.

Lights and darks have had symbolic connotations since the dawn of man. The Bible is filled with light-dark symbolism; Rembrandt and Caravaggio used light-dark contrasts for psychological purposes as well. In general, artists have used darkness to suggest fear, evil, and the unknown. Light usually suggests security, virtue, truth. Comedies tend to be brightly lighted while tragedies are usually somber, or sometimes harshly contrasting. Some movies are thematically organized around lighting motifs. Federico Fellini's *Nights of Cabiria,* for example, uses night to suggest romance, mystery, and self-deception. The bright glare of day suggests harsh reality, disillusionment, clarity. The central character vacillates between the two extremes, ending finally in a twilight world of subtle shadings of light and dark. The lights and darks are used by Fellini to convey his philosophical acceptance of life's ambiguities: humanity is neither entirely evil nor entirely virtuous, neither totally romantic nor totally practical. Life is a gray mixture of expectation and disappointment, of joy and despair.

Because of this time-honored tradition of symbolism, some directors—especially "perverse" directors like Hitchcock—will deliberately reverse light-dark expectations. Hitchcock's movies attempt to mesmerize the audience by lulling them into a false security. By using many subjective techniques—devices forcing the viewer to identify strongly with the hero—Hitchcock strips away our complacencies, often in the most terrifying manner. In *Psycho,* scenes of dark lurking shadows are shown—yet nothing happens. We laugh at

32

FIGURE 29. Z
Directed by Costa-Gavras.

When movement is from right to left, a certain sense of tension and
unnaturalness is the result, for it contradicts the eye's natural instinct to
move over an image from left to right.
Here, Costa-Gavras demonstrates one of Hitchcock's well-known theories,
that frightening events which taken place in daytime are often more terrifying
than those which occur at night, for we generally feel safe
and secure in the bright daylight.

ourselves for our paranoia. Later, when the heroine is showering in
a brightly lighted motel bathroom, a shocking outrage is committed,
against us as well as her. A similar technique is used by Costa-
Gavras in Z, when the hero is almost run down by a car in broad
daylight (Fig. 29).

Lighting can be used realistically or expressionistically. The
realist tends to favor available lighting, at least in exterior shots. Even
out of doors, however, most directors use some lamps and reflectors,
either to augment the natural light, or, on bright days, to soften the
harsh contrasts produced by the sun. With the aid of special lenses
and more sensitive film stock, some directors have managed to dispense with artificial lighting completely. Natural lighting is often
associated with a "documentary" look. The **neorealist** films of post-
war Italy were particularly associated with this look. Natural lights
often give an image a kind of hard-edged quality, an absence of
smooth modeling, and a deliberate antiromantic harshness. Boris
Kaufman's cinematography in On the Waterfront (Fig. 17) and The **33**

Pawnbroker (Fig. 18) effectively captured this unprettified look. Not all exterior shooting is necessarily hard-edged, however. Through the use of special lenses and additional lighting, John Ford and Akira Kurosawa have both been able to evoke a nostalgic romantic past while still using actual locations. For interior shots, realist directors tend to prefer images with an obvious light source—a window for example, or a lamp—or they tend to use a diffused kind of lighting with no artificial, harsh contrasts (Fig. 1). In short, the realist director does not tend to use lights and darks as his dominant contrast unless the source of light is contextually probable.

The expressionist director uses light less literally: he is guided by its symbolic implications, and will often stress these qualities by deliberately distorting natural light patterns (Fig. 6). A face lighted from below, for example, almost always appears sinister, even if the actor assumes a totally neutral expression (Fig. 30). Similarly, anything placed in front of a light source often assumes frightening implications, for the audience associates light with security, and any blockage of light is therefore a threat to this sense of safety. Welles uses this blockage technique often in *Othello.* On the other hand, in some contexts, especially in exterior shots, a silhouette effect can be soft and romantic, perhaps because the open space acts as a counter to the sense of entrapment suggested by a confined interior.

When a face is obviously lighted from above, a certain angelic effect is the result, perhaps because such lighting implies God's grace descending (Fig. 30). "Spiritual" lighting of this type tends to border on the cliché, however, and only the best lighting technicians —Raoul Coutard, Godard's favorite cinematographer, for example— have handled this technique with subtlety (Fig. 11). When a face is lighted only from the front, its sculptural contours tend to be flattened out. Such flat images are seldom found in professionally photographed films, for they tend to be associated with amateur movie lighting. Coutard has used frontal lighting with considerable subtlety, however, especially when an image is meant to convey the "two-dimensional" flatness of a character. Back lighting, which is a kind of semisilhouetting, is soft and ethereal, producing a feminine, romantic effect. It is especially evocative when used to highlight a woman's hair (Fig. 31). In the 1930s in Hollywood, this technique became nearly universal, having been popularized by the films of Ernst Lubitsch and Josef von Sternberg.

Through the use of spotlights, which permit a director to focus strong lights on relatively small areas, an image can be composed of violent contrasts of lights and darks (Fig. 6). The surface of such images seems disfigured, torn up. The expressionist director uses such violent contrasts for psychological and thematic purposes. In *Citizen Kane*, the mixture of decency and corruption in Kane is suggested often by the harshly contrasting lights: sometimes his face seems split in half, with one side brightly illuminated, the other plunged into darkness. In Ingmar Bergman's *Wild Strawberries*, the **34**

(a)

(b)

(c)

FIGURE 30. *Photos by Barry Perlus*

The lighting of a subject can be of greater importance than the subject itself. Here are several examples of how the form (lights) can alter the meaning of the content. Lighting in most movies is from above and in front (a). Lighting from below generally makes the subject appear rather sinister (b). Lighting from above often suggests spirituality (c). When the subject blocks out the light source, the audience can be made to feel insecure and trapped, for we tend to associate light with safety (d).

(d)

FIGURE 31. *The Passion of Anna*
Directed by Ingmar Bergman.

Back lighting is particularly effective in highlighting a woman's hair
(especially blondes), lending a certain halo effect.
Liv Ullmann, shown here, is perhaps Bergman's greatest actress, and has
appeared in a number of his later films.

FIGURE 32. *The Hour of the Wolf*
Directed by Ingmar Bergman.

Overexposure is a technique often used in fantasy and nightmare sequences.
The lights are so harshly overexposed in this shot that the contours and
textures of the foreground rocks and the youth's body seem almost
obliterated. The blanching contrasts produced by overexposure suggest a
sense of emotional exaggeration.

joy and innocence of childhood is suggested by brightly lit sets and light costumes; the enervating joylessness of adulthood is conveyed by somberly lit sets and dark costumes (Fig. 9). One of Griffith's most powerful images in *Birth of a Nation* shows the mangled corpses of "war's peace": the grotesquely strewn bodies are lighted in such harsh contrasts that we barely recognize what is being photographed, until in horror we realize that these are human bodies.

By deliberately permitting too much light to enter the aperture of his camera, a director can **"overexpose"** an image—producing a blanching flood of light over the entire surface of the picture. Overexposure has been most effectively used in nightmare and fantasy sequences. In Fellini's *8½*, for example, the hero's recollections of a traumatic childhood experience are shown in deliberately overexposed images. Sometimes this technique can suggest a kind of horrible glaring publicity: a sense of emotional exaggeration (Fig. 32). One sequence in Bergman's *Sawdust and Tinsel*, for example, uses overexposure to emphasize a character's anguish over a public humiliation.

COLOR

The most common dominant contrasts of a black and white film are often neutralized in a movie in color, for next to movement, color is perhaps the most immediately perceived element of a film image. Like movement, however, color can be forced to act as a subsidiary contrast, despite this tendency to dominate. Although color in film did not become commercially widespread until the 1940s, there were many experiments in color before this period. The original prints of *Birth of a Nation* (1915), for example, were tinted to suggest moods: the burning of Atlanta was tinted red, the night scenes blue, the exterior love scenes pale yellow.

For many years, the major problem with color was its tendency to prettify everything. If color enhanced a sense of beauty—in a musical, for example, or a western or historical extravaganza—the effects were often appropriate. Thus, the best commercial films of the early years of color were usually those with "artificial" or remote settings. The earliest color processes tended also to emphasize garishness, and directors seemed disinclined to tone down this obviousness. For this reason, "realistic" films—especially those dealing with contemporary subjects—were usually still photographed in black and white. Compared to the subtle color perception of the human eye, however, and despite the apparent realism of most present-day color processing, color in films is still a relatively crude approximation. Furthermore, each color process tends to "specialize" in a certain base hue—red, blue, or yellow, for example—while the other colors of the spectrum are somewhat distorted.

Psychologically, color tends to be a subconscious element in film: it is strongly emotional in its appeal, expressive and atmospheric, rather than conscious or intellectual. Psychologists have discovered that most people actively attempt to "interpret" the lines of a composition, but they tend to accept color passively, permitting it to suggest moods rather than objects. Lines are associated with nouns, color with adjectives; line is sometimes thought to be masculine, color feminine. Both lines and colors suggest meanings, then, but in somewhat different ways.

Since earliest times, visual artists have used color for symbolic purposes. Color symbolism is probably culturally acquired, though its symbolic implications are surprisingly similar in otherwise differing cultures. In general, cool colors (blue, green, violet) tend to suggest tranquility, aloofness, and serenity. Warm colors (red, yellow, orange) tend to suggest aggressiveness, restlessness, and stimulation. Many film directors have exploited these symbolic and psychological implications. Hitchcock's *Marnie*, for example, uses red to imply sexuality, violence, and danger. Each time the heroine sees red, she responds with terror. At the end of the film she learns that her irrational reaction to red is founded on a childhood trauma, involving a violent sexual experience.

Some directors deliberately exploit film color's natural tendency to garishness. Fellini's *Juliet of the Spirits*, for example, features many bizarre costumes and settings to suggest the tawdry but fascinating glamor of the world of show business. Similarly, the flashy color in Godard's *Weekend* perfectly captures the vulgar materialism of bourgeois life. Michelangelo Antonioni has actually spray-painted natural locales to emphasize the symbolic aspects of color. In *Red Desert,* for example, industrial wastes, river pollution, marshes, and large stretches of terrain were painted gray to suggest the ugliness of contemporary industrial society, and the heroine's drab, wasted existence. Whenever red appears in the film, it suggests sexual passion, yet the red—like the loveless sexuality—is a pitifully ineffectual cover-up of the pervasive gray. (See color insert, following page 112.)

Because of the predominantly emotional appeal of color, many critics believe it is ineffective for conveying precise intellectual ideas. A few directors have used color with surprising, though subtle, precision. Godard's *La Chinoise*, for example, conveys its theme primarily through color. The film deals with several French young people who live and study in a Maoist cell. Godard, himself a radical leftist, portrays the young people as basically attractive: intelligent, dedicated, idealistic. But Godard's attitude toward the youthful revolutionaries gradually becomes more ambivalent, as they become more militant. This ambivalence is reflected in his use of color. Early in the film, one of the young men, reading from Mao's Little Red Book, quotes a statement concerning the necessity that the revolutionary artist use only primary colors—red, blue, and yellow—because these are the basic, essential colors of life. The cell is accordingly painted

38

in bright shades of red, blue, and yellow, and these are the colors the revolutionaries favor in their clothing. But reality, both inside and outside the commune, is composed of other colors as well, of many ambiguous combinations and variations. Throughout the film, the primary colors are used to suggest the idealistic but oversimplified world-view of the revolutionaries; the complex and ambiguous world of reality is suggested by the other—less "pure"—colors of the natural world.

Black and white photography in a color film is often employed for symbolic purposes. Some directors alternate whole episodes in black and white with entire **sequences** in color. The problem with this technique is its facile symbolism: the bleached black and white sequences are too jolting, too obviously "symbolic," when contrasted with a scene in color. A more effective variation of this technique is simply not to use too *much* color, to let black and white predominate. In Tony Richardson's *Tom Jones*, for example, the luxuriant greens of the countryside are dramatically contrasted with our first glimpse of an 18th century London slum—drained of color, except for a few washed-out browns, blue-grays, and yellowish whites.

OPTICAL EFFECTS

Because the camera's lens is a crude mechanism when compared to the human eye, some of the most effective dominant contrasts of a film image are achieved through the distortions of the photographic process itself. Particularly with regard to size and distance, the camera lens does not make psychological adjustments, but records things literally. For example, whatever is placed closest to the camera's lens will tend to appear larger than an object at a greater distance. In the deep-focus shot of *Citizen Kane* alluded to earlier, the bottle of poison is literally larger than Kane himself, for it stands just in front of the lens, and Kane is quite distant from it. The context of the scene tells us this size difference is not literally "true," of course, but Welles is able to convey a symbolic relationship precisely through the artistic exploitation of the distorting lens.

A director can also use special lenses and **filters** to modify or distort the photographic image. Lenses and filters intensify given qualities and suppress others. Cloud formations, for example, can be exaggerated threateningly, or softly diffused, by using certain optical modifiers. Different shapes, colors, and lighting intensities can be altered through the use of special filters. The ethereal, shimmering sparkle of many of the movies of the 1930s—those of Josef von Sternberg, for example—was achieved by using special lenses and lighting techniques (Fig. 21). The extravagantly romantic haziness of many scenes in Bo Widerberg's *Elvira Madigan* were similarly the result of special filters. **39**

The **telephoto lens** is often used to get close-ups of objects from extreme distances. In effect, it works like a telescope. One side effect of this lens is its "flattening" of an image, decreasing the perception of depth (Fig. 33). Mike Nichols exploits this flattening phenomenon in one scene of *The Graduate*, when the hero (Dustin Hoffman), running desperately to rescue his girlfriend, seems to be running "in place," rather than getting to his destination. The **wide-angle lens** has a short focal length and a wide angle of view (Fig. 34). One side effect of this lens is its exaggeration of depth perception; it intensifies distortions of size and distance between planes (Fig. 33). The **fish-eye lens** is an extreme wide-angle modifier, which creates such severe distortions that the lateral portions of the image seem reflected in a sphere. John Frankenheimer, in his science-fiction film *Seconds*, used the fish eye to suggest the hero's eerie semiconscious state.

Except when a director uses deep-focus techniques, the focus of a screen image is concentrated on one spatial plane. Objects placed before or beyond that distance blur, or go into **soft focus.** Soft focus is often used for background or foreground atmospheric purposes (Fig. 21). It is also used as a neutralizing device, permitting the director to guide the viewer's eye to various distances in sequence, a technique sometimes called "rack focusing," or "selective focusing" (Fig. 35). In *The Graduate*, for instance, Nichols used a slight focus shift instead of a cut when he wanted the viewer to look first at the heroine, then at her mother, who is standing a few feet off in a doorway. This focus-shifting technique parallels the heroine's sudden realization that her mother is her boyfriend's mistress. More prosaically, a shift into soft focus has also been used to suggest drunkenness, or the loss of consciousness.

The **optical printer** is an elaborate machine that produces many special effects in the cinema. It includes a camera and projector precisely aligned, which permit the operator to rephotograph all or a portion of an existing frame of a film. **Double exposure** or the superimposition of two images, is one of the most important of these effects, for it permits the director to portray two levels of reality simultaneously. For this reason, the technique is often used in fantasy and dream sequences, as well as in scenes dealing with the supernatural. The optical printer can also produce multiple exposures, or the superimposition of many images simultaneously. Multiple exposures, are useful for suggesting mood, time lapses, and a sense of mixture—of time, places, objects, events.

40

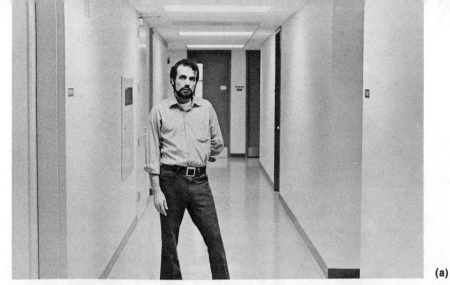

(a)

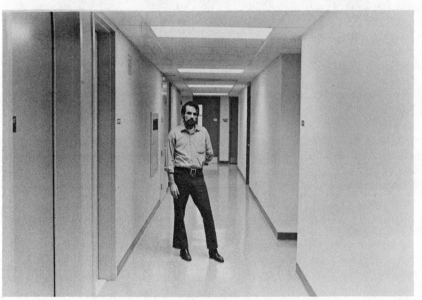

(b)

(c)

FIGURE 34. *Medium Cool*
Directed by Haskell Wexler.

The wide-angle lens not only exaggerates depth perception, but tends to distort at the edges of the image. Note how the vertical lines of the window seem to slant outward, and how the heads of the characters at the edges of the image are elongated.

FIGURE 35. *Stolen Kisses*
Directed by François Truffaut.

Through the use of shallow focus, a director can neutralize elements in the image that are not equidistant to the camera. In this illustration, the viewer is virtually forced to look at the woman, for the young man in the rear is temporarily in soft focus. This technique of neutralizing all but one distance plane is sometimes called selective focusing.

Multiple exposure techniques are often used in **montage** sequences—transitional bridges of rapidly edited images which are used to suggest the lapse of time or the passing of events. (On the Continent, "montage" usually refers to the whole complex art of editing.) In *Citizen Kane*, Welles uses a montage sequence to compress Susan Alexander's lengthy operatic tour: shots of Susan singing her heart out are superimposed and dissolved with shots of newspaper reviews, flickering stage lights, rising curtains, etc.

Negative image—the reversing of lights and darks of the positive, or finished, print—has not been much used in cinema except by avant-garde experimentalists. Movie makers apparently find this technique too flamboyant and obscure: the viewer's light-dark expectations are literally reversed, creating a sense of confusion (Fig. 36). Godard has used the technique with considerable effect in *Weekend* and *Alphaville*, where it suggests an x-ray effect, looking beneath the surface of things. Jean Cocteau has used negative images to suggest dehumanization, the pervasiveness of death and dying.

FIGURE 36. *Darby O'Gill and the Little People*
Produced by Walt Disney.

Although negative images are seldom used in motion pictures,
their use can be highly effective in sequences dealing with the supernatural.
Negative images suggest a sense of looking beneath the surface
of things, and are particularly evocative in portraying
ideas of death and dying.

FIGURE 37. *L'Avventura*
Directed by Michelangelo Antonioni.

Antonioni often uses elements from nature to suggest psychological states. Here, the turbulent ocean water and the desiccated rocks suggest the psychological dangers that the heroine (Monica Vitti) is about to expose herself to shortly before she enters into an affair with a fickle man.

TEXTURE

In referring to the "texture" of a film image, one necessarily speaks metaphorically, for texture is a tactile term, referring to the feel of a surface. But cameras can photograph the surface of objects, and occasionally the dominant contrast of a movie image is its *sense* of texture. Like color, texture tends to appeal to a viewer's emotions rather than his intellect, though—also like color—the meanings of textures can be quite precise in some contexts. In *Hiroshima, Mon Amour*, for example, Alain Resnais captured many brilliant textural effects by showing images of nude bodies partially covered by an eerie falling dust. The dust, which is eventually associated with the **44** atom bombing of Hiroshima, suggests death and its omnipresence. The beautiful smooth bodies, apparently performing the act of love, form a contradictory image, suggesting life and continuity. This texturally mixed image forms the thematic basis of the film: the conflict of the death wish and the life force within the heroine, and, by extension, in mankind itself.

Like color, texture can be used symbolically. In Robert Flaherty's *Man of Aran*, for instance, the agitated surface of the ocean suggests the sudden eruptions of violence from the elements to which the Aran Islanders are prey. Sometimes the ocean surface is gently rolling, suggesting its maternal qualities, for the ocean supplies the Islanders with their daily needs, especially food. The ocean's placidity can also be treacherously deceptive, for in one scene, a shark's fin quietly cuts across the glasslike smoothness of the water, creating a series of expanding ripples that symbolically suggest the dangers

FIGURE 38. *Fellini Satyricon*
Directed by Federico Fellini.

The works of Fellini are rich in textural effects.
Here, as is befitting a Roman orgy, the textures seem to run riot.
Note the sweating bodies of the slaves,
the smoky atmosphere, the grease-stained table,
the squishy mud floor, and the garish costumes and hair designs.

lurking just beneath the ocean's surface. Similarly, the texture of the clouds in the film is sometimes soft, caressing; at other times, they roll darkly over the heads of the vulnerable Islanders below. The roughness of the rocks suggests the slowly eroding but rugged existence of the daily life on the Island. Antonioni used many similar textural devices in *L'Avventura* (Fig. 37).

In short, in the world of film, an object is not necessarily only a thing, for objects have meanings, implications. The tactile surface of things can suggest even more meanings, sometimes independent of the object itself, or merely coincident with it. The sweat of bodies (Fig. 38), the glitter of jewels (Fig. 21), drops of water on a pane of glass (Fig. 39), or the bland smoothness of a building (Fig. 40) can suggest meanings that are dramatically more important than the object itself.

FIGURE 39. *Mississippi Mermaid*
Directed by François Truffaut.

A major difference between the stage and the screen is that in film, various impediments can be placed between the spectator and the actors for psychological and symbolic reasons.
Here, the protagonist (Jean-Paul Belmondo) is viewed through a rain-spattered pane of glass. The tearful implications of the raindrops would not be perceived by an audience at a play, for such effects are generally dependent upon the cinematic close-up.

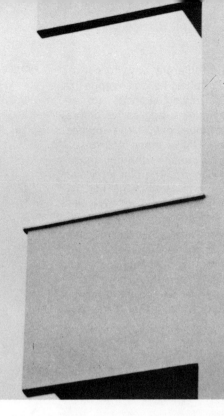

FIGURE 40. *Eclipse*
Directed by Michelangelo Antonioni.

In film, objects can be just as important as people.
Antonioni often exploits the style and design of architecture
to suggest spiritual and psychological ideas.
Some of Antonioni's images are almost exercises in pure
abstract design, as is the case here.

VARIATION AND RESTRAINT

Nearly all visual artists structure their pictures with one dominant contrast, and a series of subsidiary contrasts, which complement or counteract the dominant. In a painting or a still photograph, all the necessary meanings are contained within the single image. In a film, however, any single image can be partially incomplete, since the director has temporal and dramatic elements as well as visual ones to help convey his intentions. For this reason, a film image must sometimes be restrained, or less saturated with meanings than a painting or a still photograph. On occasion, the image will contain only subsidiary contrasts, which serve as rest areas in a movie. Such deliberate anticlimactic devices are necessary in all temporal art forms, which are structured in time, and in a series of increasing or relaxing emotional tensions. **47**

A film director has literally hundreds of different ways to convey meanings. Like the painter or still photographer, he can emphasize visual dominant contrasts. In a scene portraying violence, for example, he can use diagonal and zig-zagging lines, aggressive colors, harsh lighting contrasts, unbalanced compositions, large shapes, close-ups, extreme low angles, and so on. Unlike most other visual artists, the movie director can also suggest violence through movement, either of the subject itself or of the camera. The film artist can suggest violence through his editing. Furthermore, through the use of the sound track, violence can be conveyed by loud or rapid dialogue, harsh sound effects, and strident music. Precisely because he does have so many ways to convey a given effect, the film director will vary his emphases, sometimes stressing image, sometimes movement, other times sound. Occasionally, especially in climactic scenes, he will employ all three. Even the greatest films, then, have some images of only routine interest, for there are times when the dramatic context calls for a nonvisual dominant contrast, and the image thus serves as a temporary subsidiary contrast.

Further Reading

Alton, John. *Painting with Light.* New York: Macmillan Company, 1949.

Arnheim, Rudolf. *Art and Visual Perception: A Psychology of the Creative Eye.* Berkeley: University of California, 1954.

Bazin, André. "The Ontology of the Photographic Image," in *What Is Cinema?* Edited and translated by Hugh Gray. Berkeley: University of California, 1967. (Paper)

Clarke, Charles G. *Professional Cinematography.* Hollywood: American Society of Cinematographers, 1964.

Fielding, Raymond. *The Techniques of Special Effects Cinematography.* New York: Hastings House, 1965.

Johnson, William. "Coming to Terms with Color," *Film Quarterly,* vol. xx, No. 1, 1966. Reprinted in *The Movies as Medium,* edited by Lewis Jacobs. New York: Farrar, Straus & Giroux, 1970. (Paper)

McLuhan, Marshall. *Understanding Media.* New York: Signet Books, 1964. (Paper)

Nilsen, Vladimir. *The Cinema as a Graphic Art.* New York: Hill and Wang, 1959.

Spottiswoode, Raymond. *Film and Its Techniques.* Berkeley: University of California, 1951.

von Sternberg, Josef. "Film as a Visual Art," in *Film and The Liberal Arts.* Edited by T. J. Ross. New York: Holt, Rinehart and Winston, Inc., 1970. (Paper)

movement

The opening of a door, a hand, or an eye
can bring about a climax as thrilling
as a crash of locomotives . . . on the screen.

RICHARD DYER MacCANN

"Movies," "motion pictures," "moving pictures"—all of these phrases suggest the enormous importance of motion in film. "Cinema" derives from the Greek word for "movement." Yet oddly enough, filmgoers and critics give surprisingly little consideration to movement as meaning. Like the image itself, motion is usually thought of in terms of content: we tend to remember what happens in a scene. And rightly so. We are all concerned with the story of a film, and action *per se* is an engrossing element of movies. A great number of early films centered around a chase of some kind: the Mack Sennett comedies, for example, and the works of D. W. Griffith. Even today, many movies are structured around•the idea of a journey and what happens along the way: *Wild Strawberries, La Strada, Easy Rider.* In this chapter, however, we will concern ourselves only with the three broad types of movement within the **shot:** movement of the subject, movement of the camera, and mechanical distortions of movement through the manipulation of camera and/or projector.

MOVEMENT AND THE DOMINANT CONTRAST

Movement involves changes in time and space, and is impossible to separate from the **dominant contrast** of an image, since change inevitably alters the balance of a picture. The direction of the movement is especially important in determining its meaning. The director must decide whether motion is to be toward or away from the dominant contrast, whether the movement completes or throws off the balance of a composition. In either case, movement suggests certain **51** psychological and thematic meanings. A person throwing off the balance of a composition is creating a vacuum by upsetting the equilibrium of the status quo (Fig. 41). If balance is completed by a person's movement, he fits in by creating equilibrium where none previously existed (Fig. 42). The director must decide when to sustain balance by keeping the subject within the **frame**—that is, moving the camera with the subject's movement. At other times, the director deliberately throws off the balance by permitting the subject to move out of frame—that is, keeping the camera stationary. Movement itself can become a dominant contrast, or can create a new contrast by shifting the attention to another area of the composition.

Some directors do not plan out the movements of all their shots. Documentarists, of course, frequently are unable to control their subject matter completely. But even fiction film-makers use certain **aleatory techniques**. Particularly when improvised acting is employed in a movie, the director—who often doubles as his own cameraman—is at the mercy of chance conditions. Not only must he have an excellent eye, he must also have quick instincts, in order to be able to compose his shots on the spot. In *Shadows*, for example, John Cassavetes handled his own camera for some of the scenes, following his actors wherever their impulses led them. In order to gain a sense of documentary realism, some directors place their actors in actual locations, where the performers must interact with nonactors. The results of these chance techniques are often fresh and authentic, as in many of the crowd scenes of Haskell Wexler's *Medium Cool.*

Most directors instinctively or consciously exploit the intrinsic weight of the two-dimensional image surface. Since the eye tends to read a picture from left to right, physical movement in this direction seems psychologically natural (Fig. 13), whereas movement from the right to left often seems inexplicably tense and uncomfortable (Fig. 29). The sensitive film-maker will use these psychological phenomena to reinforce his dramatic and thematic ideas: frequently the protagonists of a movie travel toward the right of the screen, while the antagonists move toward the left. In John Huston's *Red Badge of Courage*, the protagonist moves from right to left when he runs away from a battle in fear. Later, when he courageously joins an infantry charge, his movement is from left to right.

In vertical directions, an upward movement seems soaring and free precisely because it conforms to the eye's natural path of movement (Fig. 43). On the other hand, if the movement is from top to bottom, the result is often a sensation of being cramped or squeezed (Fig. 17). Joseph Mankiewicz's *Suddenly Last Summer* exploited this psychological phenomenon effectively. Early in the film, several people are waiting for the mistress of the house (Katherine Hepburn) to descend in an elevator. Suddenly, she begins to address the visitors even as the elevator descends. Because the shot is from **low angle,** the elevator seems to be slowly crushing the visitors. During the course of the film, we discover that our first impression of the lady **52**

FIGURE 41. *Photos by Barry Perlus*

Movement in film is directed either toward or away from something: the movement thus becomes a dramatic statement.
Here, the movement of the woman throws off the balance of the picture, and since the original framing is preserved, a sense of loss or a vacuum is suggested.
If the camera panned to the right in the final frames, the balance would be corrected, thus producing a different psychological suggestion.

FIGURE 42. *Photos by Barry Perlus*

Movement into the frame can suggest integration and reconciliation.
Here, the woman's movement fills a vacuum,
and by correcting the balance of the picture, a sense of
psychological harmony is implied.

FIGURE 43. *A Woman Is a Woman*
Directed by Jean-Luc Godard.

Whimsically publicized by Godard as a "neo-realist musical,"
A Woman Is a Woman succeeded in integrating documentary realism with
the stylization required by the musical genre.
As in most Godard films, the movie is rich in allusion.
Here, one of the characters expresses the wish to appear in an
MGM musical directed by Vincente Minnelli.

FIGURE 44

The audience implicitly trusts that the camera will be aimed at the area of greatest interest—that the most important element of an image will appear near the center of the composition. By introducing movement from out of frame into the edge of the composition, a director can take his audience by surprise—a useful shock effect.

was correct, for she ruthlessly attempts to destroy the lives of several of the characters who were in this earlier scene.

Directors who want to emphasize the wildness of motion will often photograph it by stressing diagonal thrusts. Such oblique movements tend to seem out of control: like diagonal lines in a still picture, they seem to be in a state of transition. Oblique movements appear to be escaping the confines of the frame, creating a disequilibrium and sense of confusion (Fig. 12). Similarly, triangular shapes seem to move naturally when the movement is directed toward the most extreme angle. When the movement is in another direction, the result is a sense of opposition, tension, and blockage (Fig. 4).

The dominant contrast of an image is usually not too far from the middle of the screen, for this area is intrinsically more weighted than the extreme edges, which an audience considers peripheral to the center of attention. Implicitly, the audience trusts that the camera will be "aimed" directly at the area of greatest interest. Precisely for this reason, a director can concentrate his movement on the edges of the screen to catch an audience off guard—as Hitchcock often does, for instance (Fig. 44). In the **longer shots,** when a character is shown moving at the periphery of the screen, he seems some- times to be avoiding the center of human activity. In Sidney Lumet's *The Pawnbroker*, for example, the protagonist (Rod Steiger) wanders around New York City trying to avoid contact with people. This misanthropy is stressed by photographing his movements at the edges of the screen; or by showing him in the center, and the crowds of people at the edges. Either way, he seems to recoil from the center of human activity.

Orson Welles brilliantly exploits the interaction of movement with light-dark contrasts. In many scenes of *Citizen Kane*, for instance, Kane moves in and out of the light and dark areas, depending upon what he is saying, for he is an ambiguous mixture of virtue and corruption. Within the same shot, he will utter an honest sentiment in light, move toward a gray area while he reconsiders, then deliver a cynical comment from the dark. In the earlier portions of the movie, the idealistic and energetic Kane is bathed in light; as he grows older and more cynical, his slow and deliberate movements are often in semidarkness. In this and other Welles films, whole speeches are delivered from darkened areas. Even in **close-up,** Welles will counterpoint dialogue with light-dark contrasts: the slightest movement of the head can suddenly plunge part or all of the face into darkness or light, depending upon the subtle shifts in the dialogue. In film, it is usually best to trust the eye rather than the ear. In Welles' movies, the dialogue can seem sincere and honest enough, but the falseness or self-deception of the words are often betrayed by the subtle contradictions of the image and movement. The contradiction between dialogue and image–movement has become almost a standard element in the collaborations of writer Harold Pinter and director Joseph Losey—especially in *The Servant* and *Accident.*

These same generalizations about movement can apply to most dominant contrasts—color, texture, and so on. A dominant contrast in a relatively static shot can embody the primary meaning of that shot, but once movement is introduced, it inevitably "comments" on the dominant, and vice-versa. The *full* meaning of a shot, then, results from this juxtaposition: neither the dominant in the image nor the movement alone is sufficient. It is in this temporal-spatial juxtaposition that film differs from literature and most of the other visual arts.

MOVEMENT AND THE SHOTS AND ANGLES

The distance and angle from which movement is photographed determines much of its meaning. Distance and angle particularly influence the speed and intensity of movement. In general, the longer and higher the shot, the slower movement tends to appear. If movement is recorded from close and low ranges, it seems intensified and often **56** speeded up. Many viewers, oblivious to these perceptual relation- ships, tend to think of movement only in terms of gross physical action. The result has been a good deal of naive theorizing on what is "intrinsically cinematic." Such viewers tend to think that the more extravagant the movement, the more filmic it becomes. Subject matter that emphasizes **epic** events and exterior locations are pre- sumed to be fundamentally more suited to the medium than intimate, restricted, or interior subjects.

On the other hand, self-consciously highbrow viewers sometimes claim that such films are vulgar and shallow. They prefer "art" films, with their de-emphasis of action in favor of "quiet" and "subtle" subjects. Both types of viewers tend to misunderstand the nature of movement in film, though to be sure, one can use the terms "epic" and **"psychological"** in describing the *general* emphasis of a movie. But even on this general level, arguments about what is "intrinsically cinematic" are often spurious. Few would claim that Tolstoy's *War and Peace* is intrinsically more novelistic than Dostoyevsky's *Crime and Punishment*, though we may refer to one as an epic and the other as a psychological novel. In a similar vein, only a naive viewer would claim that Michaelangelo's Sistine Ceiling is intrinsically more visual than a Vermeer domestic scene. They are different, yes. But not necessarily better or worse, and certainly not through any intrinsic quality. In short, there are some good and bad epic works of art, and some good and bad psychological works. It is the treatment that counts, not the material *per se.*

But movement in film is more subtle than this, for it is necessarily dependent upon the shots and angles. The cinematic close-up can convey just as much or more movement than the most sweeping vistas in **extreme long shot.** Indeed, in terms of the area covered on the screen's surface, there is actually more movement in a close-up showing tears running down a person's face (Fig. 45) than there is in an extreme long shot of a man running thirty feet (Fig. 19). Cine- matic movement is relative. An epic film like Kurosawa's *Seven Samurai* might appear to have more movement than a claustrophobic psychological film like Carl Dreyer's *The Passion of Joan of Arc*, but in fact, Dreyer's film is photographed almost exclusively in close-up, where the movement of a feature might literally cover yards of space on the screen's surface. Yet many critics repeatedly commit the "intrinsically cinematic" fallacy, when, for instance, they dismiss excellent films like William Wyler's *The Heiress* or Fred Zinnemann's *Member of the Wedding*, on the grounds that they are "too restricted in scope" for filmic treatment.

What is usually the case in such matters is that epic and psy- chological movies employ movement in different ways, with emphasis on different shots. In general, epic films depend on the longer shots for their effects, whereas psychological films tend to employ the closer shots. Epics are concerned with a sense of sweep and breadth, psychological movies with depth and detail. Epics often emphasize **57**

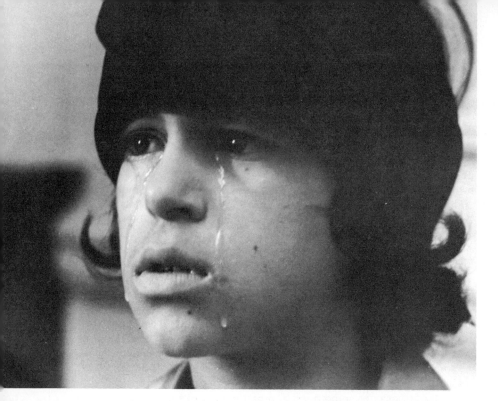

FIGURE 45. *The Wild Child*
Directed by François Truffaut.

Unlike the stage, in film movement is relative:
it is dependent upon the shot.
Even gross movements are not likely to be perceived in extreme long shot,
whereas the path of the tear in this illustration covers over
half the height of the screen.

events; psychological films, the significance and implications of events. In good movies, as in good drama, these characteristics are matters of emphasis, not exclusion. Shakespeare's *Henry V*—which in a sense is conceived in "long shot"—is not devoid of psychological detail; nor is Chekhov's *The Cherry Orchard*—conceived in "close-up"—lacking in action.

The longer shots tend to be the preferred distances for epics, but there are many psychological films that also employ these shots effectively. Antonioni, for example, often uses longer shots to suggest a sense of psychological anguish. Many of his films deal with protagonists who find themselves in a spiritual wasteland. In *Red Desert*, for instance, the neurotic heroine wanders through wasted landscapes in shot after shot, mostly in the long ranges. Antonioni's characters are usually searchers of some kind: his characters look for someone or something meaningful. Often photographed in depth, the movements of the characters seem pitifully ineffectual: the searchers seem to get nowhere—a visual metaphor for the frustrating **58** spiritual search that is going on within the protagonists. Similar techniques are used in Antonioni's *Blow-up* and *L'Avventura* (Fig. 46).

Movement is often conveyed in long shot, for it is a good compromise range between the vast distances of the extreme long shot and the disorienting details of the closer shots. Chaplin's famous dictum "long shot for comedy, close-up for tragedy" is relevant here, for comedy is often dependent upon the interaction between people and objects, people and locales, and people with each other (Fig. 4). Scenes in long shots permit actors a considerable latitude of movement. Permitting a performer this kind of spatial freedom is usually referred to as **loose framing.** The closer shots, on the other hand, are generally more confining, more **tightly framed,** for the performers have little freedom of movement (Fig. 47).

FIGURE 46. *L'Avventura*
Directed by Michelangelo Antonioni.

Movement in film is seldom random, but suggests ideas and emotions Antonioni structures some of his films around the idea of a search of some kind—a metaphor for a spiritual search for meaning or fulfillment. Here, the heroine's search for her lover in the corridors of a hotel suggests the futility of her love affair.
The endless succession of doors, fixtures, and hallways implies, among other things, the repetition of the frustration she is now experiencing.

(a)

(b)

FIGURE 47. *Photos by Barry Perlus*

The framing of a picture can totally change its meaning.
When a person is tightly framed (a), he seems to be confined,
imprisoned by both his environment and the enclosing frame.
When loose framing is employed (b), he seems to be free,
his movements are unrestricted.
Generally speaking, the closer the shot, the tighter the framing.
But framing also depends upon the *mise-en-scène.* Here, for example,
the medium close-up is more loosely framed than the long shot, where the
subject seems anchored to one position by his confining environment.

Regarding this matter of framing, an interesting comparison could
be made between two movie versions of *Hamlet.* Laurence Olivier's
film was essentially an epic, with much emphasis on costume and
setting. There are many long shots especially of the brooding castle
of Elsinore. Much is made of Hamlet's interaction with this moody
locale. Tony Richardson's version of the play was essentially a psychological study, with virtually no concern with costumes and decor. **60**

Hamlet (Nicol Williamson) is almost always seen in tightly framed close-ups. Unlike Olivier's indecisive and contemplative Hamlet, Williamson's is impulsive and rash. This impetuosity is conveyed by the sense of restriction imposed through the framing: many times Hamlet seems to be bursting the confines of the frame, nearly spilling out into the "darkness." The hand-held camera is able to keep the hyperactive prince under surveillance only with extreme difficulty.

If there is a great deal of movement in a **medium shot,** its effect on the screen will be exaggerated, perhaps even disorienting. For this reason, directors tend to employ these ranges for relatively quiet scenes. The animation of two people talking and gesturing, for example, is more than enough movement to prevent most scenes from appearing static. A memorable **two-shot** sequence in Elia Kazan's On the Waterfront takes place in the cramped back seat of a taxicab. Two brothers (Marlon Brando and Rod Steiger) engage in some masculine small talk. Before long, Brando painfully reminds the older brother that he (Brando) might have been a big-time prize fighter, had the older brother not interfered by fixing the match. The facial expressions and gestures of the two men represent the only significant movement in the scene. Yet it seems almost electric with energy, largely because of the brilliance of the two actors. Brando's pained resentment, restrained by love, is perfectly conveyed by the subtle modulations of his face. His clumsy embarrassment is reflected in his tentative hand gestures. Steiger's uptight fury gradually diminishes into remembrance and shame: wild-eyed and trembling, he avoids Brando's face. Finally, recognizing his guilt, Steiger seems almost to collapse, yet the actual movement is minimal: a sigh, and a lowering of the head. The scene is masterfully executed, with each delicate movement conveying a multitude of understated emotions.

Close shots are even more subtle in their recording of movement. The so-called "chamber films" of Bergman—The Silence and Persona, for example—are heavily dependent on close shots, for these films are restricted by cramped interiors, small casts, and static situations (Fig. 48). Robert Bresson and Carl Dreyer can extract both broad and subtle movements by photographing an expressive face in close-up. Indeed, these two directors have referred to the human face as a spiritual and psychological "landscape." In Dreyer's Passion of Joan of Arc, for instance, one of the most powerful scenes is a close-up of Joan (Falconetti) as a tear slowly trickles down her face. Expanded thousands of times by the close-up, the path of the tear represents a cataclysmic movement on the screen, far more effective than the inane cavalry charges and clashing armies of most conventional epic films (Fig. 45).

Of course, epic films can use close-ups with just as much effectiveness. In Tony Richardson's Tom Jones, for instance, one of the funniest scenes is a medium-close shot of Tom (Albert Finney) as he is being subtly propositioned by Mrs. Fitzpatrick. Tense and embarrassed, Tom smiles wanly at her, then darts a quick nervous what-am-I-to-do glance at the camera. The brilliance of the effect could only be captured at close range, for the only significant movement in the shot is Tom's eye as it turns from Mrs. Fitzpatrick to the audience.

Finally, there are times when stasis, rather than movement, forms the dominant contrast of a scene. If a setting is characterized by a great deal of movement, anything static will tend to draw the viewer's attention. Robert Flaherty's *Man of Aran* exploited this phenomenon during a storm sequence. To emphasize the stolid strength of the Islanders, Flaherty photographed an Aran woman standing rigidly at the edge of a cliff, while she scans the tortured ocean surface for her husband's boat. Despite the sense of movement in the scene—primarily from the strong winds and the sea—the dominant contrast of the sequence is focused on the woman, for she is in stark contrast to her turbulent surroundings.

FIGURE 48. *The Passion of Anna*
Directed by Ingmar Bergman.

A line of dialogue can change its meaning considerably, depending on the visuals that accompany it. If a person recites the dialogue looking off frame, as in this illustration, the words can suggest one meaning, but if the same person were to direct the dialogue toward the camera (Fig. 62), the meaning would be altered.

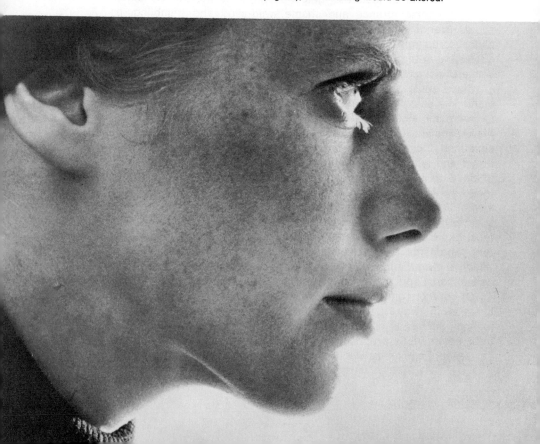

Before the 1920s, directors tended to confine movement to the subject photographed. There were relatively few who moved their cameras during a shot. **Expressionist** directors also emphasized movement through **editing.** When the German directors of the 1920s created something of a sensation by employing moving cameras, the Russian expressionist directors were among the most hostile in their reactions. Intra-shot camera movements were too distracting, they felt, too "unnatural." Most importantly, the moving camera would destroy the primacy of **editing,** which they felt was the foundation of cinematic art. To this day, many directors and critics believe that camera movements ought to be kept to a minimum, that they are permissible only in obviously necessary instances—to keep a moving subject in frame, for instance (Fig. 29).

Such German directors as F. W. Murnau and E. A. Dupont moved the camera within the shot not only for physical reasons, but for psychological and thematic reasons as well. Certainly some of these early directors probably got carried away. In Dupont's *Variety*, for instance, the camera seems never to be still, and the effectiveness of the technique eventually diminishes into tediousness. There are several instances in Murnau's otherwise fine *Last Laugh* when a straight cut would probably have been more efficient. In general, however, the German experiments of the 1920s permitted subsequent directors to use the moving camera to communicate subtleties previously considered impossible. Though editing might be faster, cheaper, and less distracting, the straight cut (that is, moving the camera *between* shots) does not always suit the purpose.

One major problem of the moving camera involves time. Films that employ this technique extensively tend to seem slow moving, since moving in or out of a scene is considerably more time consuming than a straight cut. A director must decide whether moving the camera is worth the film time involved, and whether the movement warrants the additional technical and budgetary complications. If he opts to move his camera, he must then decide how. Does he mount it on a vehicle, or simply move the camera around the axes of the tripod? Each major type of movement implies different meanings, some obvious, some subtle. The director can choose from four basic kinds of camera movements: **pans, tilts, crane shots,** and **dolly shots.** Several relatively recent innovations—the **zoom lens,** the hand-held camera, and **aerial shots**—are variations of these basic four.

PAN AND TILT SHOTS

Pan and tilt shots—those movements of the camera that scan a scene either horizontally or vertically—are taken from a stationary axis point, with the camera mounted on a tripod of some kind. Such shots are time-consuming, since the camera's movement must ordinarily be smooth and slow to permit the images to be recorded clearly. Pans are also in a sense unnatural, for when the human eye moves in a similar manner, it jumps from one point to another, and tends to skip over the intervals between points.

The most common use of a pan is to keep the subject within frame. If a man moves from one position to another, the camera moves horizontally to keep him in the center of the composition. Pans in extreme long shot are especially effective in epic films, where an audience can experience a sense of the sweep and vastness of the locale. John Ford, for example, often pans over vast stretches of desert before finally settling on some travelers as they slowly make their way across the enormous expanse of terrain (Fig. 49). But pans can be just as effective at medium and close ranges. The so-called reaction pan, for instance, is a movement of the camera away from the central attraction—usually a speaker—in order to capture the reaction of an onlooker or listener. In such cases, the pan is an effective way of preserving the cause-effect relationship between the two subjects, for a straight cut from one shot to another would tend to emphasize their separateness (Fig. 50).

Pans can also be used to emphasize solidarity and the psychological interrelationships between people. In Francois Truffaut's *Jules and Jim*, for example, the camera pans rather than cuts between three characters in a scene. A woman is loved by two men, one her husband, the other his best friend. She stands in the middle of the frame, while the men sit at either side of her. There is a genuine sense of love that binds the three together, despite their legal and moral relationships. To emphasize these complex interrelationships, the director first pans to one character, then to another, and then to a third, and back and forth again, for the duration of the shot. The characters are engaged in a rather strained conversation all the while. Since the scene is photographed from a medium-long range, the pan is too conspicuous to pass unnoticed—Truffaut's way of emphasizing the awareness of the characters of this awkward *ménage à trois*.

The **"swish" pan** (also known as a "flash" pan and a "zip" pan) is a variation of this technique that is often used for transitions between shots—as a substitute cut. What the swish pan involves is a whirling of the camera at a speed so rapid that only blurred images are recorded. Despite the fact that it actually takes more time than a cut, swish pans connect one scene with another with a greater sense of simultaneity than a cut can suggest. For this reason, flash pans **64**

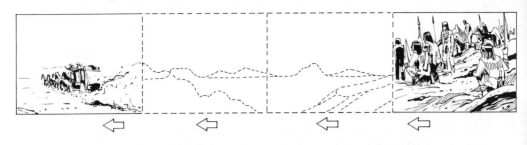

FIGURE 49

In extreme long-shot range, the pan can suggest the vastness of a location
by scanning it at length. Here, the shot opens with the Indians
looking off from the edge of a bluff, pans leftward to give
the viewer a sense of the desert terrain, and stops with the stagecoach
making its way across the locale. By cutting to separate shots
of these three elements, a director could confuse
his audience by destroying the spatial and temporal interrelationships
between the Indians, the terrain, and the stagecoach.
The panning shot, on the other hand, connects the three
elements in one continuous sweep.

are often used to connect various events at different locales which
might otherwise appear remote from each other. In *The Wild Bunch*,
Sam Peckinpah used zip pans for reaction shots within the same
scene. The effect is one of great violence, rapidity, and simultaneity.

These same general principles apply to most tilt shots, or the
vertical movement of the camera around a stationary horizontal axis.
Tilts can be used to keep subjects within frame, to emphasize spatial
and psychological interrelationships, to suggest simultaneity, and to
emphasize cause-effect relationships. Tilts, like pans, can also be
used subjectively, in **point-of-view shots:** the camera can simulate a
character's looking up or down a scene, for example. Since a tilt is a
change in angle, it is often used to suggest a psychological shift
within a character. In one scene of Vittorio de Sica's *Two Women*,
for instance, the camera photographs the heroine (Sophia Loren) at
eye level on a semideserted country road. She and her young daughter have just been brutally raped by soldiers. When a jeep load of
officers goes past, she screams hysterically at them, and finally col-
lapses on the road. As she falls, the camera slowly tilts down, suggesting the helpless vulnerability of the woman, who up to now has
been portrayed as tough, self-sufficient, and strong-willed.

FIGURE 50

At close-up range, the pan can suggest cause-effect relationships and the
solidarity of groups. Individual shots edited together, on the other hand,
would tend to suggest separateness and the individuality
of the people in a group.

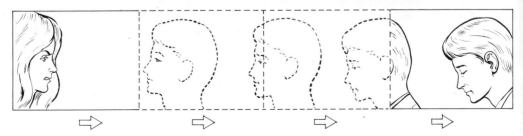

Dolly shots, sometimes called "trucking" or **"tracking"** shots, are taken from a moving vehicle ("dolly") of some kind. The vehicle literally moves in, out, or with a scene while the action is being photographed. Tracks are laid on the set to permit the vehicle to move smoothly—hence, the term "tracking shot." If these shots involve long distances, the tracks have to be laid or withdrawn while the camera moves in or out.

Today, any vehicular movement of the camera can be referred to as a "dolly shot." The camera can be mounted on a car, a train, even a horse. One of the most effective dolly shots in *Jules and Jim* was taken from a moving bicycle: the scene itself was a bicycle outing in the country, and to capture the lyrical sense of release of the characters on their bikes, Truffaut mounted the camera on a similar vehicle. A dolly need not be elaborate. To save money and to permit himself greater freedom of movement, Jean-Luc Godard will occasionally strap his cameraman in a wheelchair, and push his improvised dolly manually. Such was the case in the long tracking shot at the conclusion of *Breathless*, for example, where the camera follows the fleeing protagonist up a city side street.

Tracking is a useful technique for point of view shots—to recreate a sense of movement in or out of a scene. If a director wants to emphasize the destination of a character's movement, he is more likely to use a straight cut between the initiation of the movement and its conclusion. If the experience of the movement itself is important, the director is more likely to dolly. Thus, if a character is searching for something, the time-consuming point-of-view dolly helps to elongate the suspense of the search. Similarly, the **"pull-back dolly"** is an effective technique for surprising the character (and audience) with a sudden revelation: by moving back, the camera reveals something startling—a corpse, for example (Fig. 51).

When the camera literally follows a character, the audience implicitly assumes that it will discover something along the way. A journey, after all, usually has a destination. Antonioni sometimes exploits these expectations to convey certain philosophical themes. In shot after shot of *L'Avventura*, for example, the camera tracks after the heroine as she searches for her friend on an extinct volcano, as she walks from room to room of a great mansion, and as she searches for her lover in the labyrinthian corridors of a hotel. Precisely because we expect her to find something or someone, we experience the same sense of hopeless weariness and frustration. The tracking shots thus become metaphors for certain spiritual and psychological states: the heroine's search for clarity and meaning leads her to a succession of empty rooms and empty corridors (Fig. 46).

66

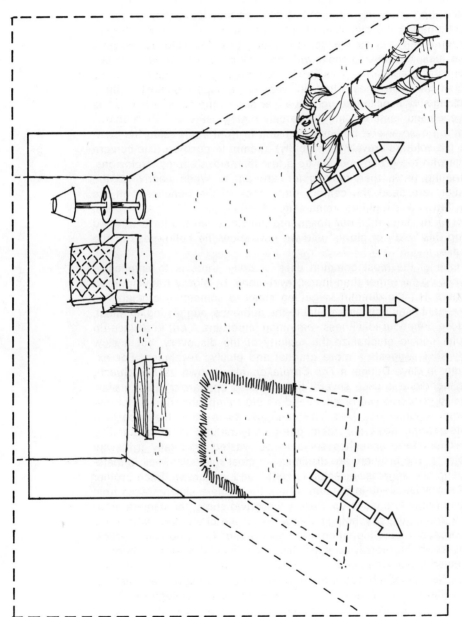

Figure 51.

The pull-back dolly begins by showing only a restricted area. Then, by withdrawing somewhat from that area, the camera reveals some important detail which acts as a sudden revelation to the viewer. This technique is especially useful in suspenseful scenes.

Some of the most stunning tracking shots in the history of film are found in Stanley Kubrick's *Paths of Glory*. The movie deals with a hopelessly futile infantry charge during World War I. The charge is ordered by an ambitious French general, who knows that most of his men will probably be wiped out as soon as they leave their trenches. To emphasize the cynicism of the general, Kubrick tracks through the long trenches as the general walks past the soldiers, wishing them luck, patronizing them with bad jokes, and uttering fatuously optimistic predictions. This is the general's "path of glory," safely behind the main lines. Then, in what is perhaps the most thrilling tracking shot ever to photograph a war scene, the camera leaves the trenches and ventures onto the fiercely raging battlefield. With bombs bursting everywhere, bodies collapsing in front and beside the camera, the soldiers bravely (or stupidly) attempt to push on. The camera stays with the group, moving up a few feet, sidestepping explosions, retreating back, then moving forward again. When nearly all the soldiers are dead, the camera turns back to the trenches with the few tattered stragglers remaining. By dollying with the soldiers, Kubrick in effect rubs our noses into the slime: we too have traveled along this "path of glory," and we now know the hollowness of the phrase.

One of the most common uses of dolly shots is to emphasize psychological rather than literal revelations. By slowly tracking in on a character, the director is getting close to something crucial. The movement itself acts as a signal to the audience, suggesting, in effect, that we are about to witness something important. A cut to a close-up would tend to emphasize the rapidity of the discovery, but a slow dolly shot suggests a more gradual and elusive revelation. For example, in Clive Donner's *The Caretaker* (also known as *The Guest*), this technique is used several times. Based on Harold Pinter's play, the film concerns two brothers and an old tramp who tries to set one brother against the other. The dialogue, as is often the case in a Pinter script, does not seem particularly helpful in understanding the characters: speeches seem to be wasted on totally irrelevant subjects. The brothers are dissimilar in most respects: Mick is materialistic and aggressive; Aston is gentle and withdrawn. Each brother has a crucial scene in the film, where the camera slowly tracks from a long range to a close-up. During these two shots, the camera gradually probes the psychological essence of the characters: with Mick, his obsessive preoccupation with "decorating" his various properties; with Aston, his horrifying experience in a mental hospital where he received shock treatments which were to make him "like other people." Neither of the speeches is really very informative, at least not on a literal level. It is in the juxtaposition of the dialogue with the implications of the dolly shot that the audience feels it has finally "arrived" at an understanding of each character.

Welles has used dolly shots to suggest the penetrating of layer upon layer of obscurities. In the famous opening of *Citizen Kane*, a

series of **dissolving** shots of Kane's fog-enshrouded mansion appear
on the screen. With each new image, the camera dollies in closer
and closer, suggesting a kind of probing effect, an attempt to get
beyond the exterior of the palatial home. Since the narrative structure
of the film is a series of investigations of Kane's "true" personality,
the dolly shots of the opening scenes are completely appropriate,
since they prepare the audience for a series of (often contradictory)
layers of truth about Kane himself.

But the purpose of a tracking shot is not always neatly explain-
able. Like many film techniques, dolly shots often work on a kind of
instinctive, irrational level. To a director, certain techniques sometimes "feel" right, even though he may be at a loss to explain why.
For example, several of the films of Max Ophüls employ tracking
shots extensively, though his reasons are not always apparent. In

FIGURE 52. *Shame*
Directed by Ingmar Bergman.

Particularly at close ranges, the hand-held camera tends to rock unsteadily,
a characteristic useful in point-of-view shots.
Here, the rocking suggests the motion of the boat.
The newsreel authenticity of this illustration is partly achieved by the
deliberately grainy texture and haphazard composition.

both his films, *Letter from an Unknown Woman* and *The Earrings of* *Mme. de. . .* , the heroine throws herself into an imprudent but glorious love affair. The camera tracks relentlessly, as the women become more deeply involved with their lovers. The tracking shots perhaps suggest restlessness, the preciousness of time's passing, the irrevocability of the women's choices. But these are rather abstract meanings, difficult to pinpoint in any given shot. Without these dolly shots, however, the films would lose much of their richness and suggestive ambiguity.

In the 1950s, the invention of a new lightweight hand-held camera permitted directors to move in or out of scenes with greater flexibility. Originally used by documentarists to permit them to shoot in nearly every kind of location, these cameras soon became the hallmark of a new movement called **cinéma vérité,** a journalistically oriented group of young film-makers which has since had a profound influence on fiction film directors. In France especially, several new directors used the hand-held camera with brilliant results. Godard, who made his film debut with *Breathless* during this period, astonished audiences with his daring use of the camera—it seemed to plunge in and out of scenes with breathtaking abandon. Godard actually shot much of his film "wild"—that is, without sound, and with no preconceived script. He simply took his small crew and cast out of doors, and photographed whatever struck him as exciting. His actors improvised on the scene, working quickly with the given conditions of each location. The result was a spontaneity of movement that would have been impossible to capture under conventional filming conditions.

Hand-held shots are often jumpy and ragged. The camera's rocking is hard to ignore, for the screen exaggerates these movements, especially if the shots are taken from close distances (Fig. 52). For this reason, directors often use the hand-held camera for point of view shots. In Mike Nichols' *The Graduate*, a hand-held shot is used to simulate the hero's attempts to maneuver through a crowded room of people. Similarly, in *Faces*, John Cassavetes used many hand-held shots to suggest an on-the-spot documentary flavor. Most cameramen, however, can manipulate a lightweight camera as steadily as a dolly if the situation requires.

CRANE SHOTS

A crane is a kind of huge mechanical arm, often more than twenty feet in length, that can lift a cameraman and camera in or out of a scene. Indeed, the crane can move in virtually any direction: up, down, diagonally, in, out, or any combinations of these. In many respects, the crane resembles those used by the telephone company to repair lines. Because of this flexibility, a crane shot can suggest a number of complex ideas. It can move from high long distances to low close ones, for example, as it does in Hitchcock's *Notorious*, where the camera moves from an extreme **high-angle** long shot of a huge ballroom to an **extreme close-up** of the hand of the heroine (Ingrid Bergman), which is clasping a small key. Crane shots can suggest sudden psychological changes, as in *The Graduate*, where the camera moves from a close eye-level shot of a woman (Anne Bancroft) back to a high-angle long shot. The movement suggests the sudden sense of desolation and humiliation the woman experiences when her lover betrays her.

Crane shots can also suggest symbolic ideas. In the penultimate shot of Lumet's *Long Day's Journey into Night*, the camera begins with a close-up and ends in an extreme long shot. The setting is the family living room, late at night. The mother, who is hopelessly addicted to morphine, is oblivious to her despairing family. She is vaguely reminiscing about her childhood experiences in a convent school, speaking more to herself than to the others. As she takes her journey into the past, the camera slowly moves back and up, from a close shot of the mother's face to a high extreme long shot of the room. At the end of the crane's movement, the entire living room is a dimly lighted white area, taking up less than a tenth of the screen, and surrounded by total darkness. The shot carries a multitude of symbolic meanings, all implied by the title. The "journey" is into the past, not only the mother's but the rest of the family's as well. The mother's journey into "night" is her increasing sense of isolation and oblivion, brought on by the drugs. The "journey" also is taken by the other members of the family, for the mother's "night" plunges the rest of the family into darkness as well. In short, the movement of the crane shot is a perfect embodiment of many of the symbolic implications of Eugene O'Neill's central metaphor.

The use of a zoom lens does not usually involve the actual movement of the camera, but its effect on the screen is very much like an extremely fast tracking or crane shot. The zoom is a combination of lenses, which are continuously variable, permitting the camera to change from close **wide-angle** distances to extreme **telephoto positions** (and vice-versa) almost instantaneously. The effect of the zoom is a breathtaking sense of being plunged into a scene, or an equally jolting sense of being plucked out of it. Zoom shots are used instead of dolly or crane shots for a number of reasons. Most importantly, they can zip in or out of a scene much faster than a vehicle. From the point of view of economy, they are cheaper than dolly and crane shots, for no vehicle is necessary. When filming in crowded locations, zoom lenses can be useful for photographing from long distances, away from the curious eyes of passers-by. With a single **71**

set-up, the zoom lens can switch from close to long shots (and vice-versa) with rapid ease. Much of the location shooting in *The Pawn-broker*, for example, required the presence of crowds. Lumet shot these scenes from long unobtrusive distances, but with the help of the zoom lens, he was able to photograph close shots as well as long.

There are certain psychological differences between zoom shots and those shots that actually involve a moving camera. Dolly and crane shots tend to give a viewer a sense of entering into or with-drawing from a set: furniture and people seem to stream by the sides of the screen, as the camera penetrates a three-dimensional space. Zoom lenses tend to foreshorten people and flatten space. The edges of the image simply disappear at all sides: the effect is one of sudden magnification. Instead of feeling as though we are entering a scene, we feel as though a small portion of a scene has been thrust toward us when we view a zoom. In shots of short duration, these differences tend to be overlooked, but in lengthier shots, the psychological dif-ferences can be crucial.

Aerial shots, usually taken from a helicopter, are really variations of the crane shot, for like the crane, the helicopter can move in virtually any direction. When a crane is impractical—usually on exte-rior locations—an aerial shot can duplicate the effect. The helicopter shot can be much more extravagant, of course, and for this reason, is occasionally used to suggest a sense of lyricism, a sweeping sense of freedom, as in the famous shot of the Beatles romping on a field in Richard Lester's *A Hard Day's Night.* In *Jules and Jim*, an aerial shot conveys Jim's transcendent sense of exhilaration when, after many years, he plans to visit his friend Jules and his wife in Germany.

MECHANICAL DISTORTIONS OF MOVEMENT

"Movement" in film is not a literal phenomenon, but an optical illu-sion. Present-day cameras record movement at twenty-four frames per second. That is, in each second, twenty-four separate still pic-tures are photographed. When the film is shown in a projector, these still photographs are "mixed" instantaneously by the human eye, giving the illusion of movement, a phenomenon called "the persist-ence of vision." By simply manipulating the timing mechanism of the camera and/or projector, a film-maker can distort "natural" movement on the screen. Even at the turn of the century, in film's infancy, Méliès was experimenting with various kinds of trick pho-tography, and though most of these experiments were largely gags and clever stunts, subsequent directors have used these discoveries with great artistic results. There are five basic distortions of this kind: **animation, fast motion, slow motion, reverse motion,** and **freeze frames.**

72

There are two fundamental differences between animation film techniques and ordinary movie methods. In animation sequences, each frame is photographed separately rather than "continuously" at the rate of twenty-four frames per second. Another difference is that animation, as the word implies, does not ordinarily involve the photographing of subjects that move by themselves. The subjects photographed are generally drawings, or static objects. Thus, in a feature length animated film, thousands of frames are separately photographed; each frame differs from its neighbor only to an infinitesimal degree. When a sequence of these frames is projected at twenty-four frames per second, the illusion is that the drawings or objects are moving, and hence, are "animated."

The common denominator of both animated and ordinary film procedures is the use of the camera, the photographic process. In a sense, animation has greater affinities with the graphic arts, whereas ordinary films have closer affinities with the legitimate theatre. But in both cases, the recording camera acts as an intermediary between the subject itself and the audience. Even animated films, however, have different emphases. Many of the features of Walt Disney, for instance, are as dramatic as ordinary fiction films. Indeed, a number of parents have considered Disney's *Bambi* too frightening and violent for children. On the other hand, some of the brilliant animated films of the Canadian Norman McLaren and the Yugoslavian "Zagreb School" are virtually abstract expressionist paintings on celluloid. Since most animated films deal with drawings or small objects, the director is able to control his product with considerably more precision than the ordinary film director. The animator is not at the mercy of the weather, the studio sets, the limitations of his actors, and so on. Perhaps for this reason, many experimental film-makers are entering the field of animation; even with 8 mm equipment and a small budget, stunning effects can be achieved in this area.

The relatively few attempts to mix animation and theatrical film techniques within the same frames have not been particularly successful. This mixture is accomplished with the aid of the **optical printer.** Two film strips are superimposed, one consisting of animated frames, the other of photographs of actual people and things. Mattes are used to block out certain areas of the real scene where the animated drawings will appear in the finished print. In Disney's *Song of the South*, this technique was used well in a few sequences, but in general, it tends to become too cute: the reality of one style contradicts the plausibility of the other. On the other hand, more successful have been the few films that have alternated theatrical scenes with animated sequences. Thus, in Tony Richardson's *Charge of the Light Brigade*, for instance, the dramatic scenes leading up to that disastrous military expedition are interspersed with satiric animated sequences, drawn in the style of Victorian political cartoons. **73**

Sequences in fast motion are obtained by photographing events at a slower rate than twenty-four frames per second. Ordinarily, the subject photographed moves at a normal pace. When the sequence is projected at twenty-four frames per second, the effect is one of acceleration, usually comic. Early silent comedies were photographed before the standardization of cameras and projectors to twenty-four frames per second, and so their sense of speed is exaggerated at present-day projector speeds. Even at sixteen or twenty-two frames per second, however, many of these early directors employed fast motion for comic effects. Without the use of fast motion, the great comedies of Mack Sennett, for example, would lose most of their vitality, and the exquisite timing of Keaton and Chaplin would be destroyed.

According to the French esthetician, Henri Bergson, when men act mechanically, rather than flexibly, comedy is often the result. Man, unlike a machine, can think, feel, and act reasonably. When his behavior becomes machinelike, we laugh at him. One aspect of machinelike behavior is speed: when a man's movements are speeded up on film, he seems inhuman, ridiculous. Dignity is impossible in fast motion, for acceleration robs man of his humanity and reduces him to an automatic mechanism that seems wild and out of control. Even when it is used for its own sake, fast motion tends to be funny. In Lester's *A Hard Day's Night*, acceleration is merely one of dozens of visual gags in the film. Other directors use the technique more organically, for thematic purposes for example, or as an aspect of characterization. The hilarious Upton Inn mixup in Richardson's *Tom Jones* is funny precisely because the fast motion captures the machinelike predictability of all the characters: Tom flies from Mrs. Waters' bed, Mr. Fitzpatrick flies off the handle, Squire Western screams for his daughter, and the servants scream for their lives. Fast motion is sometimes used to intensify the natural speed of a scene—one showing galloping horses, for example, or speeding cars.

SLOW MOTION

Slow motion sequences are achieved by photographing events at a faster rate than twenty-four frames per second, and projecting the filmstrip at the standard speed. Slow motion tends to dignify and solemnize movement. Even the most commonplace action takes on a choreographic gracefulness in slow motion. Where speed tends to be the natural rhythm of comedy, slow and deliberate movements **74** tend to be associated with tragedy. In *The Pawnbroker*, Lumet used slow motion in a **flashback** sequence, to show the protagonist as a young man on an idyllic country outing with his family. The scenes are lyric and other-worldly—too perfect to last. Luis Buñuel's *The Young and the Damned* employs this technique in a dream sequence, where the slow motion suggests a kind of hallucinatory elongation of time.

When violent scenes are photographed in slow motion, the effect is paradoxically beautiful. In *The Wild Bunch*, Sam Peckinpah used slow-motion techniques to photograph the grisliest scenes of horror —flesh tearing, blood splattering, horses toppling: an almost endless variety. The "beauty" of these scenes of ugliness suggests why the men are so addicted to a life of violence when it seems so profitless: violence becomes almost an esthetic credo, somewhat in the way that it is portrayed in the fiction of Hemingway. The violent but strangely beautiful ending of Arthur Penn's *Bonnie and Clyde* had a similar paradoxical quality: the concluding "dance" of death is a kind of preordained pattern or destiny for the protagonists.

REVERSE MOTION AND FREEZE FRAMES

Reverse motion simply involves photographing an action with the film running reversed. When projected on the screen, the sequences of events run "backward." Since Méliès' time, reverse motion has not progressed much beyond the gag stage. Lester is fond of using this technique for absurd effects. In *A Hard Day's Night* he uses reverse motion as a comic choreographic "retake," in *The Knack*, as a quick shock laugh, when an egg "returns" to its shell. Chaplin occasionally used reverse motion to suggest the almost instantaneous correction of a blunder.

A freeze frame suspends all movement on the screen. A single image is selected and reprinted for as many frames as is necessary to suggest the "freezing" of motion. By interrupting a sequence with a freeze shot, the director calls attention to an image, offering it, as it were, for the audience's delectation. Sometimes the image is a fleeting moment of poignance, which is over in a fraction of a second, as in the final shot of Truffaut's *The 400 Blows*, for example. Directors also use freeze frames for comic purposes. In *Tom Jones*, Richardson freezes the shot of Tom dangling on a rope's end, while the narrator urbanely explains to the audience why Tom should not hang.

In other instances, the freeze frame can be used for thematic purposes. The final image of Richardson's *The Loneliness of the Long Distance Runner* is frozen to emphasize the permanence of the protagonist's status at the end of the picture. Jack Clayton used

75

freeze shots in *The Pumpkin Eater* to suggest the solidification of the heroine's psychological disorder. Clayton also employs freeze shots as transitions between flashback sequences, where the technique suggests the unalterable past.

Most of the mechanical distortions mentioned above were discovered by Méliès. For many years after, they were largely ignored by the majority of commercial film-makers, until the late 1950s, when the **new wave** directors in France reintroduced them. Since the early 1960s, many of these techniques have been used indiscriminately. Zooms, freeze frames, and slow motion sequences have become almost *de rigeur* since that time. In many cases, the techniques degenerated into clichés, modish flourishes which were tacked on or zapped into the materials, regardless of whether the techniques were organic to the spirit of the subject.

Movement in film, then, is not simply a matter of "what happens." The director has dozens of ways to convey motion, and what differentiates a great director from a merely competent or poor one is not so much a matter of what happens, but how things happen—how suggestive and resonant are the movements in a given dramatic context? Or, how effectively does the form of movement embody its content? The competent director will merely put his actors through their paces, and film the action as economically, efficiently, and stylishly as possible. To the great director, economy, efficiency, and style are artistic ideals, not merely commercial ones—though of course, the two need not necessarily be in conflict.

Further Reading

Davis, James E. "The Only Dynamic Art," in *Introduction to the Art of the Movies.* Edited by Lewis Jacobs. New York: The Noonday Press, 1960. (Paper)

Deren, Maya. "Cinematography: The Creative Use of Reality," in *The Visual Arts Today.* Edited by Gyorgy Kepes. Middletown, Conn.: Wesleyan University Press, 1960.

Feldman, Joseph and Harry. *Dynamics of Film.* New York: Hermitage House, 1952.

Halas, John, and Roger Manvell. *Design in Motion.* New York: Focal Press, 1962.

Jacobs, Lewis, et al. "Movement," in *The Movies as Medium.* Edited by Lewis Jacobs. New York: Farrar, Straus, & Giroux, 1970. (Paper)

Knight, Arthur. "The Street Films: Murnau and the Moving Camera," in *The Liveliest Art.* New York: A Mentor Book, 1957. (Paper)

Lindsay, Vachel. *The Art of the Moving Picture.* New York: Liveright, 1970. (Paper)

Montagu, Ivor. "Film as Science," in *Film World*. Baltimore: Penguin Books, 1964. (Paper)

Stephenson, Ralph. *Animation in the Cinema*. New York: A. S. Barnes, 1967. (Paper)

Stephenson, Ralph, and Jean R. Debrix. "Space in the Cinema: Cutting, Camera Movement, Framing," in *The Cinema as Art*. Baltimore: Penguin Books, 1965. (Paper)

eDITING

The foundation of film art is editing.
V. I. PUDOVKIN

Physically, **editing** is simply joining one strip of film (shot) with another. Shots are joined into **scenes,** and scenes into **sequences.** On the most mechanical level, editing eliminates unnecessary time and space. Through the association of ideas, editing connects one shot with another, one scene with another, and so on. Simple as this may now seem, the convention of editing represents the first (and perhaps major) cornerstone of film art. Indeed, Terry Ramsaye, an early film critic, referred to editing as the "syntax" of cinema, its grammatical language. Like linguistic grammar, the syntax of editing must be learned—we do not possess it innately.

In only seventy short years, editing has evolved into an art of remarkable complexity, nearly each decade providing new variations and possibilities. Before the turn of the century, most movies consisted of short anecdotes, photographed in **long shot** in one **take.** When the film stock was nearly exhausted, the vignette would be quickly concluded. The duration of the shot and the scene were equal. Essentially, these early movies were little more than stage playlets on film: the camera was stationary; the actors remained in long shot; the scene ran continuously, with screen time and real time roughly the same. For example, the central idea of one early film involves a man throwing a party for several girls. The man and the girls display a number of comic "bits"—flirtations, drinks being spilled, etc. Then the vignette ends with the entire cast boisterously leaving the set.

After 1900, film-makers grew more ambitious. In France, England, and America, crude narratives made their first appearance. No longer merely vignettes, but "stories," these movies required more than one set, and more than one continuous shot. The problem was **continuity.** Odd as it may now seem to us, the film-makers of this period were worried that audiences would not see the relationship between one segment (shot) of the stories and another. To solve their problem, they may have turned to the legitimate theatre for help. Here, the curtain was an accepted **convention,** implying a transition in time and/or space. The curtain, in effect, connected the various scenes and acts to make a coherent whole. The **fade** was to film what the curtain was to drama. Quite simply, what a fade involved was the diminishing of light at the conclusion of a scene until the screen went black; the next scene would then fade in, often revealing a different location at a different time. Usually, the two scenes were unified by the presence of the same actor. As early as 1899, the Frenchman, George Méliès made a short movie, *Cinderella*, in twenty "arranged scenes."

Before long, directors began cutting within scenes as well as between scenes. The American, Edwin S. Porter, is usually credited with this innovation, though in fact, as early as 1900, the Englishman G. A. Smith inserted a **close-up** within a scene, and his countryman, James Williamson, featured an intercut chase sequence within one of his movies. These innovations were largely ignored, however, until Porter arrived at them independently somewhat later. Porter's *The Life of an American Fireman* (1902–3) pushed the concept of editing a step further. A simple story of a fireman's heroic rescue of a woman and her child, Porter's film contained seven scenes, the last of which featured three different shots: the firetruck arriving at the burning building; an interior shot of a woman and her child trapped in the burning building; and an exterior shot of the fireman carrying the woman down the ladder. (The last action was repeated in the rescue of the child.)

Traditionally, scene seven would have been filmed in long shot, showing the entire action in one continuous take. By breaking up the scene into three different shots, Porter established the shot, and not the scene as the basic unit of film construction. This new editing concept also introduced to film the idea of shifting points of view. Until that time, most movies were filmed in stationary long shot— roughly the same position that an actual observer would take. The duration of a scene would approximately correspond to that of the actual event. But with the breakup of shots into both exterior and interior positions, the "observer" is, in effect, at both places at once. Furthermore, since the time that elapses is not dependent upon the duration of the scene, a new subjective time is introduced, one dependent upon the duration of the various shots, not the actual event. **82**

The American, D. W. Griffith, has been called the father of film, not only because he consolidated and expanded earlier cinematic techniques (in addition to devising many new ones as well), but because he was the first to go beyond mere gimmickry into the realm of art. One of cinema's greatest creative geniuses, Griffith established, more than any other film maker in history, the basic language of film art. His masterpiece, *Birth of a Nation* (1915), is a virtual encyclopedia of cinematic techniques. Griffith recognized the principle of the association of ideas in the concept of editing and expanded this principle in a variety of ways. Like his predecessors, he edited to change locales, and to eliminate unnecessary time and space. He also edited for emphasis and dramatic intensity, however, and this was a major contribution.

Through the use of the close-up within the scene, Griffith managed to achieve a dramatic impact that was unprecedented in its time. Though close-ups had been used prior to this time, Griffith was the first to use a close shot for psychological rather than physical reasons. Audiences were now permitted to see the smallest details of an actor's face: no longer were the performers required to flail their arms and tear their hair. The slightest arch of an eyebrow could convey a multitude of subtle emotions. By splitting the action into a series of fragmentary shots, Griffith achieved not only a greater sense of detail, but a far greater degree of control over his audience's reactions. In carefully selecting and juxtaposing long, **medium,** and close shots, he constantly shifted the audience's point of view within the scene, excluding here, emphasizing there, consolidating, connecting, contrasting, paralleling, and so on. The possibilities were enormously far ranging. Thus, the spatial and temporal continuum of the real scene was radically altered, and replaced by a substitute continuity —the association of ideas implicit in the connected shots.

Griffith became particularly famous for his chase and rescue sequences which often ended his films. Most of these sequences featured **parallel editing**—or the alternation of shots of one scene with another, at a different location, and sometimes in a different period of time. By **cross-cutting** back and forth between the two (or three or four) scenes, Griffith conveyed the idea of simultaneous time. For example, near the end of *Birth of a Nation*, Griffith cross-cuts between four groups: a besieged group of white people trapped in a cabin, a group of white vigilantes racing to their rescue, rioting Negroes on the rampage, and the heroine being forced into an undesired marriage. In juxtaposing shots from these four scenes, Griffith managed to intensify the suspense by reducing the duration of the shots as the sequence peaked to its climax. Thus, though the sequence itself lasts twenty minutes of film time, the psychological effect of the cross-cutting (Griffith used 255 cuts, averaging five seconds each) suggests speed and tension. Generally speaking, the greater the number of cuts within a scene, the greater the sense of speed it conveys. To avoid the risk of monotony during this sequence, Griffith changed his **set-ups** (camera positions) many times: there are **extreme long,** long, medium, and close shots, varied angles, light contrasts, even a moving camera. (It was mounted on a truck.)

In his next film, *Intolerance* (1916), Griffith explored cross-cutting even further. The movie is unified by the theme of man's inhumanity to man. Rather than tell just one story, Griffith presents four different examples of intolerance: one takes place in ancient Babylon; the second deals with the crucifixion of Jesus; the third with the massacre of the Huguenots in seventeeth-century France; and the last takes place in contemporary America. The stories are not developed separately, but in parallel fashion—with scenes of one time period intercut with scenes of another. At the conclusion of the movie, Griffith features hair-breadth chase sequences in the first and last stories, a suspenseful and brutal scene of slaughter in the third, and a slow-moving tragic climax in the story of Jesus. The last sequence of the movie contains literally hundreds of shots, juxtaposing images which are historically separated by thousands of years, and geographically by as many miles—all unified by the central theme of intolerance. To this day, the film is one of the most dazzling displays of virtuosity in editing.

From its crude beginnings, Griffith expanded editing techniques to include a wide variety of functions: locale changes, time lapses, shot variety, emphasis of details, overviews, symbolic inserts, parallels and contrasts, associations, point-of-view shifts, simultaneity, and repetition of motifs. Furthermore, Griffith's method of editing was more economical, since related shots could be bunched together in the shooting schedule, regardless of their positions (or "time" and "place") in the finished film. Especially later, in the days of high-salaried stars, directors could film all of the star shots in a short period and out of sequence, leaving details (extreme long shots, close-ups of objects, other actors, etc.) to be shot at a more convenient time. Later, all the shots would be arranged in their proper sequence on the editor's cutting bench.

TIME AND SPACE

Since Griffith's editing practices were so complex, new problems arose, especially concerning time and space. The continuity of real space, of course, became fragmented and was replaced by the various shots, many of them medium and close shots. But unless the audience has a clear *sense* of space, a scene could be confusing. (Thus, the term **"jump cut"** means an editing transition that is confusing or disorienting in terms of time or place.) In order to make **84**

his transitions smooth and continuous, Griffith carefully **established**
his scenes in long shot at the beginning. Gradually he cut to medium shots, and then to close-ups. During the scene, he would cut to **"reestablishing"** shots (a return to the initial long shot) in order to remind the audience of the context of the closer shots. Until recently, this has been the editing pattern of most film sequences.

The problem of time was more difficult to solve, since its treatment in film was more subjective than the treatment of space. Movies can compress years into two film hours; conversely, films can also extend a few split seconds of time into many minutes. Generally speaking, days and years of real time are compressed into hours of screen time. There are only a handful of films that attempt to make screen time conform to real time: Agnes Varda's *Cleo from Five to Seven* and Fred Zinnemann's *High Noon* are perhaps the best known examples. Even these films cheat by compressing time in the expository opening sequences and by expanding time in the tense climactic scenes. In actual practice, time exists in a kind of limbo: so long as the audience is absorbed by the screen action, time is what the film says it is. The problem, then, is to absorb the audience.

On the most mechanical level, screen time is determined by the physical length of the filmstrip that contains the shot. This length is governed by the complexity of the image content. Raymond Spottiswoode, an early film theorist, claimed that a cut must be made at the peak of the **content curve,** that is, that point in the shot that the audience has been able to assimilate most of its meanings. Cutting before the content curve frustrates the audience's assimilation of meanings; cutting after the curve produces boredom and a sense of dragging time. Obviously, a visually complex image requires more time to assimilate than a simple one. Once any image has been established, however, a return to it during the sequence can be considerably shorter, since it works, in effect, as a reminder.

But the sensitive treatment of time in film is largely an instinctive matter, one that defies mechanical rules. Indeed, most of the great directors have edited their own films, or at least have worked in close collaboration with their editors, so crucial is this art to the success of a film. Like most great directors, Griffith had an almost unfailing sense of rhythm, and rhythm, or "pace" is what makes time in film convincing. The best edited sequences are determined by mood as well as by content. Griffith, for example, generally edited love scenes in long lyrical takes, with relatively few set-ups. His chase sequences and scenes of confusion, on the other hand, were composed of many rapid shots, jammed together. Paradoxically, the love scenes actually compressed real time, whereas the rapidly cut sequences were elongations.

There are no fixed rules concerning rhythm in films. Some editors, like Margaret Booth, cut according to musical rhythms—the march of soldiers, for example, would be edited to the beat of a military tune. This technique is also popular with many American **under-** **85**

ground film-makers, who feature rock music sound tracks. In some instances, a director will cut before the peak of the content curve. Particularly in highly suspenseful sequences, a director like Alfred Hitchcock will tease the audience by not providing enough time to assimilate all of the meanings of a shot. On the other hand, Antonioni, in many of his films, cuts long after the content curve has peaked. In *La Notte*, for example, the rhythm is languorous and even monotonous: the director attempts to create a sense of boredom and weariness in the audience—a sense of monotony that directly parallels that of the protagonists. Violent scenes are usually cut in a highly fragmented manner, but in Arthur Penn's *Bonnie and Clyde*, the exciting shoot-em-up escape sequence is photographed in long shot, with only a few cuts: this combination is what produces the scene's bizarre blend of comedy and audacity.

Sidney Lumet's *The Pawnbroker* features a kind of subliminal editing, where some shots are held on the screen for only a fraction of a second. Once again, the content and mood determine the rhythm: the central character, a Jew who has survived a Nazi concentration camp but has lost all of his loved ones, is desperately trying to repress the memories of his experiences, but the memories insistently force their way into his consciousness. Lumet suggests this psychological process by intercutting a few **frames** of the memory shots during a scene which is occurring in the present. As the past contends with the present, the flickering memory shots gradually become longer in duration, until a **flashback** sequence eventually becomes dominant, and the present is momentarily suspended. With only a few exceptions, however, it was not until the late 1950s that such unorthodox editing practices became widespread. Griffith seldom cut before the peak of the content curve, and most of his successors patterned themselves on his model.

Another manipulation of time introduced by Griffith is the flashback. In *Birth of a Nation*, he inserted "memory" shots that temporarily suspend the present. He thus established the concept of tense in the cinema—permitting future directors to interrupt the present by inserts not only of the past, but of the future as well. In Dennis Hopper's *Easy Rider*, for example, the hero (Peter Fonda) has a kind of prophetic vision of his own death. In Sydney Pollack's *They Shoot Horses Don't They?*, short **flash-forwards** of a courtroom scene are interspersed throughout the present-tense story. The flash-forwards suggest a kind of hostile determinism: like the dance contest of the story proper, the future is rigged, and personal effort is equated with self-deception.

One of the most technically complicated uses of the flashback is found in Stanley Donen's *Two for the Road*. The story of the development and gradual disintegration of a love relationship, the narrative unfolds in a series of mixed flashbacks. That is, the flashbacks are not in chronological sequence, nor are they completed in any one scene. Rather, the flashbacks are jumbled and fragmented, somewhat **86** in the manner of a Faulkner novel. To complicate matters, most of the flashbacks take place on the road, during various trips the couple has taken in the past. If each of the time periods of the film were to be designated with the letters A, B, C, D, and E, its temporal structure might be charted as follows: E (present), A (most distant past), B, C, D, B, A, C, D, B . . . ending with E. The audience gradually learns to identify each time period through various clues: the girl's hair styles, the modes of transportation, the particular crisis during each trip, and so on. In short, like Faulkner and other novelists, film-makers have attempted to crack the tyranny of mechanically measured time through the manipulation of the flashback. This technique permits an artist to develop ideas thematically rather than chronologically, and allows him to stress the subjective nature of time. In a film like Alain Resnais' *Last Year at Marienbad*, tenses are so scrambled that it becomes virtually impossible to make temporal discriminations— one of Resnais' major themes. The very flexibility of time in film makes the theme of temporality an ideal subject for the medium.

Griffith also modified time through the use of fantasy inserts. In *Intolerance*, for example, a young girl on the verge of murdering her unfaithful boyfriend imagines a scene where she is apprehended by a policeman. One of the most interesting uses of fantasy is found in Federico Fellini's *8½*. A brilliant exploration of the frustrations of the creative process, the movie centers around a film director's futile attempts to incorporate autobiographical materials in a movie he is trying to put together. The past is freely jumbled with the present, terrifying nightmares with extravagantly hedonistic day dreams, fantasy with reality, until the director (and the audience) is utterly incapable of distinguishing between them. All of these materials are "real," at least for the hero (Marcello Mastroianni), and therefore cannot be excluded or simplified in any true rendering of the artistic process. Neither an artist nor an audience can superimpose a simplistic order on what is intrinsically diffuse, contradictory, and infinitely complex.

Many pages would be required to catalogue all of Griffith's contributions to film art, but his greatest achievement lies unquestionably in his creation of a sophisticated and subtle cinematic language— the art of editing.

V. I. PUDOVKIN

Griffith was a practical artist, concerned with communicating ideas and emotions in the most effective manner possible. During the 1920s, the Soviet film-makers expanded his practices, and provided a theoretical foundation for the concept of editing, or "montage," as they called it (from the French, *monter*, to assemble.) The Russians **87** were concerned with providing an elaborate political and esthetic theory for "their" art, for Lenin saw at once the tremendous propaganda possibilities of film in a newly emerging nation, composed primarily of illiterate citizens. V. I. Pudovkin wrote the first important theoretical treatises on what he called "constructive editing." Most of his statements are explanations of Griffith's practices, but he differed with Griffith (whom he praises lavishly) on several important points.

Griffith's use of the close-up, Pudovkin claimed, was too limited: it was used simply as a clarification of the long shot, which carried most of the meaning. The close-up, in effect, was merely an interruption, offering no meanings of its own. Pudovkin insisted that each new shot must make a new point. By the juxtaposition of a series of shots, new meanings emerge. The meanings, then, are in the juxtapositions, not in one shot alone. To illustrate his point, Pudovkin quotes from the experiments of Kuleshov, his teacher and colleague. Kuleshov's experiments are now considered classics. The most impressive, and most widely known, consists of a series of juxtapositions. First, he shot a close-up of an actor with a neutral expression. He juxtaposed this with a close-up of a bowl of soup. Then he repeated the close-up of the actor, and joined it with a shot of a coffin containing a woman's corpse. Finally, he used the same actor's close-up and linked it with a shot of a little girl playing. When these combinations were shown to audiences, they exclaimed at the actor's extraordinary expressiveness in portraying pensiveness, deep sorrow, and happiness, respectively. Pudovkin's point carried. In each of the three cases, the meaning was expressed by the juxtaposition of two shots, not by the shots themselves. (Kuleshov's experiments also help to explain why film actors need not necessarily be skillful performers: in large part, they can be used as objects, juxtaposed with other objects. The emotion is in the juxtaposition, not in the actor's performance. See Chapter 5, "Drama.")

For Pudovkin, a sequence was not merely filmed, it was meticulously *constructed*. Using far more close-ups than Griffith, Pudovkin built a scene from many separate shots, all juxtaposed for one unified effect. The environment of the scene was the major source of the images, though long shots were rare. Instead, a steady series of close-ups—often of objects—provides the audience with the necessary associations to link together the overall meaning. These juxtapositions can suggest emotional and psychological states, and even abstract ideas. The effectiveness of Pudovkin's films, especially his masterpiece, *Mother*, seems to justify his theory as a major approach to film art, though perhaps none of the great Russian films of the 1920s can justify Pudovkin's rather dogmatic assertion quoted at the beginning of this chapter.

Pudovkin, and the Russian theorists in general, have been attacked on several counts. Some critics feel that the extensive use of close-ups not only clogs the pace of a film (Pudovkin's films move notoriously slowly, despite the many cuts), but also detracts from a scene's sense of **realism,** for the space-time continuum is almost totally re-arranged. But Pudovkin would claim that realism which is captured in long shot is *too* near reality. Indeed, his main criticism of Griffith was directed at his "slavish" adherence to real time and space. According to Pudovkin, the film artist must capture the essence, not merely the surface of reality, and he can do so only by conveying *expressively*—through juxtaposed close-up of objects, textures, symbols, etc.—what is an undifferentiated jumble in real life.

Similarly, some critics feel that Pudovkin and his colleagues guide the spectator too much—the choices are already made. The audience can only sit back passively, and accept the inevitable linking of associations presented to them on the screen. Political considerations are involved here, for the Russians tended to link film with propaganda, and propaganda, no matter how artistic, usually does not involve free and balanced evaluations. Anti-Russian film theorists, on the other hand, feel that an audience should not be passive, but should actively select and evaluate many of the relevant details on its own.

SERGEI EISENSTEIN

Eisenstein, another Russian theorist, and perhaps the greatest of their film-makers, believed that Pudovkin did not pursue fully the implications of editing. Like Pudovkin, he thought that each shot of a sequence ought to be incomplete, or "contributory," not self-contained. However, he criticized Pudovkin's concept of "linked" shots for being too mechanical. Eisenstein believed that editing was the cinematic equivalent of the Marxist dialectic. The conflict of two shots (thesis and antithesis) produced a wholly new idea (synthesis). Thus, in film terms, the result of a conflict between shot A and shot B is not AB (Pudovkin), but a *qualitatively* new factor, C (Eisenstein). Furthermore, transitions between shots should not be flowing, as Pudovkin suggested, but sharp, jolting, even violent. For Eisenstein, editing produces harsh "collisions," not smooth linkages. A smooth transition, he claimed, was an opportunity lost.

Editing, for Eisenstein, was an almost mystical process. He likened it to the growth of organic cells. If each shot represents a developing cell, the cut is that "explosion" which occurs when the cell splits into two. Editing is that stage when a shot "bursts"—that is, when the tensions of the shot have reached their maximum expansion. The rhythm of editing in a film should be like the explosions of an internal combustion engine, Eisenstein claimed. A great master of rhythm, his films are almost mesmerizing in this respect: shots of contrasting volumes, durations, shapes, designs, and lighting intensi- **89** ties do, indeed, collide against each other; but like objects in a torrential river, the jolting images plunge toward an inevitable destination.

The theoretical differences between Pudovkin and Eisenstein may appear to be merely academic. In actual practice, however, the two approaches produced sharply contrasting results. In Pudovkin's films, the shots tend to be additive, and they are directed toward an overall emotional effect. In Eisenstein's movies, the contrasting shots represent a series of intellectual thrusts and parries, directed toward a predominantly abstract argument. The directors' choice of narrative structures also differed. Though both artists were didactic propagandists, Pudovkin's stories did not differ radically from the kind Griffith used: the shots are determined by the context of the narrative. On the other hand, Eisenstein's stories were much more loosely structured, usually a series of semiconnected documentary episodes, which he exploited as convenient vehicles for exploring ideas and abstractions.

When Pudovkin wanted to express an emotion, he conveyed it in terms of physical images—objective correlatives—that were present in the actual locale. Thus, for example, the sense of anguished drudgery is conveyed through a series of shots showing details of a cart mired in the mud: close-ups of the wheel, the mud, hands coaxing the wheel, straining faces, the muscles of an arm pulling the wheel, and so on. Eisenstein, on the other hand, wanted film to be totally free. Pudovkin's correlatives, he felt, were too restricted by reality. Eisenstein wanted film to be as flexible as literature, particularly in its freedom to draw metaphors without respect to time and place. Film should include images that are *thematically* relevant, Eisenstein felt, regardless of whether they can be found in the locale or not. Thus, in Eisenstein's earlier films, the space-time continuum is totally destroyed, and replaced by a continuity completely dependent upon the intellectual arguments of the director.

Even in his first feature, *Strike* (1925), Eisenstein intercuts shots of workmen being machine-gunned with images of oxen being slaughtered. A very famous sequence from *Potemkin* shows three shots of stone lions, one asleep, a second aroused and on the verge of rising, and a third on its feet and ready to spring. Eisenstein considered the sequence an embodiment of a metaphor: "The very stones roar." His most radical experiments are found in *October* (also known as *Ten Days That Shook the World*). A loose documentary dealing with the earliest phases of the 1917 Revolution, the film is a perfect illustration of Eisenstein's theories in practice. An early sequence shows a statue of the czar being destroyed. Later, when Kerensky takes control, Eisenstein metaphorically describes this setback by running the statue sequence in **reverse motion.** The statue is reconstructed before our very eyes, and we thus "see" the temporary return of czarism. Many shots of Kerensky in the Winter Palace are similarly satiric: shots of Kerensky are juxtaposed with bejeweled toy peacocks, with statues of Napoleon, etc.

Brilliant as many of these scenes are, the major problem with this kind of metaphoric editing is its tendency to be obscure. Eisenstein saw no real difficulty in overcoming the spatial and temporal differences between film and literature. But the two media employ metaphors and similes in rather different ways. (See Chapter 6, "Literature.") Thus, we have no difficulty in understanding what is meant by the simile, "he's timid as a sheep." Or even the more obscure metaphor, "whorish time undoes us all." Both statements exist outside of time and place. The simile is not set in a pasture, nor is the metaphor set in a brothel. Such comparisons, of course, are not intended to be understood literally. In film, figurative devices of this kind are more difficult. Chaplin was able to express the sheep simile in the opening of *Modern Times*, but the metaphor of "whorish time" would probably be impossible to capture in film, for the materials of cinema are concrete objects. A **montage** sequence of trees in different seasons juxtaposed with images of prostitutes might be a cinematic equivalent of this metaphor, but it is doubtful if an audience would be able to decipher the comparison. The fact of the matter is that editing can produce fairly simple metaphoric comparisons, but the most expressive figurative techniques in cinema are not generally achieved through edited juxtapositions.

Eisenstein's editing theories and practices represent the most radical extreme in terms of distorting real time and space. Indeed, some of his techniques have been only recently revived. For years they remained cinematic curiosities. Even in his own day, Eisenstein was accused by hostile critics of depriving the film of its "realistic integrity." A whole counter-tradition of realistic techniques, popularized by several American directors, was brought forward by these critics as preferable alternatives to Eisenstein's **expressionistic** practices—as though film were not broad enough to accommodate more than one style.

THE REALISTIC TRADITION

Concurrent with Eisenstein, Pudovkin, and the later Griffith, directors in Germany and America were producing films that owed relatively little to the concept of editing. In Germany, G. W. Pabst developed his technique of "invisible editing," which involved cutting from one shot to another only with some physical movement of an actor. Thus, for example, a shot of an actor rising from his chair would be joined unobtrusively with another shot of the actor standing and then walking away. The Germans also took the camera off its tripod and mounted it on vehicles, thus permitting it to move in and out of a scene without the necessity of a cut. In America, three brilliant directors—Charles Chaplin, Robert Flaherty, and Erich von Stroheim—

were championed for their honesty and realism. All of them preferred long shots, very few set-ups, a stationary camera, a minimal use of close-ups, and all of them had a decided preference for showing men and their environment within the same shot. In short, all of them "respected" what André Bazin (a prominent realist critic) called "the unity of time and place."

SOUND

Expressionistic techniques of editing were altered not by the critics, however, but by technology. In the late 1920s, the first in a long series of mechanical advancements—sound—eclipsed, at least temporarily, virtually all of the advances made in the art of editing since Porter's day. With the coming of sound, films had to be more realistic, whether their directors wished them so or not, for the microphones were placed on the set itself. Sound was recorded while the scene was being photographed. Usually the microphones were hidden— in a vase of flowers, a wall sconce, etc. Thus, in the earliest sound films, not only was the camera restricted, but the actors as well, for if they strayed too far from the microphone, the dialogue could not be properly recorded.

The effects on editing of these early sound films were disastrous: synchronized sound anchored the images, so whole scenes were played with no cuts. Virtually all of the dramatic values were aural. The most commonplace sequences held a fascination for audiences: thus, if someone entered a room, the camera recorded the fact, whether it was dramatically important or not, and millions of viewers thrilled to the sound of the door opening and slamming shut. Critics and directors despaired: the days of the recorded stage play had apparently returned. (Later, these problems were solved by the invention of the "blimp," a soundproof camera housing which permits the camera to move with relative ease, and by the practice of **dubbing** sound after the shooting is completed.)

But sound also presented some distinct advantages. In realistic films especially, spoken dialogue and sound effects heightened the sense of realism considerably. Acting styles had to be more sophisticated: no longer did they have to exaggerate visually to compensate for the absence of sound. Talkies also permitted directors to tell their stories more economically, without the titles that interfered with the visuals in the silent days. The tedious exposition scenes that began most movies could also be dispensed with, for a few lines of dialogue easily conveyed any necessary information an audience would need to understand the narrative relationships.

92

The use of **deep-focus** photography, reintroduced in the late 1930s, also exerted a modifying influence on editing practices. Prior to this time, most cameras photographed only one distance range clearly. These cameras could capture a sharp image of an object from virtually any range, but other elements of the picture that were not at the same distance from the camera remained blurred, out of focus. One justification for editing was purely technical then: clarity of image. If all shots—long, medium, and close—were to be equally clear, different lens adjustments were required for each.

Two American directors, Orson Welles and William Wyler, were especially associated with deep-focus photography, and it is not coincidental perhaps, that both these men had connections with the legitimate theatre. The esthetic qualities of this process was to permit composition in depth: whole scenes could be shot in one set-up, with no sacrifice of detail, for every distance appeared with equal clarity on the screen (Fig. 1). More theatrical perhaps than cinematic, deep focus tended to be most effective when it adhered to the real time-space continuum. The dramatic effects are achieved primarily through the *mise-en-scène* or the spatial and temporal relationships within the frame) rather than through the fragmented juxtaposition of shots (Fig. 25). Some of the most effective films to use this device were Wyler's adaptations of plays—especially *The Little Foxes, The Heiress*, and *The Children's Hour*. In all these movies, Wyler tried to preserve the integrity of the dialogue sequences, without subverting his visuals, or by using them merely as illustrations of the text. Similarly, Welles, who was actually trained in the theatre, has spent much of his film career adapting plays, including two brilliant adaptations of Shakespeare: *Othello* and *Falstaff*. His 1941 masterpiece, *Citizen Kane*, was a landmark work for many reasons, but deep-focus photography was among the most important of them.

The realist critics, particularly, embraced deep-focus techniques, for inevitably, the importance of editing was thereby reduced. In-depth photography, they saw, preserved the unity of real time and space, since whole scenes could be photographed in a "mixed" shot —incorporating long, medium and close distances in one frame. Two, three, even four or five different spatial planes could be captured simultaneously. Furthermore, as Welles triumphantly demonstrated in *Citizen Kane*, the important relationship between people and their physical environment could be enhanced through the use of this technique; no longer was their interdependence fragmented by edited close-ups.

This persistent demand for "unified" space on the part of realist critics strike many people as arbitrary. But an intelligent realist critic like André Bazin was not hostile to expressionistic editing on prin-   **93**

FIGURE 53. *La Chinoise*
Directed by Jean-Luc Godard.

To emphasize fragmentation and separateness, most directors will employ
the art of editing—cutting from shot to shot. Occasionally, however,
a director will exploit the composition to achieve these ends.
Here, Godard uses the dividing wall to foreshadow the split which will soon
develop among the young people in a Maoist cell.

ciple, only when it worked against the nature of the subject. For
example, *Citizen Kane* contains some of the most dazzling edited
sequences in film history, and Bazin expressed great admiration for
these scenes. Editing emphasizes fragmentation and separateness.
In general, the realist does not disapprove of editing when it is used
to emphasize these qualities, though they can be conveyed within
the frame more effectively in some instances (Fig. 53). When the
interrelationships between two or more subjects are the emphasis
of a scene, realist directors would tend to avoid editing. For instance,
many science fiction films deal with a huge monster attacking a city.
To photograph the monster in separate edited shots would not be
nearly so frightening and real as to "imprison" the monster, city, and
inhabitants in one frame (Fig. 54). The essence of the shot is the
terror that the monster inspires in the city dwellers, and this relationship is best captured by photographing them together. One of the
most common methods of achieving this unity is to exploit the re-
sources of deep-focus photography.

   Realist critics also liked the objectivity of deep focus. Disregarding for the moment the emphatic elements of composition and
movement, details within a shot could be presented more "demo-   **94**

cratically," as it were, without the special attention that a close-up inevitably confers. Thus, realistic critics felt that audiences would be forced to be more creative—less passive—in understanding the relationships between people and things. Realistic theorists also liked the ambiguity of deep-focus films: audiences are not led by the nose to an inevitable conclusion—à la Eisenstein—but are forced to evaluate, sort out, and eliminate "irrelevancies" on their own. In short, these films are much closer to the selective processes of life as it is actually experienced, and hence, are more "realistic."

FIGURE 54

For many years, film theory was dominated by the Russian expressionists of the twenties. The art of the film, according to Pudovkin and Eisenstein, was the art of "montage," or editing. But other theorists, led by André Bazin, insisted that editing is based on an esthetic of fragmentation and disunity. Bazin pointed out that certain scenes are enhanced by keeping all the relevant elements in one frame. In the illustrations above, the fragmented images work against the sense of entrapment which is the essence of the scene. When the monster, city, and victims are all imprisoned within the same frame, the effect is more powerful than when their interrelationships are separated into individual shots. The same principle applies in less sensational scenes, where the interrelationships are more subtle (Fig. 25). Bazin and other realist critics claim that the *mise-en-scène* of such integrated shots must necessarily be more complex than in fragmented shots, in which the director need be concerned with only one element at a time.

NEOREALISM

Shortly after World War II, a movement called **neorealism** sprang up in Italy, and gradually influenced all film producing nations. The technical and philosophical implications of neorealism are discussed in the last chapter, "Theory," but it ought to be noted in passing that the movement tended to be hostile to expressionistic theories of editing. Like the American directors who favored deep focus, such Italian directors as Roberto Rossellini, Vittorio de Sica, and the early Federico Fellini, favored long or deep-focus shots, lengthy takes, and a minimal use of the cut and the close-up. The combination of deep-focus and neorealism seemed to push Eisenstein's theories even further to the background, for many of the best films of the 1940s and 50s relegated editing to relatively minor functions.

CINEMASCOPE

By the early 1950s, television was luring many moviegoers away from the theatres, and in response, Hollywood tried a series of technical innovations to entice them back. Most of them never did return, at least not habitually, despite the hoopla about 3-D, Cinerama, and CinemaScope. However, an important side effect of this economic struggle was the popularization of the new wider screen. The aspect ratio of most screens before this time was roughly 3 by 4. The new screens came in a variety of widths, ranging from 1 by 1.65 to 1 by 2.5.Wide screen has now settled to a rough ratio of 3 by 5. Like many technological innovations in film, CinemaScope provoked a wail of protest from most critics and some directors. The new screen shape would destroy the close-up, many feared, especially of the human face. There simply was too much space to fill, even in long shots, others complained. Audiences would never be able to comprehend all the action, for they would not know where to look. It was suitable only for horizontal compositions, some argued, useful for **epic** films, but incongruous for interior shots and "small" subjects. One wag claimed it was useful only for photographing funeral processions and snakes. Editing would be further minimized, the expressionists complained, for there would be no necessity to cut to something if everything was already there, arranged in a long horizontal series.

At first, the most effective wide-screen films were, in fact, westerns and historical extravaganzas. Furthermore, some movies, like George Stevens' *Diary of Anne Frank*, were disasters precisely because the director's use of wide screen seemed completely at odds with the claustrophobic mood of the story. But before long, a few directors began to use CinemaScope with more sensitivity. Like   **96** deep-focus photography, wide screen meant that directors had to be more careful in their *mise-en-scène* (Fig. 16). More relevant details had to be included within the frame, but this necessity also meant that films could be more densely saturated, and, potentially, more artistically effective. Furthermore, directors discovered that the most expressive parts of a person's face were his eyes and mouth, and consequently, close-ups that chopped off the tops and bottoms of actors' faces were not so disastrous as had been previously predicted.

Not surprisingly, the realistic critics were the first to reconsider the advantages of wide screen. Bazin liked its "authenticity" and "objectivity." Here was one step further from the "distorting" effects of editing, he pointed out: as with deep focus, CinemaScope helped to preserve "scenic unity." Close-up images containing two or more people could now be photographed in one set-up, without suggesting inequality, as deep focus often did in its variety of depth planes (Fig. 25); nor were the relations between people and things fragmented as they often were with edited sequences. Scope was also more realistic because its wide screen immersed the viewer in a *sense* of an experience, suggesting a kind of cinematic counterpart to the eye's peripheral vision (Fig. 55). All of the same advantages that had been applied to sound and deep focus were now applied to wide screen: its greater fidelity to real time and space; its detail, complexity, and density; its more objective presentation; its more coherent continuity; and its encouragement of creative audience "participation."

FIGURE 55. *Zabriskie Point*
Directed by Michelangelo Antonioni.

Realist directors and critics were among the first to champion CinemaScope, for they recognized that with the additional screen area, the *mise-en-scène* could be more densely saturated: space was less fragmented than in conventionally sized screens, or in edited sequences. Here, Antonioni exploits his fondness for architecture and corridors to suggest certain spiritual states.

Interestingly, several of Bazin's disciples were directly responsible for a return to more expressionistic editing techniques in the late 1950s and early 1960s. The influential French periodical, *Cahiers du Cinéma*, was founded by Bazin, and two of its young critics, Jean-Luc Godard and François Truffaut, eventually turned to film making, along with a number of their colleagues. Their first movies shared many characteristics with **cinéma vérité**, a documentary movement which popularized the use of a new lightweight hand-held camera, and portable sound equipment (Fig. 56). As their name suggests, the *cinéma vérité* documentarists considered themselves within the realistic film tradition. Since the hand-held camera could travel virtually anywhere, the space-time continuum was preserved by simply photographing events in one continuous take, even if this required following a subject over long distances. The technique is an extension of the **dolly shot,** of course, and in effect minimizes the need for editing. If any break in time and space is necessary, it is often performed by the

FIGURE 56. *On the set of Groupies*
Directed by Peter Nevard and Ron Dorfman.

With the introduction of new lightweight cameras and portable sound equipment, film directors have been able to travel virtually anywhere in their search for authenticity. Such equipment is often associated with the *cinéma vérité* documentary movement, but is used in fiction film making as well.

cameraman, not an editor. The major problem with this technique is that the cameraman must instinctively know where and when to start and stop his camera. **Aleatory filming** almost always requires that the film-maker be his own cameraman and editor as well as director.

Godard, Truffaut, and their colleagues were also influenced by American movies, often second-rate "B" films of the gangster variety, though these young Frenchmen transformed these old **genres** into subtle philosophical parables. Spontaneous and egocentric, these directors were eclectic in their approach to movie-making. They revived many long-discarded techniques: there are Eisensteinian metaphors, deliberate jump cuts, abrupt mood shifts, and expressionistic editing techniques that are more jolting than almost anything in Eisenstein. These techniques were not used for the sake of mere virtuosity, at least not in the best films of the *nouvelle vague,* as the group came to be called. At their best, the techniques are always appropriate to the specific dramatic needs of the moment.

The nervous editing style is particularly suited to capturing the sense of restless and rebellious youth, though it also reflects a rather complex philosophical attitude, one emphasizing the fragmentation and dislocation of contemporary life. In Godard's first feature, *Breathless*, the title seemed to refer as much to the jumpy editing as to the story itself. Indeed, the film perfectly fuses style and content: the disorienting jump cuts, the disconnected sequences, the overall plotlessness—all these reflect the sense of disorder, lack of direction, and spontaneity of the central character, a rather charming but inept gangster who self-consciously models himself on Humphrey Bogart. Many of Godard's films show a world in which all forms of established order are either irrelevant or in a state of collapse. Like their literary counterparts in the works of Camus and Sartre, the characters of these films can believe only in themselves, but their personalities are defined primarily by their actions: selfhood is an evolving thing, not a stable "given." Thus, the emphasis on improvisation, experimentation, and flexibility—in the plots, in the characterization, and in the cinematic style, particularly the editing.

But there is far more variety among the **new wave** directors than is generally conceded. Even within a film, there is often an astonishingly wide variety of techniques. Truffaut's *Jules and Jim*, for example, contains scenes of tender lyricism and liquid seductiveness that only a handful of directors would be able to equal. Yet the same film has scenes of sophisticated wit, mocking irony, and childlike simplicity. Similarly, Godard has been known to film seven-minute interview scenes in one set-up: an extraordinarily lengthy shot. Other sequences are so rapidly intercut that only fleeting glimpses of the images can be perceived. What makes so many of the new wave films attractive is this very eclecticism: realistic *and* expressionistic techniques are included in one film, according to the specific requirements of the individual scenes.

99

Within a few years, directors from other nations absorbed the lessons of the *nouvelle vague*—usually indiscriminately. Throughout the following decade, even the trashiest hack films employed the editing techniques popularized by Godard and his associates. The movies of the manic, youth-obsessed 1960s zoomed in and out, cross cut, flash cut, and jump cut—even if there was nothing in particular to zoom or cut *to*. A well written and superbly acted film like *Midnight Cowboy* was seriously flawed by John Schlesinger's zonked-out editing style—so much at odds with the intimacy and delicacy of the subject matter. In effect, the 1960s featured a style in search of content. A few directors attempted, like Godard and Truffaut, to harmonize the style with their themes: in America, Arthur Penn's *Bonnie and Clyde* and Mike Nichols' flimsy but energetic *The Graduate* are two examples. In England, Richard Lester was similarly successful, especially in his witty Beatles film, *A Hard Day's Night*, and in *The Knack*. Tony Richardson's charming *Tom Jones* was also stylistically indebted to the new wave directors.

MULTIPLE IMAGES

Multiple images, widely seen at Expo 67, will probably be the next modification of editing. What this process involves is the literal fragmentation of different images on the screen at the same time. The technique itself is not new—nor are the concepts of multiple screens and multiple projectors—but it was not until the late 1960s that commercial film-makers were willing to experiment with the concept. Its relative success in such Hollywood films as *Grand Prix, The Thomas Crown Affair*, and *The Boston Strangler* may mean that multiple image represents the wave of the future.

Unlike most of the technological developments prior to this time, multiple image film-making does not intensify a movie's sense of realism, as the term has been used in this book, but tends to emphasize the expressionistic aspects of film art. Like Eisenstein's theory of editing, its principal esthetic effect involves the idea of fragmentation. In this case, however, the images are not fragmented in a sequence, but simultaneously (Fig. 57). Multiple-image film-making thus far has not been particularly impressive artistically, but its potential for the future is awesome. All the enormous complexities that now go into the making of a single-image movie could be multiplied by as many images as are on the screen, not to speak of the complexities introduced by the interrelationships between these images.

The possibilities are staggering. This technique could conceivably show past, present, future, and fantasy simultaneously. It could show

100

FIGURE 57. *Photos by Barry Perlus*

Multiple images employ the esthetic of fragmentation more radically than conventional editing, for some elements of the same frame may be taken from the past, future, or the imagination. The space-time continuum is totally destroyed and rearranged to suggest thematic rather than spatial or temporal interrelationships.

many different points of view of an action at the same time. Motivation could be as complex as the number and quality of images on the screen, with the added advantage that they would be apparent at the time of the relevant action. Thus, to give a crude but simple hypothetical example, if the major image on the screen were to show a man contemplating murder, other images could show his motivations. Perhaps one image would be a flashback of some humiliating encounter with the intended victim. Another image might be a fantasy scene, illustrating the murderer's projected hopes for the future. Still another might be a contrasting flash-forward, illustrating what will, in fact, happen to him. And so on, for as many images the director may require. Naturally, a new set of conventions would have to be established, in order to permit an audience to be able to distin- **101** guish the different time and space contexts. The number, design, and duration of the multiple images would also be variable, according to the specific needs of a particular scene. Editing such films would be infinitely more complex, for each individual image sequence would have to be edited in coordination with many others, all of them with differing rhythms, **dominant contrasts,** designs, and **content curves.** At least for the immediate future, the importance of editing in film art seems assured.

Further Reading

Barr, Charles. "CinemaScope: Before and After," in *Film: A Montage of Theories.* Edited by Richard Dyer MacCann. New York: E. P. Dutton, & Co., Inc., 1966. (Paper)

Bazin, André. "The Evolution of the Language of Cinema," and "The Virtues and Limitations of Montage," in *What is Cinema?* Edited and translated by Hugh Gray. Berkeley: University of California Press, 1967. (Paper)

Booth, Margaret. [Interview], in Kevin Brownlow, *The Parade's Gone By . . .* New York: Ballantine Books, 1969. (Paper)

Eisenstein, Sergei. *Film Form.* New York: Harcourt, Brace and Co., 1949. (Paper)

———. *Film Sense.* New York: Harcourt, Brace and Co., 1942. (Paper)

Gessner, Robert. *The Moving Image.* New York: E. P. Dutton & Co., Inc., 1968.

Jacobs, Lewis, "Art: Edwin S. Porter and the Editing Principle," "D. W. Griffith: *The Birth of a Nation* and *Intolerance*," in *The Rise of the American Film.* New York: Teachers College Press, 1968. (Paper)

Montagu, Ivor. "Rhythm," in *Film World.* Baltimore: Penguin Books, 1964. (Paper)

Pudovkin, V. I. *Film Technique and Film Acting.* Translated and edited by Ivor Montagu. London: Vision, 1954. (Paper)

Reisz, Karel. *The Technique of Film Editing.* New York: Hastings House, Publishers, 1968. (Paper)

sound

Cinematic sound is that which does not simply add to, but multiplies, two or three times, the effect of the image.

AKIRA KUROSAWA

There are three types of sound in film: sound effects, music, and language. These can be employed independently or in any combination. They can be used **realistically** or **expressionistically.** Realistic sound tends to be **synchronous:** that is, the sounds correspond to the images, and are often recorded simultaneously with them. Many exposition sequences, for example, use synchronized sound (dialogue) with corresponding images (**two-shots**). Even **long** and **extreme long shots** are sometimes shot synchronously: to capture the actual noise of traffic in an urban location, for example. Expressionistic sound tends to be **nonsynchronous:** that is, the sounds are detached from their sources, often acting in contrast with the image, or existing as totally separate sources of meaning.

THE EARLY PERIOD

In 1927, when *The Jazz Singer* ushered in the "talkie" era, many critics felt that sound would deal a deathblow to the art of the film, but in fact, the setbacks were temporary, and today sound is one of the richest sources of meaning in film art. Actually, there never really was a "silent" film, for virtually all movies prior to 1927 were accompanied by some kind of music. In the large city theatres, full orchestras provided atmospheric background to the visuals. In the small towns, a piano was often used for the same purpose. In many theatres, the "Mighty Wurlitzer" organ, with its bellowing pipes, was the standard musical accompaniment. Music was played for practical as well as artistic purposes, for these sounds muffled the noises of **105** the patrons, who were occasionally rowdy, particularly when entering the theatre. Once the audience was settled, musical accompaniment filled the vacuum of silence in the hushed theatre.

Most of the early "100% talkies" were visually dull, since the equipment of the time required the simultaneous recording of sound and image. The camera was restricted to one position, the actors could not move far from the microphone, and **editing** was restricted to its most minimal function—primarily scene changes. The major

FIGURE 58. On the set of *The Hour of the Wolf*
Directed by Ingmar Bergman.

Under ideal studio conditions, most directors still prefer the large blimped cameras that have been used since the thirties.
(Bergman working at the camera.)

FIGURE 59. On the set of *Medium Cool*
Directed by Haskell Wexler.

Even on location, most directors prefer to record the sound.
(The overhead boom, of course, would not appear in the frame.)
Note the technician's hands which pull the dolly in this traveling shot.
Wexler (at the camera) began his career as a cinematographer.

source of meaning was in the sound, especially the dialogue. The
images tended merely to illustrate the sound track. Before long,
adventurous directors began experimenting. The camera was housed
in a soundproof "blimp," thus permitting the camera to move in and
out of a scene silently (Fig. 58). Soon, several microphones, all on
separate channels, were placed on the set. Overhead sound **booms**
were constructed to follow an actor on a set, so that his voice was
always within range, even when he moved about (Fig. 59).

Despite these technical advances, the Russian expressionistic directors remained hostile to the use of realistic (synchronous) sound recording. Eisenstein and Pudovkin issued a manifesto, reasserting their faith in the primacy of editing, but they saw great possibilities in the use of sound if it were not used synchronously. They advocated the alternating use of sound and image, with each conveying different —not duplicating—meanings. Sound, especially music, should be used as an aural counterpoint to the images. Realistic or synchronized sound, on the other hand, would destroy the flexibility of editing, and thus kill the very soul of film art. The proper use of language in film, Eisenstein claimed, was in the narrated monologue, not dramatic dialogue. The monologue would replace the expository titles of the silent film, giving the images an uninterrupted dominance. This preference for the monologue reflected the Russian bias toward documentary film, whereas dialogue tended to be associated with the film as an aspect of drama.

Even directors of more theatrical biases, however, were opposed to strictly realistic uses of sound. The French director, René Clair, came to the same conclusions as the Russians. Sound should be used selectively, not indiscriminately. The ear, he believed, is just as selective as the eye, and sound could be edited just as the images could. As early as 1929, he praised a Hollywood musical, *Broadway Melody*, for its imaginative experiments in sound. He observed that the film let us *hear* a door slam, so the director wisely chose not to show us the action as well. In this, and in other instances, sound could be used to replace the **shot.** Even dialogue sequences need not be totally synchronous, he claimed, for sound can act as a **continuity** device, once the relationship between image and sound has been made clear. Thus, sound could replace Griffith's establishing long shots, permitting the camera to roam at will.

Clair made several comedies with music illustrating his theories. In his *Le Million*, for example, music and song often replace dialogue. Language is juxtaposed ironically with nonsynchronous images. Many of the scenes were photographed without sound, and later **dubbed** when the edited sequences of the images were completed. These charming films had virtually all of the visual freedom of the pre-sound era, and none of the stolid literalness that ruined most early talkies. Indeed, the pattern established by Clair, though ahead of its time, eventually became a major approach in sound film production.

Several American directors also experimented with sound in its first years of use. Lewis Milestone added sound effects of bombs bursting and guns firing without corresponding visuals in *All Quiet on the Western Front*. Like Clair, Ernst Lubitsch used sound and image nonsynchronously to produce a number of witty and often cynical juxtapositions. Rouben Mamoulian used dialogue as a continuity **108** device for the present, while the visuals portrayed events of the past. In short, by the early 1930s, the practice of dubbing sounds after the images had been photographed liberated the camera from the tyranny of strict synchronization.

ADVANTAGES OF SOUND

Once these initial problems were overcome, the enormous advantages of sound became apparent. Acting styles became more natural, for performers no longer needed to compensate visually for the lack of dialogue. Like stage actors, film stars realized that the subtlest nuances of meaning could be conveyed through the voice. The moveable camera is a further advantage for the screen actor, for if he is required to mutter under his breath, for example, he can do so *naturally*, photographed in **close-up;** he need not, like the stage actor, mutter in stage whisper, a convention in the legitimate theatre.

In the silent days, directors had to use titles to communicate nonvisual information: dialogue, exposition, abstract ideas, etc. In some films, these interruptions nearly ruined the delicate rhythm of the visuals. Dreyer's *Passion of Joan of Arc*, for example, is clogged by an irritating series of explanatory titles which convey the dialogue. Other directors avoided titles by dramatizing visually as much as possible. This practice led to a galaxy of visual clichés. Early in a film, for example, the villain might be identified by showing him kicking a dog; the heroine, by flooding her with "spiritual" lighting, and so on.

Furthermore, as John Grierson has pointed out, sounds which are detached from their sources can take on additional meanings. For example, the sound of a distant foghorn can suggest loneliness and isolation, the roar of a jet engine can convey images of height and power. Even in nondialogue sequences, sound eliminates the need for what Clair called "inflated visuals." Without sound, virtually all the necessary meanings have to be included in the images. Indeed, this problem is the basis of one expressionistic theory of art: that art forms thrive on their limitations. Rudolf Arnheim, for example claimed that the art of the film is possible precisely because it is not like reality. With no sound, the film artist must convey all his meanings with images, just as literary men must communicate their sense of reality with words, composers with sounds, and so on. (See Chapter 7, "Theory.") But by mixing sounds and images, film is not necessarily more "like reality," as subsequent directors were to demonstrate. Sound allowed directors to expand their range of possibilities, and permitted them to convey meanings with a whole new set of juxtapositions, not all of them by any means the same as those found in reality.

In some respects, 1941 was a watershed in the history of the sound film, for this was the release year of Orson Welles' *Citizen Kane.* Here was the *Birth of a Nation* of its era—bursting with visual brilliance in nearly every shot, the movie featured a sound track so complex that the film world seemed to gasp in astonishment. Coming from the legitimate theatre and radio, Welles brought to this film a range of virtuoso sound techniques that dazzles audiences even today. The dialogue alone was literate, subtle, and yet flamboyantly theatrical. While the camera seemed to leap over time periods and different locales, the sound track formed the continuity for whole scenes. One famous scene, for example, shows Kane listening to a song sung by Susan Alexander, a girl he has just met, who will eventually become his mistress, and later his second wife. The scene is set in her dingy apartment. While the song continues on the sound track, the image **dissolves** to a parallel shot, revealing Kane in an opulent apartment, where an elaborately bedecked Susan finishes her song at a grand piano. In a matter of seconds, Welles establishes the relationship between Kane and his mistress, using only the song to bridge the enormous time-space gap. In another episode, Welles employs a dissolve and **montage** sequence of Susan on her disastrous operatic tour. On the sound track, her aria can be heard, distorted into a screeching dismal wail.

In an opening sequence of the film, dialogue is spoken through an echo chamber, to suggest the hollowness of Kane's onetime guardian, whose papers are stored in a tomblike archive. To demonstrate Kane's gradual estrangement from his first wife, Welles featured a series of breakfast scenes, while on the continuous sound track, Kane and his wife engage in a series of exchanges, beginning with some honeymoon sweet talk, and ending with a furious quarrel. The entire sequence contains only some thirty or so lines. The film's very structure is based on a series of visual flashbacks, while five informants speak of their present day opinions of Kane's paradoxical personality. Throughout the movie, Welles juxtaposes words, sound effects, and music with images of such complexity that many meanings are conveyed simultaneously.

In his next film, *The Magnificent Ambersons,* Welles developed his technique of "sound montage," where dialogue between several groups of characters is recorded simultaneously. One of the most brilliant episodes is the leavetaking scene at the final Amberson ball. The sequence is shot in **deep focus,** with expressionistic lighting contrasts; the dialogue of one group of characters gently overlaps that of another, which in turn overlaps with a third group. The effect is hauntingly poetic, despite the relative simplicity of the words themselves. The quarrels among the Amberson family are often recorded in this same manner. Welles' actors do not patiently **110**

wait for cues: accusations and recriminations are hurled simultaneously, as they are in real life. The violent words, often irrational and
disconnected, spew out in spontaneous eruptions of anger and frustration. As in many family quarrels, everyone shouts, but no one
listens. Robert Altman used a similar technique for comic purposes
in some scenes of M*A*S*H.

Welles also was a pioneer in sound "distance" recording, though
probably for financial rather than strictly artistic reasons. Until the
1950s, the distance between the camera and subject was paralleled,
in effect, by the sound. Thus, if the camera was a long distance from
the subject—in **extreme long shot,** say—dialogue would not be com-
prehensible to an audience. In long shot, dialogue might be heard,
though perhaps slightly muffled by the distance. In **medium shot,** the
same dialogue would be crisp and clear. In close-up, sounds would
seem very intimate: even a whisper could be recorded clearly. Particularly in Europe, Welles has not always been able to record sound
as carefully as we would wish, primarily because of budget limitations. In *Falstaff*, for example, he often uses extreme long and long
shots, while the dialogue seems at "close-up" range. Part of his problem was simply not enough time (or money) to shoot all the necessary footage. Because many of his actors are high-salaried stars
who can afford to work with him only for a few weeks, Welles is often
required to use stand-in actors. Because they are stand-ins, he must
photograph them from long distances, so that audiences will not
recognize the ruse. When the dialogue—recorded prior to shooting
by the original actor—is combined with these long-distance images,
many audiences find the discrepancy disorienting. Since the 1950s,
such image-sound discrepancies have become more common, even
when there are no budgetary problems. John Schlesinger, for example, used long shots and "close-up" sound in *Midnight Cowboy*, to
emphasize the insectlike insignificance of his two protagonists in
New York City. The sound, in such instances, serves as a continuity
device, while the audience is forced to scan the image in order to
find the source of the dialogue.

SOUND EFFECTS

Though the primary function of sound effects is generally believed
to be atmospheric, they can also be surprisingly precise sources of
meaning in film. Directors like Ingmar Bergman and Michelangelo
Antonioni will spend nearly as much time with their sound effects as
they do with their music and dialogue. The eerie remoteness of
forest sounds in Bergman's *The Magician* was captured only after
many hours of painstaking sound recording. Similarly, in *L'Avventura*,
Antonioni went to great lengths to recreate the desolate whine of the   **111**

wind as it swept over an extinct volcano. In this same film, the insistent monotonous pounding of the ocean's waves suggested the gradual spiritual erosion of the heroine.

Sound effects can also act to expand an image—to remind the audience of the context of a scene. In Stanley Kubrick's *Paths of Glory*, for example, the sounds of guns and cannons are constant reminders to the soldiers in the trenches of the dangers they must face when they enter the battlefield. Far away sounds can suggest a sense of distance between locations, both literal and symbolic. In *Long Day's Journey into Night*, for example, the remote foghorn reminds the characters of the psychological journey each will take before the night is out. Though they all desire the oblivion of forgetfulness, the foghorn brings them back to the reality of the present, which has been shaped by the past.

Sound effects can evoke terror in suspense films and thrillers. Since we tend to fear what we cannot see, directors like Hitchcock and Fritz Lang will sometimes use nonsynchronous sound effects to strike a note of anxiety. The sound of a creaking door in a darkened room can be far more fearful than an image of someone stealing through the door. In Lang's *M*, the child murderer is identified by a tune he whistles off screen. During the early portions of the movie, we never see him, we only recognize him by his sinister tune. Similarly, the most terrifying suspense sequences often occur when we hear but cannot see the source of a threat.

In Hitchcock's *Psycho*, the sound effects of shrill bird noises are used for transitions, for associations, for characterization, and for thematic purposes. A shy and appealing young man (Anthony Perkins) is associated with birds early in the film: he stuffs various birds as a hobby, and his own features are intense and rather hawklike. Later in the film, when a brutal murder is committed, the sound track plays shrill music mixed with bird screeches. The audience assumes the murderer is the boy's mother, but the bird noises have been associated with the boy. One of Hitchcock's recurrent themes is the transference of guilt. In this film, the transfer is rather complex: the boy has dug up his long-dead mother's body and "stuffed" it. Often he dresses himself up in her clothes. While the audience thinks it sees the mother killing two victims, it has in fact seen the schizo-

Red Desert

The films of Michelangelo Antonioni are as notable for what is left out of them as for what is put in. Many of the frames from *Red Desert* seem only partly filled, and details are kept to a minimum. The color in this film is austere and restrained: we expect and wish for more. Antonioni uses color to convey symbolic ideas rather than to enhance a sense of realism or to emphasize the picturesqueness of the setting. The world of *Red Desert* is without sunlight and joy; it is strewn with debris, and living organisms are slowly choking on the poisonous wastes of technology and industry. To be "well adjusted" in this world is to be profoundly corrupted. *Note:* These stills are taken directly from a print of the film and are uncropped and unretouched. Hence, a few scratches show up.

Giuliana (Monica Vitti) is seen with her young son, wandering aimlessly over the bleak industrial terrain. She buys a partly eaten sandwich from a factory worker, then withdraws anxiously to eat it behind a tangle of leafless bushes. The left half of the frame is "empty," suggesting a kind of vacuum in Giuliana's existence.

Giuliana wanders through her husband's factory. The symbolic motif of iron pipes is introduced: they suggest the veins and arteries of "living" machines. The blue boiler of this shot dominates the frame, crowding Giuliana's figure to the right.

Giuliana, outside the shop she is planning to open. (She wants to paint the walls either blue or green, "because they are restful.) Antonioni spray-painted the fruit white (!) and the locale in various shades of gray. Giuliana, no longer in her green coat, begins to blend in with the surroundings. The bold geometrical shapes and minimal movements in this shot suggest an abstract painting of gray textures.

Giuliana, in the red room of a shack near the polluted canal. She and her husband are with several couples, crowded on the floor. This "orgy" sequence is charged with eroticism, but as the garish red of the walls suggests, the sexuality of the scene is forced, a too insistent cover-up of the ubiquitious gray.

...I want to make love!

Giuliana's husband and companions, as seen from her point of view, isolated in the thick smog. Again, Antonioni keeps color, movement and details to an austere minimum. As in all these frames, he exploits the full range of the wide screen. The figures seem suspended like grim statues in a featureless void.

Corrado (Richard Harris), a business associate of Giuliana's husband, seems more sensitive and responsive than the other men of the film. He has just finished a sales pitch to some laborers, trying to persuade them to work in an Argentina factory. The setting is a warehouse, filled with large empty blue bottles—a symbol of the drab uniformity and regimentation of the workers. Corrado stands behind the bottles, surveying them thoughtfully.

Giuliana recounts a fable to her son, a wishful fantasy where the sun always shines, the colors are vibrant, and the young heroine is happy in nature. This is the only sequence in the movie where color is used at full saturation, yet its very vividness suggests unreality. Significantly, even in an idealized fantasy, Giuliana imagines herself alone.

Giuliana, in desperation, visits Corrado at his hotel. They lie on his bed, separated by the red pipe of the bed's footboard. The imagery of the factory has invaded the bedroom. She seems caged by the pipe, fearful of being forced into the "darkness" below the frame. The eroticism of the sequence is desperately neurotic: Giuliana both desires and fears Corrado's sexual advances.

Giuliana's hand writhes in a gesture of agony and ecstacy. This brief (42 frames) shot symbolizes her sexual climax. The formal manipulation of shapes, colors, and textures is characteristic of Antonioni's minimal technique: even the most intimate human experience is reduced to a stark abstract pattern.

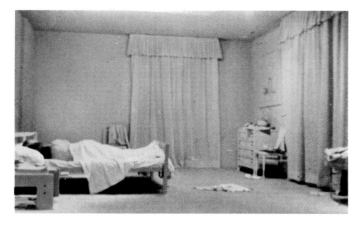

After the love act, Corrado's white room turns pink—a metaphor for Giuliana's realization that Corrado is different from her husband only in degree, not in kind. The pink room is a variation of the loveless eroticism of the red shack—hence, the significance of the title. As in most of Antonioni's films, sex solves nothing: it brings little comfort, and simply complicates an already complex problem. The deathly stillness of this frame is emphasized by the repetition of vertical and horizontal lines.

Giuliana, wandering along the waterfront. In the foreground lies a heap of castoff machine parts and industrial debris. The red background is the side of a huge ship. Giuliana, in the midground, seems trapped by the weirdly coiled pipes of the rubbish pile. In a desperate desire to escape, she asks a Turkish sailor if she can depart with the ship, but neither speaks the other's language.

The concluding shot of the film. Giuliana, again wearing her green coat, walks through the industrial landscape with her son. He asks how the birds manage to fly through the sulphurous smoke of the factory chimneys. She then tells him a symbolic parable of how the birds must contrive to fly around the poisonous smoke as best they can. The yellow smoke and the factory go into soft focus, while Giuliana looks back at them anxiously the frame still half-empty.

phrenic boy as his other self—his mother. The sound effects of the bird noises offer early clues to this psychological transference.

Sound effects can also serve symbolic functions. Symbolic sounds can be determined by the dramatic context, as they are in Luis Buñuel's *Belle de Jour*, for example, where the sounds of jingling bells are associated with the heroine's sexual fantasies. Other symbolic sound effects are more immediately clear. In Bergman's *Wild Strawberries*, for instance, the protagonist, an elderly professor, has a nightmare. The surrealistic sequence is virtually silent, except for the insistent sound of a heart beat—a *momento mori* for the professor, a reminder that his life will soon end.

Silence in a sound film works somewhat like black and white in a color film: it is conspicuous, and tends to form the **dominant contrast.** Any significant stretch of silence in a sound film creates an eerie vacuum—a sense of something impending, about to burst. Arthur Penn exploited this phenomenon in the conclusion of *Bonnie and Clyde.* The lovers stop on a country road to help a friend (actually an informer) with his car, which has presumably broken down. Clumsily, the "friend" scrambles under the car. There is a long moment of silence. The lovers exchange puzzled, then anxious glances. Suddenly the sound track roars with the noise of machine guns, as the lovers are brutally cut down by policemen hiding in the bushes. In Bergman's *The Silence*, the great many stretches of quiet paradoxically communicate a vast number of fears, anxieties, and frustrations.

MUSIC

Music is one of the most abstract of media, tending towards pure form. It is very difficult, for example, to speak of the "content" of a musical phrase. When merged with lyrics, music acquires more concrete meanings, for words, of course, have more specific referents than musical sounds alone. Both words and musical notes convey meanings, but again, each in a different manner. Music, with or without lyrics, can be more specific when juxtaposed with film images. Even in the "silent" years, film directors were aware of the intensifying powers of music, and used it primarily to emphasize the emotional impact of their scenes.

But music in film is not necessarily mere background filler, despite the fact that most films employ music primarily as a **subsidiary,** rather than a dominant, contrast. Indeed, Pudovkin and Eisenstein insisted that music in film must never serve merely as accompaniment: they felt that the music must retain its own line, its own integrity. The film critic Paul Rotha claimed that music must even be allowed to dominate the image on occasion. In short, the use of music in film is surprisingly varied. Many directors still use it as an intensifier of the image, and as background atmosphere. Some film- **113** makers insist on purely descriptive music—a practice referred to as "mickeymousing." Descriptive scores employ music as a kind of literal equivalent to the image: if a character stealthily tiptoes from a room, for example, each step has a musical note to emphasize the suspense. Some directors would hold that film music should not be "too good," lest it detract from the images. Most of the great directors, however, disagree with these views. For them, the music of even the greatest composers can be used in film. Furthermore, music can be used for contrasting purposes as well as emphatic ones. Indeed, some directors employ it as a totally separate source of meaning.

In the best films, music—whether an established work or an original score—is never a careless matter. Nor is film composing a job for hacks, for the list of composers who have worked directly in film is a long and impressive one, including Darius Milhaud, Arthur Honegger, Paul Hindemith, Dimitri Shostakovitch, Arnold Schoenberg, Sergei Prokofiev, William Walton, Benjamin Britten, Aaron Copland, Quincy Jones, The Modern Jazz Quartet, Virgil Thompson, Kurt Weill, Vaughan Williams, Richard Rodgers, Leonard Bernstein, and Malcolm Arnold, to mention only some of the best known.

THE MUSICAL

Many of the first successful talkies were musicals. Beginning with *The Jazz Singer* and the early Clair sound films, the musical has become one of the most enduring and popular film **genres,** with a different set of **conventions** from other types of movies. Most importantly, the principal *raison d'être* of the genre is music (and usually dance), not the narrative structure or the fidelity to everyday life as it can be observed. The music is not an incidental or subsidiary concern of this genre, for as in opera or ballet, the narrative and dramatic elements are often mere pretexts for the production numbers in a musical.

The major meanings of a musical are found in sounds, song lyrics, dances, and a set of stylized conventions that have grown up around the genre. When people want to communicate ideas and emotions, they do so with song and dance—like Donald O'Connor's brilliantly satiric and wistful "Keep It Gay" routine in *Singin' in the Rain*, for instance. A number of musicals—those of Clair, for example, or the Rogers-Astaire movies of the thirties—are also surprisingly sophisticated in their use of nonmusical elements, especially the snappy dialogue and the meticulously worked out plots.

Because the musical is fundamentally a stylized genre, the few attempts at realistic musicals have been rather unfortunate. In real life, people seldom burst out in song or dance, and certainly not with **114**

FIGURE 60. *West Side Story*
Directed by Robert Wise.

Most musicals employ stylized studio sets, in keeping with the artificiality of the genre. When actual locations are used, the contrast between the realism of the set and the stylization of the songs and dances can be jarring, as was often the case in *West Side Story.* (But see Fig. 43.)

the finesse of a Gene Kelly. Thus, a musical like *West Side Story*, which uses some actual New York City locations, seems weirdly incongruous, despite the general admiration the film received in its original showings (Fig. 60). On the other hand, if the locale of a musical is actually romantic, the effect can be exhilarating, for wide open locations can help to liberate the camera. Several numbers in *Gigi*, for example, were magnificently exuberant, for the Parisian locales were as glamorous as any studio set, and considerably more spacious. In general, however, the best musicals (and most of them are American) tend to use studio sets, not actual locales. Godard's *tour de force, A Woman Is a Woman*, is a conspicuous exception, an experiment he referred to as "a neo-realist musical" (Fig. 43). Generally speaking though, the unreal world of a musical film must be stylistically consistent, or the audience will not be able to suspend its disbelief: graceful ballets and musical duets are jarring in the grim slums of West Side New York. In short, the musical is basically an expressionistic genre, and it is not surprising to find that realistic film theorists either ignore the musical, or make an exception of it.   **115**

A director does not need any technical expertise to use music effectively. As Aaron Copland has pointed out, a director must know what he wants from music *dramatically*: it is the composer's business to translate these dramatic needs into musical terms. Directors and composers work in a variety of ways. Most composers begin after they have seen the **rough cut** of a film—that is, the major footage of a movie before the editor has tightened up the slackness between shots. Some composers do not begin until the film has been totally completed, except for the music. Alfred Hitchcock, on the other hand, works with his composers before the shooting even begins. In most of Hitchcock's films, the design, movements, editing, and sounds (including music) are worked out in the script-writing stage. The actual shooting, editing, and sound recording, according to Hitchcock, are merely technical matters.

In *Alexander Nevsky*, Eisenstein and Prokofiev worked out a kind of "audio-visual score," in which the line of the music corresponds to the movement of the images set in a row. Eisenstein's essay, "Form and Content: Practice," relates how Prokofiev avoided purely "representational elements" in the music (mickeymousing). Instead, the two artists worked together closely, concentrating sometimes on the images first, other times on the music. The result was what Eisenstein called "vertical montage," where the line of notes on the staff, moving from left to right, parallels the movements or major lines of the images, which, set side by side, also "move" from left to right. Thus, if the lines in a series of images move from lower left to upper right, the notes of music would move in a similar direction on the musical staff. If the lines of a composition were jagged and uneven, the notes of music would also zig-zag in a corresponding manner (Fig. 61). It is difficult to know how influential this kind of audiovisual composition has been, for there are few discussions of music in film that have gone into such visual detail. William Walton's music for Lawrence Olivier's *Henry V* seems indebted to this technique, and probably most film composers have used it at least occasionally.

FUNCTIONS OF MUSIC

Beginning with the opening credits of a movie, music can serve as a kind of overture, to suggest the general mood or spirit of the film as a whole. John Addison's opening music in *Tom Jones* was a witty, rapidly executed harpsichord piece. The harpsichord itself, of course, is especially associated with the eighteenth century, the period of **116** the film. The occasionally jazzy phrases in the tune suggested a kind of sly twentieth-century overview—a musical equivalent to the **new wave** flamboyance of Richardson's visual techniques.

Certain kinds of music can suggest certain locales, classes, or ethnic groups. The rock songs of Dennis Hopper's *Easy Rider* are not merely modish flourishes; they reflect the drug culture of the two protagonists, a culture that is viewed with hostile suspicion by most of the conventional characters in the film. John Ford's westerns almost always feature simple, sentimental folk tunes that are associated with the American frontier of the late nineteenth century. Richly nostalgic, these songs are often played on frontier instruments —a plaintive harmonica, or a concertina. Similarly, many of the Italian **neorealistic** films feature sentimental folk songs: simple, melodic, strongly emotional, these tunes are particularly associated with the urban culture of working-class Italians.

Music can also be used as foreshadowing, particularly when the dramatic context does not permit a director to prepare an audience for an event. Hitchcock, for example, will often accompany an apparently casual sequence with "anxious" music—a warning to the audience to be prepared. Sometimes these musical warnings are false alarms; other times, they explode into frightening crescendos. Similarly, when actors are required to assume restrained or neutral expressions, music can suggest their internal—hidden—emotions. Bernard Herrmann's music functions in both of these ways in Hitchcock's *Psycho*.

Music can convey sudden emotional shifts within a continuous scene. In John Huston's *Red Badge of Courage*, for example, the protagonist (Audie Murphy), in an irrational outburst of daring, snatches the flag from a dying comrade, and dashes forward onto a raging battlefield. To emphasize the boy's sudden surge of patriotism, the scene is accompanied by a spirited—if not slightly satiric— rendering of Yankee fighting songs. Suddenly, the charging boy stumbles next to a wounded Confederate standard bearer, writhing in pain on the ground, his flag in tatters. With this image, the music abruptly shifts to an agonizing dirge, and gradually transforms into a grotesque distortion of "Dixie." The "heroic" excitement of the protagonist's charge might easily have overshadowed the poignance of the wounded Confederate soldier, but with the aid of the music, the audience as well as the protagonist is suddenly brought to a grim halt.

Music can also function as an ironic contrast to a sequence. Indeed, in many cases, the predominant mood of a scene can be neutralized or reversed with contrasting music. In *Bonnie and Clyde*, the robbery scenes are often accompanied by spirited banjo music, giving these sequences a jolly sense of fun. More satirically, a scene from Kenneth Anger's *Scorpio Rising* shows a Hell's Angel motorcyclist putting on his elaborate riding gear. The scene is almost solemnly ritualistic, but the feminine fastidiousness of the young man **117**

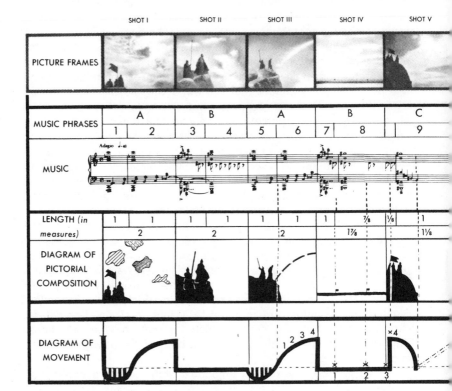

FIGURE 61. *"Audio-visual score" from Alexander Nevsky*
Directed by Sergei Eisenstein, music by Sergei Prokofiev.

The music composer need not always subordinate his talents to those of the film director. Here, two great Russian artists coordinate their contributions into a totally fused production.

is satirized by the banal tune, "Blue Velvet," which plays on the sound track. The homosexual undertones of his life style are emphasized by the line "she wore blooo velll-vet. . . ." Contrasting music need not always be satiric, however. Pier Pasolini's *Accatone* concerns the life of a neurotic ne'er-do-well, but his innate dignity is insistently reaffirmed by the swelling grandeur of Bach's organ music, which accompanies the visuals. Similarly, in Penn's *Alice's Restaurant*, the cheerful lyrics of the title song ("You can get anything you want at Alice's Restaurant") are ironically juxtaposed with a long slow **tracking shot** of Alice staring desolately past the camera.

Characterization can be suggested through musical motifs. In Fellini's *La Strada*, the pure, sad simplicity of the heroine (Giulietta Massina) is captured by a melancholy tune she plays on a trumpet. This theme is varied and elaborated upon in Nino Rota's delicate **118**

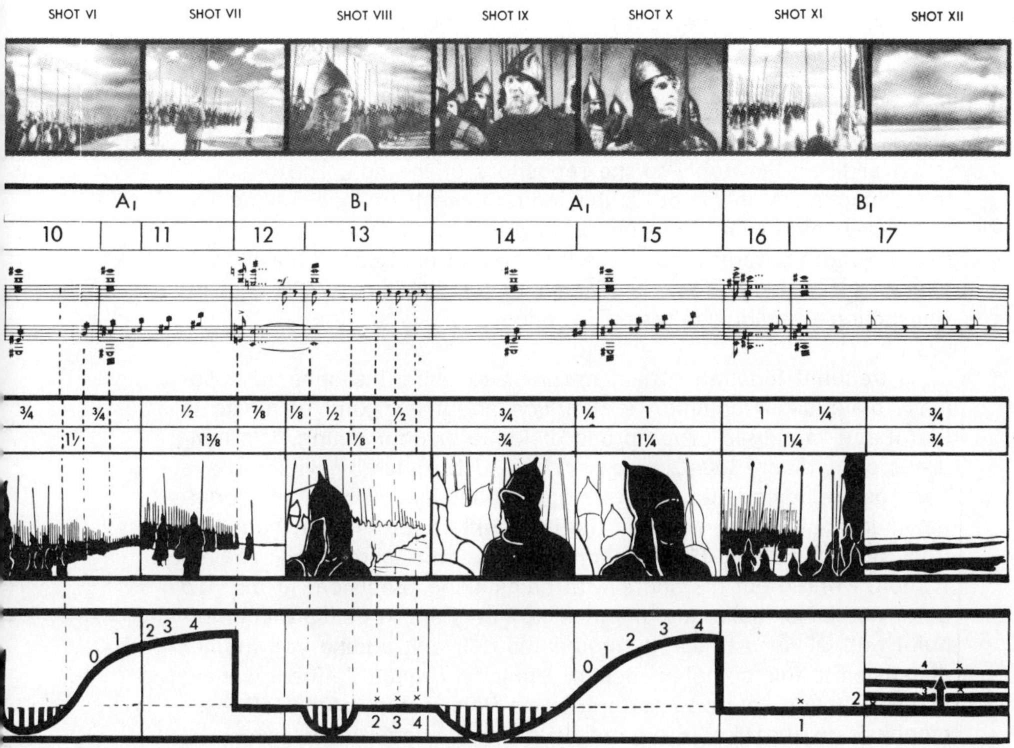

SHOT VI SHOT VII SHOT VIII SHOT IX SHOT X SHOT XI SHOT XII

A_1		B_1		A_1		B_1	
10	11	12	13	14	15	16	17

| ¾ | ¾ | ½ | ⅞ | ⅛ | ½ | ½ | ¾ | ¼ | 1 | 1 | ¼ | ¾ |
| 1½ | | 1⅜ | | | 1⅛ | | ¾ | | 1¼ | 1¼ | | ¾ |

score, suggesting that even long after her death, her spiritual influence is still pervasive. Bernard Herrmann's flamboyant score for *Citizen Kane* employs motifs in a more complex manner. Specific musical phrases are used to identify the major characters. These motifs are dropped, picked up again, and woven into elaborate combinations. The "Rosebud" motif, for example, is introduced early in the film, with Kane's death. The motif is reintroduced each time the reporter questions several of Kane's former associates about the significance of the word "Rosebud." In the finale, the musical phrase swells grandly into dominance, as the audience (but not the characters) finally discovers the mystery of "Rosebud."

Music can even be used to communicate the major theme of a film. Hopper's *Easy Rider* begins with the two likeable protagonists selling cocaine in order to stake themselves to a journey they plan to take to New Orleans. The visuals during this sequence are not particularly condemnatory, but on the sound track, Steppenwolf's sinister rock tune "The Pusher" makes it clear what we are to think of the transaction. ("But the pusher don't care if you live or die— goddamn the pusher.") The lyrics also refer to hard drug pushers **119** as having "tombstones in their eyes." This motif is also developed visually, for several times during the course of the film, the two protagonists find themselves in cemeteries or among tombstones. The final song of the film, Roger McGuinn's "Ballad of Easy Rider," explicitly develops this motif of death, with its emphasis on cleansing water, rivers, and freedom. The heroes can be free only in death, for the river flows inevitably to the repository of the sea. The death of the protagonists, in effect, is the indirect result of their selling the cocaine—which might possibly bring death to its users. When Wyatt (Peter Fonda) bitterly recognizes that he and his buddy "blew" their chance for real freedom, he seems to be alluding to the corrupt transaction—paradoxically, the economic basis of their idealistic search.

A frequent function of film music is to underline speech, especially dialogue. A common assumption about this kind of music is that it acts merely to prop up bad dialogue or poor acting. The hundreds of mediocre love scenes performed to quivering violins have perhaps prejudiced many viewers against this kind of musical accompaniment, but in fact, some of the most gifted actors have benefited from it. In Olivier's *Hamlet*, for example, the composer, William Walton, worked out his score with painstaking precision. In the "To be or not to be" soliloquy, the musical notes act in delicate counterpoint with Olivier's brilliantly modulated delivery, adding yet another dimension to this complex speech. Similarly, Franco Zeffirelli wanted two very young actors to perform in his *Romeo and Juliet.* Zeffirelli's emphasis in the film is on believability the naturalness, which at times forced him to minimize the highly stylized language. Indeed, the young principals recited their dialogue almost as though it were prose in some scenes, but Nino Rota's excellent score helps to restore the artifice to the speeches, emphasizing certain rhythms, underlining key phrases, and unifying the halts and pauses with the words. In short, the film exploits the naturalness of prose phrasing in the dialogue delivery, while the rhythm of the language is preserved by the musical accompaniment.

Like many other elements in film, music is not always easy to explain. Indeed, it is often deliberately ambiguous. For example, in *Breathless* and *La Chinoise*, Godard uses Mozart's *Clarinet Concerto*, at times almost independent of the images. Mozart's music is considered by many to be the perfection of ordered elegance. Perhaps Godard uses this music as a metaphoric device, to suggest the desire on the part of the characters to construct a similar order—a life style, in effect, that parallels the disciplined precision of Mozart's music. Buñuel's *Viridiana* features the triumphant strains of Handel's "Hallelujah Chorus" during the credit sequence. The effect seems ludicrous and disquieting—and perhaps a little blasphemous—though it is difficult to know why exactly, for the images give no hint of the philosophical cynicism the director later reveals in his handling of the story.

A common misconception, held even by otherwise sophisticated moviegoers, is that language in film cannot be as subtle or complex as it is in literature. The fact that Shakespeare has been successfully brought to the screen—with no significant diminishment in either the language or the visuals—should stand as an obvious contradiction to this notion. In fact, a good number of great films are not particularly literary, but this is not to say that movies are incapable of literary distinction, only that some film directors wish to emphasize other aspects of their art. Those film critics who dismiss "literary" movies as "uncinematic" find themselves in the questionable position of condemning Welles, Bergman, Losey, Bresson, Richardson, Olivier, and Resnais—to mention only the most prominent film directors of literary sympathies.

In some respects, language in film can be more complex than in literature. In the first place, the words of a film, like those in the theatre, are spoken, not written, and the human voice is capable of far more flexibility than the cold printed page. The written word can only crudely approximate the nuances and connotations of spoken language. Thus, to take a crude example of no literary merit, the meanings of the words "I will see him tomorrow" seem obvious enough in written form. But an actor can emphasize one word over the others, and change the meaning of the sentence considerably:

I will **see** him tomorrow.
I will see him **tomorrow.**
I will see him tomorrow.
I **will** see him tomorrow.
I will see **him** tomorrow.

Of course, a novelist or poet could emphasize a few words by italicizing them, but unlike the actor, literary men do not generally emphasize words in every sentence. On the other hand, an actor routinely goes through his speeches to see which words to stress and how, and which to "throw away," and how—in each and every sentence. With a gifted actor, the written speech is a mere blueprint, an outline, compared to the complexities of the spoken speech. A performer with an excellent voice—an Alec Guinness, for example—could wrench ten or twelve meanings from this simple sentence, let alone a Shakespearean soliloquy.

Written punctuation is also a crude approximation of speech rhythms. The pauses, hesitancies, and rapid slurs of speech can be only partially suggested by punctuation:

I will . . . see him—tomorrow.
I will see him: tomorrow!
I will . . . see him—tomorrow?

121

And so on. But how is one to capture all the meanings that have no punctuation equivalents? Even professional linguists, who have a vast array of diacritical marks to record speech, recognize that these symbols are primitive devices at best, capable of capturing only a fraction of the subtleties of the human voice. An actor like Laurence Olivier, for instance, has built much of his reputation on his genius for capturing the little quirks of speech—an irrepressible giggle between words, for example, or a sudden vocal plummeting on one word. Or a gulp or an hysterical upsurge in pitch. Indeed, the gamut of sounds and rhythms in Olivier's delivery suggests the virtuosity and richness of a musical instrument. But these are merely some of the advantages of language that film enjoys over literature—advantages shared, in large part, by the legitimate theatre.

As an art of juxtapositions, film can also extend the meanings of language by contrasting spoken words with images. This same sentence acquires quite different meanings when the image shows the speaker smiling, for example, or frowning, or looking determined. All sorts of juxtapositions are possible: the sentence could be delivered with a determined emphasis; but an image of a frightened face (or eye, or a twitching mouth), can modify the verbal determination, or even cancel it out. The juxtaposed image could be a reaction shot—thus emphasizing the effect of the statement on the listener. Or the camera could photograph an important object, implying a connection between the speaker, the words, and the object. If the speaker is photographed in long shot, his juxtaposition with his environment could also change the meanings of the words. The same line spoken in close-up would emphasize yet different meanings.

The advantages of simultaneity also extend to other sounds. Music and sound effects can modify the meanings of words considerably. This same sentence spoken in an echo chamber will have different connotations from the sentence whispered intimately. If a clap of thunder coincided with the utterance of the sentence, the effect would be different from the chirping of birds, or the whining of the wind. Since film is also a mechanical medium, the sentence could be modified by a deliberate distortion in the sound recording mechanism. In short, depending upon the vocal emphasis, the visual emphasis, and the accompanying sound track, this simple sentence could have dozens of different meanings in film, some of them impossible to capture in strictly literary media.

Some directors are expanding their techniques to include written language as well as spoken. Godard, for example, likes to make visual puns, like "cinemarxist." He also inserts written quotations between shots, often to exploit the very coldness and impersonality of the printed word (see frontispiece). In his *Les Carabiniers*, for example, two stupid and greedy soldiers send back a series of post-cards to their family. The handwritten postcards are inserted between horrifying scenes of killing and destruction: the immediacy and human misery of these scenes are juxtaposed with the cool, detached descriptions of the events on the postcards. After the audience has experienced the viciousness of war, the "objectivity" of the written descriptions seems inadequate to the point of immorality. (A sardonic McLuhanesque comment, perhaps, on the differences between literary and visual media in their treatment of the same content.)

The advantages of language—whether spoken or written—are indispensable to the film artist, and not merely for the director of literary tastes. As Clair foresaw many years ago, language permits a director more visual freedom, not less. Because speech can reveal a person's class, occupation, prejudices, etc., the director does not need to waste time establishing these facts visually: a few lines of dialogue can convey all that is necessary, thus freeing the camera to go on to other matters. Even an essentially antiliterary film like *Easy Rider* uses speech to establish important nonvisual information, for there are many instances where language is the most economical and precise way of conveying meanings in film.

THE MONOLOGUE

The monologue is most often associated with documentaries, where an unseen narrator provides the audience with factual information which accompanies the visuals. Most documentary theorists are agreed that the one cardinal rule in the use of this technique is to avoid duplicating the idea in the image. The commentary should provide only that information which is not apparent on the screen. In short, the audience is provided with two separate kinds of information, one concrete (visuals), the other more abstract (narration). The *cinéma vérité* documentarists have extended this technique to include interviews. Thus, instead of an anonymous narrator, the sound track conveys the actual words of the subjects of the documentary—slum dwellers, perhaps, or students. Occasionally, the camera focuses on the speaker, but most of the time, it roams in search of appropriate visuals.

It was Orson Welles who introduced "documentary" narration to fiction films. Early in *Citizen Kane*, after the protagonist has died, a simulated *News on the March* sequence recounts the highlights of Kane's public life. This sequence sets up most of the major characters and themes that are developed later in a series of interview flashbacks. In *The Magnificent Ambersons*, Welles sets the mood of the film with a charming and nostalgic series of fashion tableaux, accompanied by Welles' witty commentary on "the good old days." The use of an offscreen narrator is now a commonplace in fiction films. Haskell Wexler's *Medium Cool*, for example, uses the monologue—indeed many sound techniques—with almost Wellesian complexity. The very title of the film is an ironic play on words. Television, in McLuhan's terms, is a **"cool"** medium, one with a low density of information, requiring a certain audience participation to fill in the gaps to produce a totality of meaning. But TV is also "cool" in the sense that it is uninvolving emotionally, detached, and—ultimately —immoral.

For instance, in one scene, the matter-of-fact objectivity of a TV reporter's voice as he describes the riot during the Chicago Convention of 1968 is juxtaposed with scenes of violent police brutality outside the convention hall. In another scene, the impassioned words of Martin Luther King can be heard from a TV set, while the visuals concentrate on the protagonist and his girlfriend. The TV documentary, with its slick commentary, deals with the extraordinary courage and commitment of the recently murdered King, while the protagonist callously remarks how much he loves to shoot film. Wexler also uses the monologue as a **flash-forward.** Near the end of the film, the hero and his girl are shown speeding down a highway. On the sound track, the cool detached voice of a TV newsman announces an automobile accident that critically injures the protagonist, and kills his girlfriend. Soon "after," the accident occurs on the screen.

The interior monologue is one of the most valuable tools of the director, for with it, he can convey what a character is thinking. Originally a dramatic and novelistic device, the interior monologue is in fact frequently used in cinematic adaptations of plays and novels. Bresson's *Diary of a Country Priest*, for example, preserves a good deal of the language of Bernanos' novel. Many of the episodes in the film are tied together by the young priest's diary entries, which are recited on the sound track. Bernanos' novel is highly "visual," but even more abstract literary styles can be translated on the screen. John Frankenheimer's *The Fixer*, based on Malamud's novel, is successful because the visuals always retain their independent interest, while the sound track conveys some of the abstract and speculative thoughts of the protagonist (Alan Bates).

The soliloquy—a device borrowed from the theatre—is another variation of the monologue. Before Olivier entered the film world, most soliloquies were delivered as they are on stage: that is, the microphone "overhears" a character literally talking to himself, while the camera records the scene. Olivier's *Hamlet* introduced a more filmic soliloquy. In the "To be or not to be" speech, several of the lines are "thought," not spoken. Suddenly, at a crucial line, Olivier spews out the words in exasperation. With the use of the sound track, both thoughts and speech can be combined in interesting new combinations, with new, and often more subtle, emphases. In *Richard III*, the villain Richard (Olivier) brazenly directs his soliloquies to the camera—forcing us to be his confidants. (And thereby suggesting that we are, in a sense, his accomplices.) Bergman uses a similar technique in the *Hour of the Wolf* (Fig. 62).

Richardson's *Tom Jones* employs the monologue in a number of interesting variations. John Osborne's script provides for an off- **124**

FIGURE 62. *The Hour of the Wolf*
Directed by Ingmar Bergman.

Direct camera address is seldom used in films, for it tends to remind the viewer of the presence of a camera. In some instances, however, addressing the camera can be likened to the theatrical soliloquy, and can suggest a rapport or intimacy between a character and the audience.

screen narrator who is nearly as witty and urbane as Fielding's, though necessarily less chatty. This narrator sets up the story, provides us with thumbnail sketches of the characters, connects many of the episodes with necessary transitions, and comments "philosophically" on the escapades of the hero. Another device Richardson employs is the aside. Borrowed from the threatre, the aside is a quick, pithy remark that is addressed to the audience by a character who momentarily ignores the other characters present. In one scene of the film, Tom asks Sophy if she can provide a domestic position for his secret mistress, Molly Seagrim. He laments that Molly's father has many hungry daughters to feed. Then, in an impish *double-entendre*, he turns to the camera and says, "Most hungry—I can vouch for it." During another sequence in the film, Squire Allworthy unravels to Squire Western the complicated history of Tom's birth and present status. But before Allworthy can begin his history, his voice fades and Mrs. Waters turns to the camera and explains these same facts in a charming and admirably succinct manner.

125

One of the major differences between stage dialogue and screen dialogue is the degree of density. One of the necessary conventions of the theatre is articulation: if someone or something is bothering a character, we can usually assume that he will *talk* about the problem. The theatre is a visual as well as aural medium, but in general, the spoken word is dominant: we tend to hear before we see. If information is conveyed visually in the theatre, it must be larger than life, for most of the audience is too distant from the stage to perceive visual nuances. The convention of articulation is necessary, therefore, to compensate for this visual loss. Like most artistic conventions, stage dialogue is not usually realistic or natural, even in so-called "realistic" plays; for in real life, people do not articulate their emotions and ideas with such precision. In film, the convention of articulation can be relaxed. Since the close-up can show the most minute detail, verbal comment is often superfluous. This greater spatial flexibility means that film language does not have to carry the heavy burden that stage dialogue does. Indeed, since the image conveys most of the dominant meanings, dialogue in film can be as realistic as it is in real life.

One of the major problems in adapting plays for the screen is determining how much of the dialogue is necessary. George Cukor's version of Shakespeare's *Romeo and Juliet* was a conservative film adaptation. Virtually all the dialogue was retained, even the exposition and purely functional speeches of no particular poetic merit. The result was a respectful but often tedious film, where the visuals tended merely to illustrate the language. Often the images and dialogue contained duplicate information, producing an overblown, static quality that actually contradicted the swift sense of action in the stage play.

Zeffirelli's film version of this play was much more effective. Verbal exposition was cut almost completely, and replaced (just as effectively) by visual exposition. Single lines were pruned meticulously from some of the speeches, if the same information could be conveyed by images. Most of the great poetry was preserved, but often with nonsynchronous visuals, to expand—not duplicate—the language. The close-ups looked like a series of exquisite Renaissance portraits. The camera recorded the most intimate details of the lives of the lovers, the sound track picked up the most delicate sighs. The fight scenes were more thrilling than any stage presentation could ever hope to be, for the camera raced and whirled with the combatants. In short, Zeffirelli's film, though technically less faithful to the stage script, was actually more Shakespearean in spirit than the scrupulously literal version of Cukor.

Film dialogue does not necessarily have to conform to natural speech patterns. If dialogue is stylized, the director has several **126** options to make it believable. Like Olivier, he can emphasize an intimate style of delivery—sometimes even whispering the lines. Welles' Shakespearean films are characterized by a booming theatricality: the expressionistic stylization of the images in *Othello* conforms with the artificiality of the language. Zeffirelli "prosifies" much of Shakespeare's dialogue, using music to underline the rhythms of the language. Alain Resnais' incantatory sound rhythms in *Hiroshima, Mon Amour* are in perfect accord with the formalized patterns of the visuals. Generally speaking, if dialogue is nonrealistic, the images must be stylistically consistent—sharp contrasts of style between language and visuals can produce jarring (and sometimes comic) incongruities.

Some directors have deliberately used realistic dialogue as a device which obscures rather than clarifies. Joseph Losey, in collaboration with the playwright Harold Pinter, has used language to suggest the evasion of communication. In Pinter's plays for the stage, dialogue is often a kind of "cross-talk," a way of concealing certain fears and anxieties. This technique works more effectively in film, where close-ups can convey the real meanings behind words more subtly than an actor on a stage. Losey's *The Servant*, for example, revolves around a fierce struggle for dominance between an upper-class Englishman and his manservant. The conflict is conveyed visually, especially through the use of extreme angles; Pinter's dialogue is scarcely ever directly concerned with the struggle. Indeed, speech is employed to mask rather than illuminate the real nature of the conflict.

In the late 1960s, overlapping sound was popularized by Mike Nichols' *The Graduate*. This technique involves the recording of a sentence of dialogue while the director **jump cuts** from one image to another during the middle of the sentence. The jump usually involves one synchronous shot with a nonsynchronous one. The technique produces a deliberate sense of disorientation and confusion in the audience. For example, in *The Graduate*, the hero (Dustin Hoffman) spends most of his time either lounging by his parents' swimming pool or sleeping with his middle-aged mistress in a hotel room. In one sequence, the scene ends with a shot of the nude hero lying on top of his mistress. Suddenly, the sound track booms with his father's voice: "Ben, just what do you think you're doing?" During the sentence, the camera has jump cut to another shot of the hero, but when we get our bearings, we realize that he is sprawling on a rubber raft in his pool at home. The comedy results from the audience's confusion over the jump cut, for the viewer mistakenly assumes, of course, that the hero has been discovered *in flagrante delicto* by his father. Wexler also used this device in *Medium Cool*, where frivolous or inane speeches overlap with grimly contrasting visual images—a society matron's complacent description of her country retreat, for example, overlaps with shots of Chicago slum tenements.

Foreign language films are shown in this country either in a dubbed version, or in the original language, with subtitles. Both methods have obvious limitations. Dubbed movies often have a hollow tinny sound, where only the dialogue and gross sound effects are recorded. Furthermore, in most cases, the dubbing is performed by actors of abilities inferior to the originals. Even when the actor is the same—Sophia Loren, for example, dubs her own English—the nuances of the original speech are lost. Dubbed films also tend to lack sound "texture"—the subtleties of the sound effects are usually only approximated, thus robbing the sound of its suggestiveness and complexity.

On the other hand, dubbed films permit the audience to concentrate on the visuals, rather than the subtitles. Because some foreign language films have been highly successful in this country, dubbing has been much improved, for mass audiences tend to prefer this technique to subtitles. For many years, post-synchronized sound has been a major practice in Italy, including even the Italian dialogue. Not surprisingly, some of the best foreign language dubbing has been found in Italian movies. Luchino Visconti's *The Damned*, for example, had an international cast, consisting of Englishmen, Germans, and Italians. The film was released in several languages, and the English language version was reasonably effective in its dubbing. The trend towards internationalization in casts probably means that dubbing will be the wave of the future, at least for popular foreign films. Most experienced filmgoers still prefer titles, however, despite their disadvantages. Particularly where sound is a major source of meaning, titles permit the viewer to hear what the *director* wished us to hear, not what some technician—however clever—decided we would settle for.

Further Reading

Clair, René. "The Art of Sound," in *Film: A Montage of Theories*. Edited by Richard Dyer MacCann. New York: E. P. Dutton, & Co., Inc., 1966. (Paper)

Eisenstein, Sergei. "Form and Content: Practice," in *Film Sense*. New York: Harcourt, Brace and Co., 1942. (Paper)

————, V. I. Pudovkin, and G. V. Alexandrov. "A Statement on the Sound Film," in *Film Form*. New York: Harcourt, Brace and Co., 1949. (Paper)

Eisler, Hanns. *Composing for the Films*. New York: Oxford University Press, 1947.

Jacobs, Lewis. "Refinements in Technique," in *The Rise of the American Film*. New York: Teachers College Press, 1968. (Paper)

Johnson, William. "Face the Music," in *Film Quarterly*, vol. xxii, No. 4, 1969.

Knight, Arthur. "The Movies Learn to Talk," in *The Liveliest Art*. New York: A Mentor Book, 1957. (Paper)

Kracauer, Siegfried. "Dialogue and Sound," and "Music" in *Theory of Film*. New York: Oxford University Press, 1960.

Manvell, Roger, and John Huntley. *The Technique of Film Music*. New York: Focal Press, 1957.

Springer, John. *All Talking, All Singing, All Dancing!* New York: Citadel, 1966.

Stephenson, Ralph, and J. R. Debrix. "The Fifth Dimension: Sound," in *The Cinema as Art*. Baltimore: Penguin Books, 1965. (Paper)

Drama

*The function of the cinema is to reveal,
to bring to light certain details that the stage
would have left untreated.*

ANDRÉ BAZIN

Many audiences cling to the naive belief that theatre and film are two aspects of the same art, the only major difference being that drama is "live," while movies are "recorded." Certainly there are undeniable similarities between the two arts. Most obvious, perhaps, is that both employ action as a principal mode: what people *do* is a major source of meaning. The theatre and the movies are also collaborative enterprises, involving the coordination of writers, directors, actors, and technicians. Drama and film are both social arts, performed before groups of people, and experienced publicly as well as individually.

TIME AND SPACE

But films are not mere recordings of plays. The language and materials of the two media are fundamentally different, particularly in their treatment of space and time. Theatrical time generally corresponds to real time. That is, the amount of dramatic time that elapses during a **scene** (the basic unit of construction in the theatre) is roughly equal to the length of time the scene takes to perform. To be sure, some plays traverse many years, but in general, these years transpire "between curtains." We are informed that it is "seven years later," either by a stage direction or by the dialogue. The cinematic **shot** (the basic unit of construction in film) can lengthen or shorten time more subtly, since the average shot lasts only ten or fifteen seconds. Drama has to chop out huge blocks of time between the relatively few scenes and acts; films can expand or contract time between the hundreds of shots.

FIGURE 63

Somewhat like painting, the theatre is a synthetic art, and includes all
the relevant variables within the frame (the proscenium arch or its
equivalent). We do not imagine that the action is continued in the
wings or dressing rooms of the theatre. The proscenium arch is
permanent: when its contents no longer serve the playwright's needs, the
scene is concluded and a new time and/or place is presented.

Space in the theatre is also dependent upon the basic unit of
the scene. Theatrical space is continuous: the action takes place
on a stage area, which has specific limits, usually defined by the
proscenium arch. A synthetic art, theatre confines all the relevant
meanings within this given area: the action is not "continued" in the
wings and dressing rooms of the theatre (Fig. 63). The "proscenium
arch" in film is the **frame**—a masking device that isolates objects
and people only temporarily. As an analytical art, film deals with a
series of space "fragments." Beyond the frame of a given shot,
another aspect of the action waits to be photographed (Fig. 64).
A close-up of an object, for example, is generally a detail of a subsequent long shot, which will give us the context of the close-up
(Fig. 59). In the theatre, it is much more difficult to withhold information in this manner.

The relationship between the audience and the work of art is
also different in the two media. In the theatre, the members of the
audience remain in a stationary position: the distance between the
stage and audience is constant. To be sure, the actor can move close
to an audience, but compared to the fluid space of the cinema, distance variation in the legitimate theatre is negligible. The film viewer,
on the other hand, identifies with the camera's lens, which permits
him to "move" in any direction, and from any distance. An **extreme
close-up** allows him to count the lashes of an eye (Fig. 24); the
extreme long shot permits him to see miles in each direction (Fig. 19).
In short, the cinema has the advantages of **editing** and the moving
camera. Most theatrical equivalents to these techniques have been
crude at best.

These spatial differences do not necessarily favor one medium
over another. In the theatre, space is three-dimensional, occupied
by tangible people and objects, and hence, is more **realistic,** since
our perception of space and volume is essentially the same as it is
experienced in real life. The living presence of actors, with their

FIGURE 64

As an analytical art, film tends to chop up time and space into fragments.
The frame is a temporary masking device which isolates only a small portion
of the setting. Beyond the frame, another aspect of the action waits
to be photographed. The basic unit in film is the shot;
in the theatre, the scene.

subtle interactions—both with other actors and the audience—is impossible to duplicate in film. Movies provide us with a two-dimensional *image* of space and objects, and no interaction exists between the screen actors and the audience. For this reason, nudity, for example, is not so controversial an issue on the screen as in the theatre, for on stage, the naked people are real, whereas on film, they are "only pictures." The stage performer interacts with his viewers: he must establish a delicate rapport with each new audience. The screen actor, on the other hand, is inexorably fixed on celluloid: he cannot adjust, for the worlds of the screen and the audience are not connected and continuous as they are in the theatre.

Because of these spatial differences, the viewer's visual participation is different in each medium. In the theatre, an audience generally must be more active. Since all of the visual elements are provided within a given space, the viewer must sort out what is essential from what is incidental. Disregarding for the moment the importance of language in the theatre, drama is a **cool** medium visually—that is, the audience must fill in certain meanings in the absence of visual detail. A film audience, on the other hand, is generally more passive. All the necessary details are provided by **close-ups** and by edited juxtapositions. Film, then, is a **hot** medium—that is, the pictures are highly saturated with meanings, requiring little or no filling in of information. These generalizations are relative, of course. Realistic film directors tend to be more theatrical in their handling of space, forcing their audiences to participate more than they would in viewing an **expressionistic** or highly fragmented film.

CONVENTIONS: ACTION AND LANGUAGE

Though both drama and film are eclectic arts, the theatre is a narrower medium, one specializing in spoken language. That is, most of the meanings in the theatre are found in "highly saturated" words. For this reason, drama is generally considered a writer's medium. This primacy of the text is what makes drama a kind of special branch of literature. The theatre, then, tends to be "hot" verbally, and "cool" visually: a critic once observed that a blind man could still grasp the essentials of most stage plays. Film, on the other hand, is generally considered a visual art, and a director's medium, for it is the director who creates the images. Most films are "hot" visually, and "cool" verbally: the same critic observed that a deaf man could still grasp most of the essentials of a film. (These generalizations are also relative, for some films—many of Welles' movies, for example—are "hot" verbally as well as visually.)

But the relationships between the two media are more complicated than this. Both arts depend upon certain **conventions**, some **136** of them verbal, some visual. In the theatre, the two major sources of meaning are action and dialogue: we observe what people do and what they say. The action of a play is no mere illustration of the words. Hedda Gabler's burning of Lövborg's manuscript, for example, embodies "meanings" that cannot be adequately paraphrased in language. The contrast between what people say and do is a common source of irony on the stage: Chekhov built several of his plays around this ironic contrast. Even in a "talky" play like Shaw's *Man and Superman*, the audience delights in watching Ann Whitefield vamping John Tanner, while he talks on and on.

Action, in the theatre, is restricted primarily to **long shots,** to use a cinematic metaphor. That is, because of the distance between audience and stage, only fairly large actions are effective: the duel between Hamlet and Laertes, Amanda helping Laura to dress, in *The Glass Menagerie*, and so on. Extreme long shot ranges—to continue the cinematic metaphor—must be stylized in the theatre: the epic battles of Shakespeare's history plays, for example, would appear ridiculous if staged realistically. Likewise, close-up actions would be missed by most audiences unless they were exaggerated and stylized by the actors: Hamlet's distaste for Claudius must be expressed visually either by exaggerated facial expressions, or by the prince's larger-than-life gestures and movements. Except in the most intimate theatres, close-up actions in the drama must be verbalized. That is, the subtlest actions and reactions of stage characters are usually conveyed by language rather than by visual means. We know of Hamlet's attitude toward Claudius primarily through Hamlet's soliloquies and dialogue. On the close-up level of action, then, what we see on stage is often not what people do, but what people *talk* about doing, or what's been done.

Because of these visual problems, most plays avoid extreme long shot and close-up actions, restricting themselves to the **medium-long shot ranges.** Once outside these ranges, the theatre must resort

FIGURE 65

The film is a more comprehensive art than the theatre in portraying events realistically. The camera can show an action that takes place on a few square inches, or it can view events from miles way. The legitimate theatre can show events realistically only in the medium-long-shot range. Beyond these ranges, the drama must resort to certain conventions: stylized tableaux and ballets, or the convention of articulation.

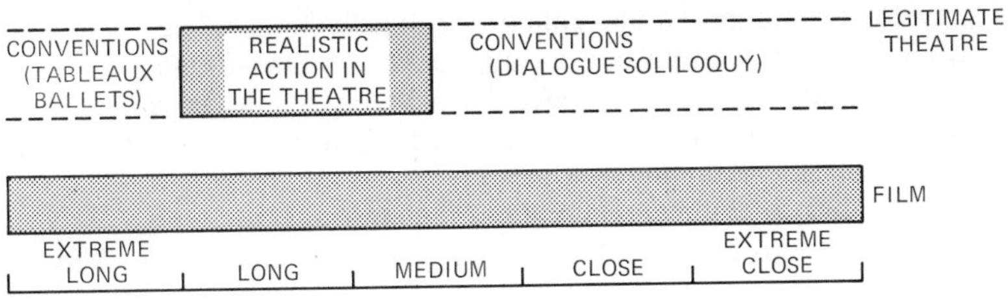

CONVENTIONS (TABLEAUX BALLETS)	REALISTIC ACTION IN THE THEATRE	CONVENTIONS (DIALOGUE SOLILOQUY)	LEGITIMATE THEATRE

FILM

EXTREME LONG	LONG	MEDIUM	CLOSE	EXTREME CLOSE

to unrealistic conventions: to ballets and tableaux for extreme long shot actions, to the convention of verbal articulation for close-up actions. The film, on the other hand, can move easily among all these ranges. For this reason, the cinema often dramatizes the action that takes place on the stage only "between the curtains" (Fig. 65). This is not to say that the cinema does not have its own conventions. The moveable camera, expressionistic sound, and editing are just as unrealistic as the conventions of the legitimate theatre. In both cases, the audiences accept these conventions as the rules of the game.

There is a certain obviousness in the theatre for precisely these reasons. Most dramatic plots, for example, involve a clear-cut, linear conflict between a protagonist and an antagonist: between Antigone and Creon, Lear and his two daughters, Stanley Kowalski and Blanche Dubois. A clear problem or conflict is presented early in the play; this conflict intensifies progressively over the course of the ensuing scenes, resulting finally in a climactic confrontation where either protagonist or antagonist triumphs. Not all plays conform to this Aristotelian structure of action, but a surprising number of them do, even a delicate "nontheatrical" play like Chekhov's *The Cherry Orchard*, where the protagonists are the members of the Ranevsky family, and the antagonists are the forces of a changing society, which ultimately deprive the family of their orchard, their estate, and a whole way of life.

In the cinema, the dramatic or Aristotelian mode is only one of several that can be employed, though it is easily the most popular, especially in America. Because of the freedom, both in time and space, cinema can employ a number of other modes and structures as well: the **epic** (*Birth of a Nation*), the lyric (*Easy Rider*), the stream-of-consciousness (Buñuel's *An Andalusian Dog*), the documentary (*Man of Aran*), even the essay (Godard's *Masculine-Feminine*). In short, film can dispense with overt conflicts, climaxes, and even plots, for cinematic action can be theatrical or nonthreatrical with equal ease.

The human being is central to the esthetic of the theatre: words must be recited by people, conflicts must be embodied by actors. The film is not so dependent upon humans. The esthetic of film is based on photography, and anything that can be photographed can be the subject matter of a film (Fig. 40). In general, drama tends to emphasize man's relationships to men; the film can also deal with man's relationships to things (Fig. 29). For this reason, perhaps, adapting a play to the screen, while difficult, is hardly impossible, for much of what the stage can do can be duplicated on the screen. To adapt most films to the stage, however, would be much more difficult. Movies with exterior locations would be almost automatically ruled out, of course. But even films with interior locations would probably be impossible to translate into theatrical terms. True, the words would present no problem, and some actions would be transferable. But how would one deal with the time dislocations of Resnais' *Last Year at Marienbad*? Or the kaleidoscopic dislocations of space in a Richard Lester movie? Theme and characterization in Losey's *The Servant* are communicated primarily through the use of camera angles—impossible to duplicate in the theatre. The theme of Bergman's *The Silence* is conveyed primarily through images of empty corridors, doors, and windows. How could one transfer this technique to the stage?

Nor is the best method of adapting a play for the screen necessarily to "open it up"—to substitute exterior locations for interiors. Cinema does not always mean extreme long shots, sweeping **pans,** and flashy editing. Alfred Hitchcock once observed that many filmed versions of plays fail precisely because the tight, compact structure of the original is lost when the film director "loosens it up" with inappropriate cinematic techniques. Particularly when a play emphasizes a sense of confinement—either psychological or physical— the best adaptors respect the spirit of the original by finding filmic equivalents. Tony Richardson's *Hamlet* is photographed almost exclusively in medium shots and close-ups. All the sets are confining interiors, except one, where the camera is at a longer distance: the scene fails precisely because it violates the sense of psychological and spiritual claustrophobia that is so carefully preserved in the rest of the film.

THE DIRECTOR

In the mid-1950s, the French periodical, *Cahiers du Cinéma*, popularized the **"auteur" theory,** a view which stressed the dominance of the director in film art. According to this theory, whoever creates the image is the true "author" of a film. The other collaborators (writers, cinematographer, actors, editor, etc.) are merely his technical assistants. No doubt the *auteur* critics exaggerated the primacy of the director, particularly in America, where most film directors have been at the mercy of the studio system, which emphasizes group work rather than individualism, "stars" rather than directors, and box-office success rather than artistic distinction. If a director could control the financing of a film—that is, act as his producer as well as director—then he might be freer to control the final product. Some of the best films of John Huston, William Wyler, and Alfred Hitchcock, for example, were produced as well as directed by these men.

Despite the distortions of the *auteur* critics, they are essentially correct: most good films *do* seem attributable primarily to their directors. To refer to a movie as good "except for its direction" seems as contradictory as referring to a play as good "except for its script." **139**

To be sure, we can enjoy a poorly directed movie, or a badly written play, but what we enjoy are usually the secondary aspects of the art —an effective single performance, or a suggesitve set, or an interesting costume. Such enjoyable elements generally represent the individual triumph of a gifted interpretive artist (actor, set designer, costumer) over the mediocrity of the dominant artist—the director in film, the writer in the theatre.

The theatrical director, then, is essentially an interpretive artist. If we see a rotten production of *King Lear*, we do not dismiss the play, but only a specific interpretation of the play. True, the stage director creates certain patterns of movement, appropriate gestures, and spatial relationships, but all of these are implied in the author's text. The theatrical director's relation to the text is similar to the stage actor's relation to a role: he can add much to what is written down, but what he contributes is usually secondary to the text itself —an improvisation, as it were, which is circumscribed by the limits set down by the author.

These conditions generally do not hold true with film directors. In the first place, some directors hardly bother with a script. Godard, for example, often begins a movie with only a few ideas jotted down on a scrap of paper. Other directors serve as their own writers: this is true of many of Bergman's films, for example. Still others depart radically from their scripts once they are on the set: Antonioni and Fellini have done this with most of their films. The majority of great film-makers have had some hand in the writing of their movies. Surprisingly few major directors depend entirely upon others for their scripts. Joseph Losey and Harold Pinter, Marcel Carné and Jacques Prévert, and Vittorio de Sica and Cesare Zavattini are perhaps the most famous director-writer teams. In most cases, however, even when the director takes no formal part in the writing, the "author" of a film is generally still its director, for it is he who creates the images. The writer, in most of these instances, describes the content of the images, just as a pope might have suggested the subject matter of a fresco to Michelangelo. In short, the film does not generally have a text in the same sense as the theatre. The dramatic script is like a music score; the cinematic script (if one exists) is more like a description of a painting.

The stage director is a kind of go-between for the author and the production staff. That is, the director is responsible for the general interpretation of the script, and usually defines the limits for the other interpretive artists: actors, designers, technicians. The director must see to it that all the production elements are harmonized and subordinated to his overall interpretation. His influence tends to be stronger during rehearsals than in the actual performance. Once the curtain opens before an audience, he is powerless to control what then takes place.

On the other hand, the screen director has a good deal more control over the final product. He too dominates the preproduction

activities, but unlike the stage director, he controls virtually every
aspect of the finished work as well. The degree of precision a film
director can achieve is impossible on the stage, for the movie director can rephotograph people and objects until he gets exactly what
he wants.

The differences in control and precision can be best illustrated
perhaps by examining their handling of the *mise-en-scène*, the arrangement of volumes within a given space. The stage director is
much more restricted: he must work within one stationary set per
scene. All patterns of movement and spatial relationships take place
within this given area. Since this is a three-dimensional space, he
has the advantage of depth as well as breadth to work with. Through
the use of platforms, he can also exploit height on the stage. The
theatrical director must use certain space conventions to assure
maximum clarity. Thus, with a proscenium stage, the audience pre-
tends it is peeping into a room where one wall has been removed.
Naturally, no furniture is placed against this "wall," nor do actors
turn their backs against it for very long periods, for their dialogue
would not be audible (Fig. 63). If a thrust stage is used, the audience
surrounds the acting area on three sides, forcing the performers to
rotate their movements and speeches, so that no side is neglected.
Again, this convention is necessary to assure maximum clarity.

In the cinema, the director converts three-dimensional space into
a two-dimensional image of space. Even with deep-focus photography, "depth" is not literal. But the flat image has certain advantages.
Since a camera can be placed virtually anywhere, the film director
is not confined to a stationary set with a given number of "walls."
The **eye-level** long shot more-or-less corresponds to the theatrical
proscenium arch. But in film, the close-up also constitutes a given
space—in effect, a cinematic "roomlet," with its own "walls" (the
frame). Each shot, then, represents a new given space, with different
(and temporary) confines. Eisenstein referred to this kind of volume
arrangement as the "mise-en-shot." Furthermore, the moveable
camera permits the director to rearrange his "walls" many times for
maximum expressiveness, with no sacrifice of clarity. Thus, in film,
a character can enter the frame from below, from above, from any
side, and from any angle. By **dollying** or **craning,** a camera can also
take us "into" a set, permitting objects to pass us by. Because of the
audience's identification with the camera's lens, the viewer in the
cinema is, in a sense, mobile.

Since the stage director's *mise-en-scène* is confined to the unit
of the scene, a certain amount of compromise is inevitable. He must
combine a maximum of expressiveness with a maximum of clarity—
not always an easy task, especially in realistic productions. The film
director has to make fewer compromises of this sort, for he has a
greater number of "scene-lets" (shots) at his disposal. He can give
us a half dozen shots of the same object—some emphasizing clarity,
others emphasizing expressiveness. Some shots can show a char- **141**

acter with his back to the camera: the sound track guarantees the clarity of his speech. A character can be photographed through an obstruction of some kind (Figs. 14, 39). Sidney Lumet photographed his protagonist (Rod Steiger) through wire cages in *The Pawnbroker*. Haskell Wexler photographed some action through glass panes in *Medium Cool*. Eisenstein occasionally had one actor block out another by having the first stand before the camera. Such "impediments" are usually employed for symbolic reasons, but since the cinematic shot need not be lengthy, clarity can be suspended temporarily in favor of expressiveness.

These generalizations are postulated upon the assumption that the stage is essentially realistic, whereas the cinema is basically expressionistic. But the differences are relative, of course. Indeed, a good argument could be made that Strindberg's expressionistic plays—*The Dream Play*, for example—are more fragmented and subjective than a realistic film like Chaplin's *Gold Rush*, which emphasizes the continuity of time and space. Certainly it is true that most realistic film directors (the Italian **neorealists,** for example) treat time and space theatrically, while some expressionistic dramatists (the Absurdists, for example) handle time and space cinematically. In each case, however, we use the terms "theatrical" and "cinematic" as metaphors: when all is said, the differences in time and space remain fundamental.

ACTING

Space and time differences also determine the differences between stage-acting and screen-acting. The essential requisites for the stage actor are that he be seen and heard clearly. Thus, the ideal theatrical actor must have a flexible, trained voice. Most obviously, his voice must be powerful enough to be heard even in a theatre containing thousands of seats. Since language is the major source of meaning in the theatre, the nuances of the dialogue must be conveyed through vocal expressiveness. An actor's voice must be capable of much variety: he must know which words to stress, and how; how to breathe properly for different types of lines; when to pause, and for how long; how fast or slow a line or speech ought to be uttered. Above all, the stage actor must be totally believable, even when reciting dialogue that is highly stylized and unnatural.

Since the theatre is not a "hot" medium visually, physical requirements are less exacting than in films. Most obviously, the actor must be seen—even from the back of the auditorium. Thus, it helps to be tall, for small actors tend to get lost on a large stage. It also helps to have large and regular features, though makeup can cover a multitude of deficiencies. For this reason, casting a forty-year old **142** actress as Juliet is not necessarily a disaster in the theatre, for if the actress is in reasonably good physical shape, her age will not show beyond the first few rows of seats. Because of the low visual saturation in the theatre, actors can play roles ranging twenty or thirty years beyond their actual age, providing their voices and bodies are flexible enough.

The stage actor's entire body is always in view, and for this reason, he must be able to control it with some degree of precision. Such obvious activities as sitting, walking, and standing are performed differently on the stage than they are in real life. An actor must usually learn how to dance a little, how to fence, and how to move in period costumes naturally. He must know what to do with his hands—when to let them hang, and when to use them for an expressive gesture. Furthermore, an actor must know how to adjust his body to different characters: a twenty-year old youth moves differently from a thirty-year old man; an aristocrat moves differently from a clerk of the same age. The body must communicate a wide variety of emotions in pantomime: a happy man even stands differently from a dejected man, or a fearful one. And so on.

Theatrical acting is temporally continuous: the performer must build—scene by scene—toward the climactic scene near the end of the play. Usually the stage actor begins at a relatively low energy level, then increases this energy with each progressive scene, until, in the climax, the energy reaches its bursting point, then quickly tapers off in the resolution of the play. In short, the actor generates in psychic energy the play's own structure. Within this overall structure, the stage performer "builds" within each scene, though not every scene is automatically played at a greater intensity than its predecessor, for different plays "build" in different ways. What is essential for the stage actor is to sustain an energy level for the entire duration of a scene. Once the curtain rises, he is alone on the stage: mistakes are not easily corrected, nor can a scene be replayed or cut out.

FILM ACTING

In general, the film actor can get along quite well with a minimum of stage technique. The essential requisite for a performer in the movies is what Antonioni calls "expressiveness." That is, he must *look* interesting. No amount of technique will compensate for an inexpressive face. Indeed, a good many film directors do not want actors in the conventional sense. Robert Bresson, for example, feels that a film can be made by "bypassing the will of those who appear in them, using not what they do, but what they *are*." Antonioni agrees: "Film actors need not understand, but simply be." Eisen- **143** stein also avoided professionals. Why use an actor to impersonate a peasant, he once asked, when one can go out and photograph a real peasant?

The practice of typecasting is virtually universal in the cinema for these very reasons. An actor is often cast because he looks the role, not necessarily because he has the technical skills to fit into it. Certain film stars have made very comfortable incomes playing essentially the same roles in film after film: John Wayne, Gary Cooper, James Stewart, Doris Day, Thelma Ritter, Marilyn Monroe. Indeed, in America particularly, films are often tailor-made to fit certain stars, who commonly reject any role that does not fit their type. The great actor-stars (Marlon Brando and Bette Davis, for example) have usually commanded sufficient prestige that they could insist upon a wider variety of roles, but until recently, such performers have been the exceptions to the rule.

Though it is a much abused practice, typecasting is not so simple-minded as it may seem. George Cukor's version of *Romeo and Juliet* is a good case in point. The film boasted some of MGM's most "distinguished" (i.e., stage-trained) performers. Leslie Howard played Romeo, Norma Shearer Juliet, John Barrymore was Mercutio. On stage, it would have been a stunning production, for Shakespeare's language was recited beautifully. But the film abounded in visual absurdities: Juliet had clearly not seen thirteen for many years; Romeo was middle-aged and balding; Mercutio was paunchy and fiftyish. That such mature people would behave so childishly made the whole dramatic action seem ludicrous. Thirty years later, Franco Zeffirelli filmed the same work, using teenagers in the major roles: the movie was a brilliant success, in large part because the director cast his principals according to type.

Acting in film is almost totally dependent upon the director's approach to his materials. In general, the more realistic the director's techniques, the more he has to rely upon the abilities of his actors. Such directors tend to favor long shots, which keep the actor's entire body within the frame. This is the camera distance that corresponds to the proscenium arch of the legitimate threatre. The realist also tends to favor shots of long duration—thus permitting an actor to sustain a performance for relatively lengthy periods: editing is kept to a minimum. In short, the more realistic the directorial techniques, the more theatrical are the acting techniques. From the audience's point of view, it is easier to evaluate acting in a realistic film than in an expressionistic movie, for we are permitted to see sustained scenes without interruptions, or "distractions" from the camera. Indeed, the camera remains essentially a recording device.

The more expressionistic the director, the less likely he is to value the actor's contribution. For Bresson, for example, the actor is not an interpretive artist, but merely one of the "raw materials" of the cinema. Indeed, Bresson avoids professionals precisely **144**

FIGURE 66

The effect of a line of dialogue can be altered considerably
by the setting in which the line is spoken.
Imagine the line "I will see him tomorrow" recited in these three contexts.

because they tend to want to convey emotions through acting. Like DRAMA Pudovkin, Bresson feels that emotions and ideas in film should not be communicated theatrically, but cinematically—by juxtaposing shots to produce linked associations. Thus, in his *A Gentle Woman*, a fierce domestic conflict is conveyed almost exclusively through the use of images of doors and windows, juxtaposed with the neutral expressions of his two (amateur) leading actors. In this same film, a suicide is portrayed through a sequence of nontheatrical images: the young wife is shown in long shot looking from a balcony; next, a medium shot of a balcony chair tipping over; next, a shot showing the empty balcony; finally, a shot showing a delicate scarf floating upwards in the air beyond the balcony's railing.

Antonioni has stated that he uses his actors only as a part of the composition—"like a tree, a wall, or a cloud." Many of the major themes of Antonioni's films are conveyed through long shots, where the juxtaposition of people and their settings are used to suggest complex psychological and spiritual states. Perhaps more than any other contemporary director, Antonioni is sensitive to how meanings change, depending upon the *mise-en-scène*. Thus, the significance of a line of dialogue can be totally changed when it is uttered by an actor standing before a brick wall, or on a deserted street (Fig. 66). Antonioni has also pointed out that a line spoken by an actor in profile may have a totally different meaning from one delivered at full face (compare Figs. 48 and 62). Mike Nichols used these techniques in a powerful scene from *The Graduate*. A middle-aged woman (Anne Bancroft) has just been betrayed by her young lover (Dustin Hoffman). In confused bewilderment, she leans against a wall in her house, as the camera swiftly cranes back and up. The image of the collapsed pale woman, dwarfed by a vast expanse of the sterile white wall, is far more effective in communicating her sudden sense of desolation than if the scene had been acted theatrically.

Though he is by no means a total expressionist, some of Alfred Hitchcock's most stunning cinematic effects have been achieved by minimizing the contribution of actors. In a movie called *Sabotage*, Hitchcock was working with Sylvia Sidney, a stage actress, who burst into tears on the set, because she was not permitted to act a crucial scene. The episode involved a murder, where the sympathetic heroine kills her brutish husband in revenge for his murder of her young brother. On stage, of course, her feelings and thoughts would be communicated by the actress' exaggerated facial expressions. But in real life, Hitchcock has observed, people's faces don't reveal what they think or feel. For a number of reasons, Hitchcock preferred to convey these ideas and emotions through edited juxtapositions (Fig. 67).

The setting for the scene is a dinner table. The heroine looks at her husband, who is eating, as usual. Then a close-up shows a dish containing meat and vegetables, with a knife and fork lying next to it; the wife's hands are seen behind the dish. Hitchcock then cuts **146**

to a medium shot of the wife thoughtfully slicing some meat. Next, a
medium shot of the brother's empty chair. Close-up of the wife's
hands with knife and fork. Close-up of a bird cage with canaries—
a reminder to the heroine of her dead brother. Close-up of wife's
thoughtful face. Close-up of the plate and knife. Suddenly a close-up
of the husband's suspicious face: he notices the connection between
the knife and her thoughtful expression, for the camera pans, rather
than cuts, back to the knife. He gets up next to her. Hitchcock quickly
cuts to a close-up of her hand reaching for the knife. Cut to an
extreme close-up of the knife entering his body. Cut to a **two-shot**
of their faces, his convulsed with pain, hers in fear. Cut to a medium
shot, in which his dead body drops out of the frame.

One of Hitchcock's recurrent themes is the idea of complicity.
By forcing the audience to identify with his heroes, he involves us
in their behavior; in effect we share the responsibility for certain
questionable acts. Hitchcock encourages this identification by ex-
ploiting the star system (In *Rear Window*, for example, we become
Peeping Toms, primarily because wholesome James Stewart is
engaged in this questionable act as a relief from boredom while
convalescing in bed.) In *Sabotage*, Hitchcock wanted the audience
to identify with the heroine: we must somehow excuse her act of
murder by participating in it. He forces this identification by frag-
menting the sequence at the dinner table. Like the heroine, we too
connect the knife with the dead brother and the guilty husband. The
knife gradually seems to acquire a will of its own, a kind of destiny.
Before we (or the heroine) realize what is happening, the knife is
in the husband's body—almost as though it were predestined to find
its home there. The revenge is complete, yet we do not really blame
the distraught wife, for in effect we have helped commit the act. When
Miss Sidney saw the finished product, she was delighted with the
results, and exclaimed at Hitchcock's brilliance. The entire scene,
of course, required virtually no acting in the conventional sense.

In actual practice, the majority of film directors' attitudes to
actors are not so simplistic. Nor do directors approach every film
with the same attitudes: in some movies, they will use predominantly
realistic techniques, in other films, expressionistic. In *Rope*, for
example, Hitchcock includes virtually no edited sequences; in
Psycho, the most effective scenes are highly fragmented. Men like
Elia Kazan and Ingmar Bergman, who are distinguished stage directors as well as film-makers, will vary their techniques considerably,
depending upon the dramatic needs of the film. Nor is there any
correct approach to filming a scene: a director like Bergman might
convey a specific idea through acting (Fig. 68), whereas Carl Dreyer
might approach the very same idea through editing or composition.
Each version could be effective: whatever *works* is right.

But whether the director is a realist or expressionist, the differences between film acting and stage acting remain fundamental.
For example, a performer in film is not so restricted by vocal require- **147**

FIGURE 67. Sequence from _Sabotage_
Directed by Alfred Hitchcock.

Through the art of editing, a director can construct a highly emotional
"performance" by juxtaposing shots of his actors with shots of objects.
In scenes such as these, the actor's contribution tends to be minimal: the
effect is achieved through the linking of two or more shots.
This associational process is the basis of Pudovkin's
theory of "constructive editing."

FIGURE 68. *The Passion of Anna*
Directed by Ingmar Bergman.

Many directors, particularly those who, like Bergman,
work in the legitimate theatre as well as the cinema,
will permit their actors nearly as much histrionic freedom
in films as they do in the theatre.

ments, since sound volume is controlled electronically. Marilyn Monroe's small breathy voice would not have projected beyond the first few rows in the theatre, but on film it was perfect for conveying that childlike vulnerability that gave her performances such poetic delicacy. Some film actors are popular precisely because of the offbeat charm of their voices: James Stewart's twangy nasality, for example, is an essential aspect of his country-boy unpretentiousness. Since acting in movies is not so dependent upon vocal flexibility, many performers have succeeded despite their wooden, inexpressive voices: Gary Cooper, John Wayne, Gregory Peck.

Even the quality of a movie actor's voice can be controlled mechanically. Music and sound effects can totally change the meaning of a line of dialogue. Through electronic devices, a voice can be made to sound garbled, or booming, or hollow. Indeed, Antonioni claims that language in film is primarily pure sound, and only secondarily meaningful dialogue. Since much of the dialogue in a film is **dubbed,** a director can rerecord a line until it's perfect: sometimes he will select one or two words from one recorded **take,** and blend **150** them with the words of another, or even a third, or fourth. This kind of synthesizing can be carried even further—by combining one actor's face with another actor's voice.

Similarly, the physical requirements for a film actor are different from those for a stage performer. The movie actor does not have to be tall, even if he is a leading man type. Alan Ladd, for example, was a short man: 5 feet, 2 inches tall. His directors simply avoided showing his body full, unless there was no one else in frame to contrast with his height. He played love scenes standing on a box, his body cut off at the waist. **Low-angle shots** also tended to make him seem taller. A film actor's features do not have to be large, only expressive—particularly the eyes and mouth. An actor who moves badly is not necessarily at a disadvantage in film. The director can work around the problem by not using many long shots, and by photographing the actor *after* he has moved. Complicated movements can be faked by using stuntmen or doubles. Elaborate sword fights, for example, are usually performed by specially trained stuntmen, dressed like the principal actors. These shots are intercut with closer shots of the leading actor, and the edited juxtaposition leads the audience to assume that the main performer is involved in all the shots. Even in close-up, the film actor's physical appearance can be changed through the use of special lenses, **filters,** and lights.

Since the shot is the basic building unit in film, the movie actor does not have to sustain a performance for very long—even in realistic films, in which the takes can run to two or three minutes. In an expressionistic movie—in which shots can last for less than a second—one can scarcely refer to the performer's contribution as acting at all: he simply *is.* Furthermore, the shooting schedule of a film is determined by economic considerations. Thus, the shooting of various sequences is not always artistically logical. An actor may be required to perform the climactic scene first, and low-keyed exposition shots later. The screen actor, then, does not "build" emotionally, as the stage actor must. The film performer must be capable of an intense degree of concentration—turning emotions on and off for very short periods of time. He is almost totally at the mercy of his director, who later constructs the various shots into a coherent performance. Some directors have tricked actors into a performance. Hitchcock and Antonioni, for example, have deliberately lied to their actors, asking for one quality in order to get another.

Since acting in the cinema is confined to short segments of time and space, the film performer does not need a long rehearsal period to establish a sense of ease with other actors, the set, or his costumes. Sometimes the film performer has not even seen the set when he arrives at the studio or on location; yet he is expected to pretend he has been living there all his life. Unlike the stage actor, he does not have to establish an intimate rapport with other performers: sometimes he has not even met his co-actors. Many directors do not **151** bother rehearsing some scenes, especially for shots of brief duration. Actors occasionally do not know their lines: this is remedied by having a prompter on the set, or by writing the lines on a blackboard off frame, where the actor can read them. Furthermore, a film actor is expected to play even the most intimate scenes with dozens of technicians on the set, working or observing. He must seem totally at ease, even though the lights are unbearably hot, and his running makeup must be corrected between shots. Since the camera distorts, actors are required to perform some scenes unnaturally: in an embrace, for example, the lovers cannot really look at each other, or they will appear to be cross-eyed on the screen. In point-of-view shots, an actor must direct his lines at the camera, rather than at another actor. Much of the time, the screen actor has no idea what he is doing, or where a shot might appear in the finished film, if indeed, it appears at all, for many an actor's performance has been left on the cutting room floor. In short, the lack of theatrical **continuity** in the cinema places the film actor almost totally in the hands of the director.

COSTUMES AND MAKEUP

In the most sensitive films and plays, costumes and makeup are not merely frills added to enhance an illusion, but aspects of character and theme. The style of a costume can suggest certain psychological states. In Jack Clayton's *The Pumpkin Eater*, for instance, the hair styles and costumes of the heroine (Anne Bancroft) are used to convey her sense of freedom or frustration. Whenever she is happy—usually when she is pregnant or with her young children—her costumes are casual and a bit sloppy, her hair loose and wild. When she feels unhappy and useless, her costumes are neat, fashionable, yet oddly sterile. One especially effective outfit of this sort is a smart tailored suit, and a severe Garbo-type hat which conceals her hair. The effect is somewhat like a chic straitjacket.

Depending upon their cut, texture, and bulk, certain costumes can suggest agitation, fastidiousness, delicacy, dignity, and so on. Costumes, then, are media, especially in the cinema, where a close-up of a fabric can suggest meanings that are independent even of the wearer. One of the directors most sensitive to the meanings of costumes was Sergei Eisenstein. In his *Alexander Nevsky*, the invading German hordes are made terrifying primarily through their costumes. The soldiers' helmets, for example, do not reveal the eyes: two sinister slits are cut into the fronts of the metal helmets (Fig. 69). Their inhumanity is further emphasized by the animal claws and horns the officers have at the top of their helmets as insignia. The highly ornate armor they wear suggests their decadence and machinelike

152

FIGURE 69. *Alexander Nevsky*
Directed by Sergei Eisenstein.

In both theatre and film, costumes are media: they convey information by
suggesting ideas and emotions. Eisenstein's costumes often
violate historical accuracy in order to suggest a kind of symbolic truth.
Here, the ruthless mechanization of a medieval horde of
German soldiers is conveyed by the metal helmets which
dehumanize the invaders by obscuring the features of their faces.

impersonality. An evil churchman is costumed in a black monk's
habit: the sinister hood throws most of his hawklike features into
darkness. In contrast, Nevsky and the Russian peasants are costumed in loose and flowing garments. Even their war armor reflects a
warm, humane quality. Their helmets are shaped like Russian church
onion domes, and permit most of the features of the face to be seen.
Their chain mail reminds the viewer of the fishing nets of the earlier
portions of the film, where the peasants are shown happiest at their
work repairing their fishing apparatus (Fig. 22). In Eisenstein's *Ivan
the Terrible*, the evil boyars are portrayed as animal-like, especially
the boyar princess, whose bulky black headdress, cape, and dress   **153**

suggest a huge, sinister vulture. Ivan, on the other hand, is Christ-like, with his simple flowing hair, beard, and unpretentious white robes.

Fellini's costumes in *Juliet of the Spirits* are deliberately garish. The gaudy reds and yellows, the elaborate feather boas, and the fantastic extravagance of the women's outfits especially, are used to convey the vulgar, show-biz world of the heroine's husband—a world that combines the worst features of a circus and a nightmare. Color symbolism is used by Franco Zeffirelli in *Romeo and Juliet*. Juliet's family, the Capulets, are characterized as aggressive parvenues: their colors are appropriately rich reds, yellows, and oranges. Romeo's family, on the other hand, is older and perhaps more established, but in obvious decline. They are costumed in blues, deep greens, and purples. These two color schemes are echoed in the liveries of the servants of each house, which helps the audience identify the combatants in the brawling scenes. The color of costumes can also be used to suggest change and transition. The first view of Juliet, for example, shows her in a vibrant red dress. After she marries Romeo, however, her colors are in the blue spectrum. Line as well as color can be used to suggest psychological qualities. Verticals, for example, tend to emphasize stateliness and dignity (Lady Montague); horizontal lines tend to emphasize earthiness and comicality (Juliet's nurse).

Perhaps the most famous costume in film history is Chaplin's Charlie the tramp outfit. The costume and makeup perfectly convey the complex mixture of vanity and clumsiness that make Charlie so universally appealing. The moustache, derby hat, and cane all suggest the fastidious dandy. The cane particularly is used to give the impression of self-importance, as Charlie swaggers confidently before a hostile world. But the baggy trousers, several sizes too large, and belted by a piece of rope, the oversized shoes, the too tight coat —all these suggested Charlie's insignificance and poverty. Chaplin's view of mankind is symbolized by that costume: self-deceived, vain, absurd, and—finally—pathetically vulnerable (Fig. 20).

Makeup in the cinema is generally more subtle than on stage. The theatrical actor tends to use makeup primarily to enlarge his features so that they will be seen from long distances. On the screen, makeup tends to be more understated, though Chaplin used stage makeup for the tramp character, since he was generally photographed in long shot. Even the most delicate changes in makeup can be perceived in the cinema. Mia Farrow's pale green face in Roman Polanski's *Rosemary's Baby*, for example, was used to suggest the progressive corruption of her body while she is pregnant with the devil's child. Similarly, the ghoulish makeup of the actors in Fellini's *Satyricon* suggested the degeneracy and death-in-life of the entire Roman population of the period. In *The Graduate*, Anne Bancroft is almost chalk white in the scene where she is betrayed by her lover.

In *Tom Jones*, Richardson used elaborate, artificial makeup on the city characters like Lady Bellaston, to suggest their deceitfulness and **154** decadence. (In the eighteenth-century comedy of manners, cosmetics are a favorite source of imagery to suggest falseness and hypocrisy.) The country characters, on the other hand, especially Sophy Western, are more naturally made up, with no wigs, no powder, and a minimum of cosmetics.

SETTINGS

In the best films and stage productions, the setting is not merely a backdrop for the action, but an extension of the theme and characterization. Like lights, costumes, and makeup, settings are "media." They not only tell us what the tastes and habits of the characters are, they can be used also to suggest certain symbolic ideas, especially in the film. Sets can be realistic or expressionistic, depending upon the nature of the work of art. In either case, however, stage sets need not be so detailed as film sets, for the audience is too distant from the stage to perceive many small details. The stage director generally must work with fewer sets, usually one per act, and thus, he must inevitably settle for less precision and variety than a comparable screen director, who has virtually no limits of this kind, especially if he is shooting on location.

Spatial considerations force the stage director to make constant compromises with his sets. If he uses too much of the upstage (rear) area, the audience would not be able to see or hear well. If he uses high platforms to give an actor dominance, the director then has the problem of getting his actor back on the main level quickly and plausibly. The stage director also must use a constant-sized space: his settings are confined to "long shots": if he wants to suggest a vast field for example, he must resort to certain conventions. He can stage an action in such a way as to suggest that the playing area is only a small corner of the field. Or he can stylize his set with the aid of a cyclorama, which gives the illusion of a vast sky in the background. If he wants to suggest a confined area, he can do so only for short periods, for an audience grows restless when actors are restricted to a small playing area for long periods. Stage directors can use vertical, horizontal and oblique lines in a set to suggest psychological states, but unlike the film director, they cannot cut out these lines (or colors, or objects) in scenes or speeches where they are inappropriate.

The film director has far more freedom in his use of settings. Most importantly, of course, the cinema permits a director to shoot out-of-doors—an enormous advantage. The major works of a number of great directors would have been impossible without this freedom: Eisenstein, Griffith, Chaplin, Kurosawa, Fellini, Antonioni, de Sica, Godard, Truffaut, Renoir. Antonioni often structures his films **155** around a location. In *Red Desert*, for example, the main "character" of the film is really the polluted industrial wastelands of Ravenna, a northern Italian city. In *Zabriskie Point*, the middle portion of the film takes place in Death Valley, which Antonioni uses as a metaphor for the sterility of contemporary America. Epic films would be virtually impossible without the extreme long shots of vast expanses of land: the poetry in the epic films of John Ford, for example, is largely found in the exquisite photography of the American plains, mountains, and deserts.

Exterior locations can also be used to suggest a sense of progression or development. In Fellini's *La Strada*, for instance, the protagonist and his simple-minded female assistant are shown as reasonably happy as they travel together from town to town with their theatrical act. After he abandons her, he heads for the mountains. Gradually, the landscape changes: the trees are stripped of their foliage, snow and dirty slush cover the ground, the sky is a murky gray. The changing setting becomes a metaphor for the protagonist's spiritual condition, and nature itself seems to grieve when the helpless girl is left to die alone.

In *Tom Jones*, Richardson employs a progressive drainage of color in his settings to suggest the moral qualities of the three main locations: the Allworthy estate, the road to London, and London itself. Brilliant colors are used to suggest the full-bodied richness of Tom's early life in the country. As he gets closer to the city, the color becomes more diffuse, more grayish and sickly. London itself is virtually colorless, save for the gaudy clothes of the rich and powerful. The cinema, then, is an ideal medium for dealing with the themes of man's relationship to nature. Such themes are rare in the theatre, but in film they are commonplace: *Easy Rider, Gold Rush, Blow-up, Two Women, Alice's Restaurant, The Rules of the Game.* The list is a long and distinguished one.

Even with interiors, the film can get more mileage from its settings. On the stage, a setting is generally admired with the opening of the curtain, then quickly forgotten as the actors take over as the center of interest. In the movies, however, a director can keep cutting back to his setting to remind the audience of its significance. Indeed, the setting in a film can be likened to a character—as is Kane's opulent palace, Xanadu, in Welles' *Citizen Kane.* The palatial estate is used to externalize Kane's fantastic wealth and growing dominance over others. During the course of his life, he keeps adding more and more clutter to the palace. Even his second wife is essentially an object to be stored in his vast warehouse. The castle is a bizarre mixture of styles and periods—just as Kane's personality is an inconsistent blend of psychological contradictions. Finally, the mansion becomes a grotesque prison, for Kane discovers too late that a man can become possessed by his possessions.

A film can fragment a set into a series of shots, now emphasizing one aspect of a room, later another, and so on. In Losey's *The* **156**

Servant, a stairway is used as a major thematic symbol. The film deals with a servant's gradual control over his master. Losey uses the stairway as a kind of psychological battlefield, where the relative positions of the two men on the stairs give the audience a sense of who is winning the battle. Losey also uses the rails on the stairway to suggest prison bars: the "master" of the house is often photographed from behind these bars. In John Frankenheimer's *All Fall Down*, the separate rooms and corridors of a house are used to suggest the emotional fragmentation of a family. The father is usually seen in the cellar, the mother on the ground floor, the two sons in the upper bedrooms. The family connects emotionally only for short periods, usually in the corridors of the house.

Even the furniture of a room can be exploited for psychological and thematic purposes. In his book, *Lessons with Eisenstein*, Vladimir Nizhny describes how Eisenstein discussed at length the significance of a table for a set. The class exercise was centered around an adaptation of Balzac's *Père Goriot*. The scene takes place at the dinner table, which Balzac describes as circular. But Eisenstein convincingly argues that a round table is wrong cinematically, for it implies equality, with each person linked in a circle. To convey the highly stratified class structure of the boarding house, Eisenstein suggests the use of a long rectangular table, with the mistress of the house at the head, the favored tenants close to her sides, and the lowly Goriot alone, near the base of the table (Fig. 70).

Such careful attention to the details of a set often distinguishes a master of film from a mere technician, who settles for only a general effect. Indeed, some directors feel that the set is so important that they will even construct different versions for a separate shot. In *The Graduate*, Nichols wanted to underline the sudden sense of loss and insignificance of Anne Bancroft when she is exposed by

FIGURE 70

The objects of a set are often used to convey symbolic ideas.
Eisenstein pointed out how a circular table suggests social equality,
with no seat dominating. A rectangular table tends to
suggest social stratification, with a "head" at one end and positions of less
social importance descending from this dominant seat.

Dustin Hoffman. To convey the effect more forcefully, a separate set was constructed, with an oversized doorway towering above her. With the camera at a **high angle,** a vast expanse of white wall to one side, and a huge empty doorway at the other side, Miss Bancroft was literally reduced to insignificance.

The setting of a movie—far more than in any play—can even take over a film. In Kubrick's *2001: A Space Odyssey*, the director spends most of his time lovingly photographing the instruments of a space ship, various space stations, and the enormous expanses of space itself. Indeed, the few people in the film seem almost incidental, and certainly far less interesting than the real center of concern—the setting. It would be impossible to produce *2001* on the stage: the "language" of the film is not theatrically convertible. And though the movie is perhaps an extreme instance of how the cinema communicates, it represents, nonetheless, a logical extension of Bazin's observation, quoted at the head of this chapter.

Further Reading

Antonioni, Michelangelo. "Two Statements," in *Film Makers on Film Making.* Edited by Harry M. Geduld. Bloomington: Indiana University Press, 1969. (Paper)

Bazin, André. "Theater and Cinema," in *What Is Cinema?* Edited and translated by Hugh Gray. Berkeley: University of California Press, 1967. (Paper)

Carrick, Edward. *Designing for Moving Pictures.* London: Studio, 1947.

Eisenstein, Sergei. *Notes of a Film Director.* Moscow: Foreign Languages Publishing House, no date.

Lindgren, Ernest. *The Art of the Film.* London: George Allen and Unwin Ltd., 1948.

Macdonald, Dwight. "Our Elizabethan Movies," in *Film and the Liberal Arts.* Edited by T. J. Ross. New York: Holt, Rinehart and Winston, Inc., 1970. (Paper)

Nicoll, Allardyce. *Film and Theatre.* New York: Crowell, 1936.

Nizhny, Vladimir. *Lessons with Eisenstein.* Translated and edited by Ivor Montagu and Jay Leyda. New York: Hill and Wang, 1969. (Paper)

Panofsky, Erwin. "Style and Medium in the Moving Pictures," in *Film: An Anthology.* Edited by Daniel Talbot. Berkeley: University of California Press, 1966. (Paper)

Pudovkin, V. I. *Film Technique and Film Acting.* Translated and edited by Ivor Montagu. New York: Grove Press, 1960. (Paper)

LITeraTure

The film-maker/author writes with his camera
as a writer writes with his pen.

ALEXANDRE ASTRUC

It has been variously estimated that from one-fourth to one-fifth of all feature films have been literary adaptations. Nor has the relationship between movies and literature been one way: many commentators have remarked upon the cinematic qualities of much contemporary fiction and poetry, including Dos Passos' *U.S.A.*, Joyce's *Ulysses*, and Eliot's "The Love Song of J. Alfred Prufrock." The relationship between the two media can be traced back almost to film's infancy. At the turn of the century, Georges Méliès was using literary sources as a basis for several of his movies. Griffith claimed that many of his cinematic innovations were in fact taken straight from the pages of Dickens. In his essay, "Dickens, Griffith, and the Film Today," Eisenstein shows how Dickens' novels provided Griffith with a number of techniques, including equivalents to **fades, dissolves, frame compositions,** the breakdown into **shots,** special modifying lenses, and—most importantly—the concept of **parallel editing.** Eisenstein even converts Chapter XXI of *Oliver Twist* into a shooting script, to demonstrate Dickens' "cinematic" sensibility.

Until recently, most commentators have tacitly assumed that literature is the superior art form because of its greater breadth, its ease in treating both concrete objects and abstract ideas. Film, with its esthetic based on photography, has generally been thought to be restricted to the treatment of concrete objects only. But the problem is more complex than this. Different media appeal to different senses, and satisfy different needs. To assert the superiority of one art over another is an exercise in irrelevance, unless one restricts such comparisons to analogous techniques and problems. Michelangelo's Sistine Ceiling and Mozart's Symphony no. 40 are both masterpieces, but their appeal and methods of communication are simply not comparable. Although film and literature have far more in common, some fundamental differences also exist between these two media, some favoring literature, others favoring film.

In the opinion of most commentators, the flexibility of the literary trope—figurative language—is the major advantage of poetry and fiction over film. Through the uses of images, similes, metaphors, and symbols, the writer is able to combine ideas and objects in an almost infinite variety. For example, most similes and metaphors compare an abstract quality or condition with a physical object, such as Burns' famous line, "my love's like a red, red rose, that's newly sprung in June." For the present, we will confine ourselves only to the concrete image of the rose, which is used to clarify and intensify the abstraction, "love."

Burns' image is vivid, it's true, but a cinematic image is more vivid. After all, the term "imagery" is itself a metaphor when applied to language: that is, the word "rose" is merely a sign—like "x"— which refers to a concrete object. But the photographic image of a rose is more explicit, it is a picture-sign. The word "rose," though relatively concrete, tends to evoke the general concept of "rose-ness," rather than a specific rose. In short, a literary "image" must be imagined in the mind of the reader. The word is an intermediary between the perceiver and the object. Because it is not as explicit as a film image, the word-picture can suggest certain desirable ambiguities which may or may not be present in a literal photograph. But because of its explicitness, the cinematic image is more immediate and vivid. Each medium, then, has certain strong points and weaknesses. In general, however, literature that is highly imagistic and descriptive can be duplicated with comparative ease in the cinema.

Pudovkin was the first film-maker to formulate a self-conscious theory of metaphor in film. The juxtaposed shots of an **edited** sequence, Pudovkin felt, could serve as a cinematic equivalent to the literary trope. According to his theory, a shot of two lovers spliced with a shot of a rose could produce Burns' simile in filmic terms. The theory works reasonably well, provided the appropriate objects of comparison arise naturally from the setting. Certainly this kind of juxtaposition is the most common type of editing trope found in film, but it is sadly limited when compared to the flexibility of literary tropes. In the hands of an imaginative director, however, this juxtaposing technique can be highly effective. In Hitchcock's *Shadow of a Doubt*, for example, a man's reaction to some shattering information is conveyed through metaphoric editing. The suave villain (Joseph Cotten) is about to begin his breakfast. While the information is conveyed verbally, Hitchcock cuts to a **close-up** of an egg being punctured by a knife. By showing the yellow of the egg oozing out, Hitchcock wittily communicates the murderer's sudden sense of fear and vulnerability.

162

Similarly, in Joseph Losey's *The Servant*, the eroticism of a sequence is conveyed by juxtaposing shots of a sexy seductress, a tense but aroused young man, and a kitchen faucet dripping water. As the scene grows more intense, the sounds of the dripping water grow louder. The **cross-cutting** builds up the tension until it is almost unbearable. Suddenly the young man turns to the sink and tightens the handles of the faucet in an almost hysterical attempt to stop the dripping. The gesture is a metaphor for the young man's mental attempt to "shut off" his aroused sexuality. As an art of juxtapositions, the film can produce this type of metaphor with considerable ease.

But literary metaphors are usually more complex than Burns' simple comparison, and Pudovkin's linked juxtapositions. Eisenstein recognized this fact, and attempted to expand the uses of metaphor in film. His basic disagreement with Pudovkin concerned the sources of comparison. Cinematic metaphors need not be drawn from the setting of a film, Eisenstein believed. Like literary tropes, virtually any comparison can be introduced in a film, irrespective of its source. One of Eisenstein's most famous noncontextual tropes occurs in *October (Ten Days That Shook the World)*, in which the director satirizes the fears and anxieties of an antirevolutionary politician by intercutting shots of a "heavenly choir" of harpists with shots of the politician delivering his speech. The row of pretty blonde harp players is brought in "from nowhere": that is, they are certainly not found in the locale (a meeting hall), but are introduced solely for metaphoric purposes. (See Chapter 3, "Editing.")

Eisenstein felt that editing tropes might go even further than this. In his essay, "The Cinemagraphic Principle and the Ideogram," he describes how the Chinese ideogram began as a picture language, which gradually was able to develop abstract words by joining two graphic characters. For example, the picture-character for "heart," when joined with the character for "knife," could produce the abstraction "sorrow." Eisenstein believed that editing tropes might work in the same way. His theory seems a trifle far-fetched, possibly because we are unused to this particular convention in film. In literature, "iron horse" is an acceptable metaphor for train to most of us because of its familiarity. To those unfamiliar with Anglo-Saxon poetry, however, the striking kenning "bone-house" (for human body) might also appear far-fetched. Many people are inclined to dismiss such innovations as obscure and pretentious when they are first introduced, just as many of Eliot's original readers were exasperated by the obscure "metaphysical conceits" of his early poetry.

Since the late 1950s, some film-makers, following the example of Jean-Luc Godard and other **new wave** directors, have begun to employ Eisensteinian editing tropes with greater frequency. These practices have been facilitated by the fact that many movies since this period have cast plots aside. Freed from the rigors of tight narrative structures and conventional story telling, these directors have enjoyed greater freedom to develop ideas metaphorically, without regard to setting and strict logic.

Even popular films have begun to employ editing tropes with success—Stanley Kubrick's *2001: A Space Odyssey*, for example. The film is constructed in three parallel episodes, each dramatizing a giant leap in intelligence. The first section deals with a group of anthropoid apes, who are the first to discover that large thighbones can be used as weapons—in effect, as primitive machines. At the conclusion of part one, the ape leader joyously hurls a thighbone up in the air. As it sails through the sky, Kubrick match cuts to a shot of a space ship, shaped like the bone, traveling effortlessly through space. The year is now 2001, and the ape's primitive machine has "evolved" into a fantastically complex mechanism.

Part three of the film takes us "beyond Jupiter," where the fourth dimension reduces our concept of the space-time continuum to an irrelevancy. The astronaut is shown to be a prisoner or a scientific subject of some kind. He lives in a zoo-laboratory, which is decorated in a weird version of Louis XIV furniture (an ironic parallel to a human's attempt to make animals "at home" in a zoo). Before our eyes, the hero begins to age, and while eating in one room, he sees himself dying in another. At last, his corpse seems to be observed by a mysterious monolith—a superior form of intelligence. The final images of the film are taken from out in space, showing a new planet, a kind of placenta. Within the placenta is a fetus, which has the features of the astronaut.

Kubrick parallels the complexity of his metaphors with the complexity of each civilization. The comparison of the thighbone with the space ship is a relatively simple analogy. In some respects, it is a Pudovkin-style juxtaposition, paralleling one kind of intelligence with another: that is, the scientific wonders of the space ship are logical outgrowths of man's first "machine," the thighbone. The embryo image, however, is less literal, and not derived from the setting. The comparison of the fetus–planet with the space ship and thighbone is, in fact, an Eisensteinian trope, as intriguing and richly ambiguous as virtually any in literature.

Editing tropes are almost certain to be expanded and explored by future film-makers. For the present, however, there are some kinds of literary metaphors that seem beyond the capabilities of this cinematic technique. Shakespeare's "sluttish time" (Sonnet 55), for example, probably could not be produced through an edited juxtaposition. His "summer's lease" (Sonnet 18) might be photographable, but it is doubtful that an audience could grasp its meaning. Because words can be juxtaposed with greater emotional logic than pictures, literature enjoys a far greater freedom than the cinematic equivalent of editing. But editing is only one kind of trope in film, and not necessarily the most important. While it is clear that film cannot use all the devices of literature, it can use a great many **164** of them. In addition, of course, the cinema can use almost the whole language of painting and photography, the whole language of music, most of the language of theatre, and a good deal of dance. Indeed, there are an enormous number of techniques found in movies that have no literary equivalents.

INTRA-SHOT TROPES AND THE METAPHORIC CAMERA

Perhaps the major function of figurative language in literature is to convey general and abstract ideas more concretely, more vividly. As we have seen, concreteness is no problem in film, for the visual image is explicit. Cinematic metaphors, then, tend to work in the opposite direction: they make the specific more general, more abstract. As Alexandre Astruc observes in his essay, "La Caméra-Stylo," the traditional problem of film has always been how to express thought and ideas. The invention of sound, of course, was an enormous advantage to the film-maker, for with spoken language, he could express virtually any kind of abstract thought. But film directors also wanted to explore the possibilities of the image as a conveyor of abstract ideas. The editing trope was only one technique that enlarged the director's possibilities of expression. The metaphoric use of the camera and the intra-shot trope permitted him even more expressive range.

A word on metaphors and symbols: sometimes fine distinctions are made between the two terms, when in fact there is a considerable gray area between them. In film, the distinctions are even more blurred than in literature. A metaphor is usually defined as a figure of speech in which a term is transferred from an object or idea it ordinarily describes to another object or idea. It is an implicit comparison or analogy, such as "devouring love," which links the term "devouring" (ordinarily associated with eating and animals) to the abstraction "love."

A symbol is generally defined as something that represents something else (as well as being a thing in itself) by association or resemblance. Often a concrete object is used to represent something intangible. A flag, for example, can represent a nation, its people, and its ideals. In actual practice, a symbol is often also a metaphor and vice-versa, for both techniques imply a comparison or parallel between two (or more) literally unlike things. Generally, a metaphor tends to strike us with its dissimilarities—a yoking together of two things not ordinarily associated. The symbol, on the other hand, tends to emphasize similarities—extensions or layers of meaning beyond the literal level. But these are generalizations only. Is the ice of Dante's final circle of Hell a metaphor or a symbol? And what of **165**

the clothes images in Carlyle's *Sartor Resartus*? In short, there is
much overlapping between the two terms, more than is generally
admitted. What concerns us for the present, however, is that both
of these analogical techniques are used in movies to aid the film-
maker in dealing with general and abstract ideas.

Virtually every cinematic technique can be employed figuratively.
Beginning with the shot itself, the amount of space permitted within
the frame can convey a number of symbolic ideas (Fig. 47). In *The
400 Blows*, for example, Truffaut uses **long shots** and **loose framing**
as metaphors of freedom which the young protagonist enjoys while
he cavorts on the city streets, away from the restrictive control of
his parents and teachers. In the scenes featuring authority figures,
the camera moves into the closer ranges—usually **tightly framed
medium shots**—where the youngster seems pinned down, confined
(Fig. 14). A particularly effective use of this metaphoric technique
is found in the interview scene between the boy and the reform
school psychologist. As the questions of the anonymous psychologist
are heard on the sound track, the camera (at medium shot) seems
riveted to one position, mercilessly keeping the boy under surveillance as he answers the questions.

The symbolic suggestions of colors, lines, and angles have
already been discussed (Chapter 1, "Picture"), but we might note
in passing that we often create metaphors when we describe these
elements verbally. Red is not literally "aggressive," for example, nor
are horizontal lines "resting," except in a figurative sense. Similarly,
extreme angles often portray a metaphoric rather than a literal reality.
In Hitchcock's *Notorious*, for instance, a Nazi spy (Claude Rains)
realizes that he has married an American agent, and can do virtually
nothing to correct his blunder. Hitchcock conveys Rains' sense of
entrapment and self-contempt metaphorically: with a **high angle,**
tightly framed **extreme close-up.** The shot, in effect, shows us the
way he sees himself.

Light and dark images are among the most often used in literature
to convey symbolic ideas. Much of the richness of Hawthorne's *The
Scarlet Letter*, for example, is due to the author's extraordinary
sensitivity to the metaphoric implications of light and the lack of it.
In literature, the writer must deal with such images singly, and in
sequence. In the forest scene of *The Scarlet Letter*, for instance,
Hawthorne devotes several paragraphs to describing the effects of
the lights and darks on the major characters of the scene. In the
cinema, such symbolism is almost an inevitability, for every scene
must be lighted, merely as a practical necessity. In the hands of a
master—a Josef von Sternberg or an Orson Welles—light and dark
symbolism can add layers of meanings to the content of the images.
Furthermore, the film director can employ such symbolism more
densely and throughout his work. A single shot can do the work of
many pages, for the film-maker can include as many lighting contrasts within the shot as he wishes (Fig. 25).

LITERATURE

Dissolves, **double exposures,** and **montage shots** are often used metaphorically, since each of these techniques involves the super-imposition and implied paralleling of two or more images. In *All Fall Down*, John Frankenheimer used a series of dissolves and double exposures as metaphors for the act of love. Echo, the heroine (Eva Marie Saint), falls in love with a callous opportunist (Warren Beatty). Earlier in the film, Beatty has engaged in a number of sordid affairs with other women. To emphasize the difference in his attitude toward Echo and to preserve the ethereal purity of the heroine, Franken-heimer poeticizes their liaison. While they are in each other's arms, the camera moves closer for each dissolve, until finally the screen is filled with a lyrical montage of close-ups of the lovers kissing passionately. Frankenheimer is thus able to suggest the sexual union of the two lovers without cheapening the heroine and without resort-ing to visual or verbal clichés.

Directors frequently exploit the symbolic implications of objects. In film, as in literature, a thing is often more than a thing. Within certain contexts, it can suggest emotions and ideas as well. In Antonioni's *Eclipse*, the final image is a shot of an ultramodern street-lamp, which the camera **dollies** in on. The film concludes with the lamp's blinding glare filling up the screen. The image is a metaphor, suggesting the sterility of the central love affair and its final eclipse at the end of the film. Mirrors are among the most commonly used metaphoric objects in film, perhaps because they permit a director to show two selves simultaneously and naturalistically—without re-sorting to special effects photography (Fig. 71). In *Psycho*, Hitch-cock used a number of mirror shots to suggest the schizophrenia of the central character (Anthony Perkins), and the self-division of several of the other characters as well.

Some of the most richly suggestive metaphors using settings and objects are found in Bresson's *Diary of a Country Priest.* Themati-cally, the movie can be likened to Gerard Manley Hopkins' "Terrible Sonnets," for it deals with a young priest's frustrating attempts to succeed at his vocation, and his equally desperate desire to under-stand an apparently perverse God. The priest's increasing sense of despair is suggested by the many long and extreme long shots of him walking over the bleak landscape, which is stripped of all foliage. Silhouetted against the skies, the black branches of the huge denuded trees resemble hundreds of crooked fingers, supplicating the unresponsive heavens for leaves. In other shots, these trees resemble tautly stretched nerve endings, straining to connect with the ashen vacuum above.

Movement can also be employed metaphorically. We have seen how **slow motion, fast motion,** and **freeze frames** can suggest a dance, a machine, and a solidification, respectively (Chapter 2, "Movement"). Dolly and **crane shots** are often employed symbolically. At the conclusion of *Two Women*, Vittorio de Sica combines the motifs of windows, lights and darks, and a crane shot to form a highly

167

FIGURE 71. *Medium Cool*
Directed by Haskell Wexler.

Mirror shots are often used in film to suggest self-division
and themes of illusion vs. reality. Here, the mirror shot is more complex,
for it introduces a character who is not literally present in the frame.

complex cluster of ideas. From the beginning of the film, the fierce
maternality of the heroine (Sophia Loren) is established by showing
her constantly fussing over her young daughter's comfort and safety.
During a bombing raid, she quickly pulls down the shutters of her
shop windows, then throws herself over her daughter's body to
protect her. Several times during the film, the mother is shown clos-
ing more windows in order to shield her daughter from the dangers
and discomforts of the outside. In one scene, the daughter's loveli-
ness is likened to the promise of Italy's post-war future. Throughout
the film, the mother connives against her neighbors in order to
provide for herself and her girl. Late in the movie, while the two are
walking on a deserted road, they decide to rest in a bombed-out
church. Several times, de Sica cuts to the huge bomb holes in the
ceiling and floor of the building.

Suddenly swarms of Algerian soldiers flood the church. They knock the two women to the floor and brutally rape them. While the shrieking girl is held down by several soldiers, the first assaulter mounts her body. Suddenly the camera **zooms** to the face of the horrified girl: the shot is a metaphor of sexual penetration. When the women recover, the daughter feels that her life has been permanently defiled. She accuses her mother of selfishness and moral irresponsibility, for, had they gone in search of a comrade as the daughter had wished, perhaps the rape might have been avoided.

The symbolic strands of the film are brought together in the final crane shot. After a furious quarrel, the two women embrace each other in tears, drawing their only comfort from the fact that they have at least survived, while others (including the comrade) have died in the war. The shot is a reversal of the metaphor of penetration: the camera slowly withdraws, pulling back from the two women, and from the locale itself. The craning stops at extreme long shot range, leaving only a small circle of light, masked by a vast expanse of blackness. The symbolic implications of the final shot are several: the shrunken circle of light suggests survival and the tenuousness of life. It is a window of life, overlooking a sea of blackness—the blackness of death, suffered by many of their countrymen. The black mask also seems to suggest the uncertainty of the future. The circle of light implies, too, the bombed hole of the church, and of course the loss of innocence—the scar of the rape. The final crane shot is deliberately ambiguous, suggesting both positive and negative ideas.

The allusion is a common type of literary analogy. It is an implied or indirect reference, usually to a well-known event, person, or work of art. Some commentators hold that the film does not often employ allusions because of its ease in showing things directly. But moviemakers, like literary authors, have discovered that an indirect allusion is often more suggestive than an explicit reference. The richness of allusions depends upon implication, not directness (Figs. 11, 43). Dennis Hopper's *Easy Rider* contains several allusions to historical persons and events from American history. The leading character's name, Wyatt (Peter Fonda), seems to be an allusion to Wyatt Earp; his contentious side-kick, Billy (Dennis Hopper), dresses in a buckskin jacket, suggesting Wild Bill Hickok. The young people of a hippie commune dress in Indianlike outfits. We learn that they almost starved the previous winter, but now they are planting corn for the winter ahead. Wyatt expresses the opinion that they will "make it," but the clothing allusion suggests the opposite: like most of the American Indians of the past, the hippies will either starve or be destroyed. *Easy Rider*, despite its apparent simplicity, employs a wide range of metaphors, symbols, and allusions. The movie draws heavily from popular myths, American history, and American literature, including Whitman's *Leaves of Grass* and Twain's *Huckleberry Finn*.

In short, both film and literature depend upon certain figurative devices to convey ideas and emotions, for both are arts of juxtaposi-

169

tion and analogy. In literature, words cán be joined with each other to produce a wide variety of meanings. In film, shots can be juxta- posed in a similar, though more limited, manner, for as we have seen, editing is not so flexible as linguistic syntax. But movies can employ symbols and metaphors within the shot and through the use of the camera itself. The juxtapositions possible in film are enormous: objects, people, settings, costumes, makeup, colors, lights, **filters,** movements, framing, sound effects, music, spoken language. Fur- thermore, unlike literature, film can employ a number of different tropes simultaneously. In one shot alone, a film-maker can create metaphors and symbols from the lighting, the color, the angle, the framing, the costuming, and so on. Of course, most directors do not employ tropes in such density, but in good films, as many as five or six simultaneous metaphors can be used in one shot. The notion that film is limited in its artistic expression when compared with literature is both snobbish and parochial. Indeed, the composer, Ralph Vaughan Williams, observed that "the film contains potentialities for the com- bination of all the arts such as Wagner never dreamed of."

JEAN COCTEAU

A number of film-makers have attempted even more ambitious tech- niques than have those directors mentioned above. Jean Cocteau was perhaps the greatest of these. He has been called "the father of the new wave," and Godard referred to him as a "bard," and a "film poet." An extraordinarily gifted man, Cocteau also distinguished himself as a painter, poet, critic, dramatist, and novelist. He did not neatly compartmentalize his various activities: to him, all artists were "poets," whether they wrote with words, sounds, or images. Never one to disparage one art in favor of another, Cocteau felt that each form of poetic expression had its specialty. The film poet, for exam- ple, simply wrote with the "ink of light." He believed that the cinema was a first-rate vehicle for ideas, permitting the poet-director to take the viewer into realms that previously only sleep and dreams had led him to. As this statement suggests, Cocteau was among the first, along with the early surrealists, to employ the stream-of-conscious- ness in film.

Cocteau was always deceptively matter-of-fact about his movies. Like many French artists, he detested phony romanticism, and al- ways claimed that he was a "realist." But to Cocteau, like Méliès before him, "reality" in film need not be the same reality as that on the street corner. Cocteau was concerned with the internal realities —the realms of the psyche and the soul, particularly of the artist. His monumental "Orpheus Trilogy," consisting of The Blood of a

Poet (1930), *Orpheus* (1950), and *Testament of Orpheus* (1960) is an exploration of the mysteries of poetic creation: what a poet is, how he creates, what he creates from. Like *Birth of a Nation, Citizen Kane,* and *Open City*, the Orpheus Trilogy is a landmark achievement, and has influenced countless other directors.

"The more one touches mystery," Cocteau claimed, "the more important it becomes to be realistic." The esthetic of film is based on photography, and what can be photographed *exists*, at least in some form. Thus, to take one of Cocteau's recurring film images, if the poet enters a mirror, we cannot deny what we have *seen*. What is involved here, of course, is the literalizing of a metaphor. A verbal paraphrase of the scene might be: "poetic creation is like entering a mirror." Or, to convert the simile to a metaphor: "poetic creation is entering a mirror." In a whimsical dialogue exchange from *The Blood of a Poet*, a statue tells the poet to walk through a mirror. "But one can't go into mirrors," he answers. "I congratulate you," the statue responds dryly, "you wrote that one could go into mirrors and you didn't believe it." The poet then walks through the mirror, into another world.

Many of Cocteau's most brilliant effects are literalized metaphors. Technically, they were achieved through trick photography. The mirror shot, for example, was accomplished by placing the camera on its side. The floor was then made to look like the wall, and the wall the floor. A vat of reflective liquid was placed on the floor; the edges of the vat suggested the frame of the mirror. Various props (chairs, etc.) were nailed on the wall above the vat. When the actor plunged into the reflective surface of the liquid from above, the entire scene looked as though he were entering a mirror, once the shot was projected right side up. *The Blood of a Poet* is a fascinating excursion into another world—yet it is always a "real world," in Cocteau's sense of the term, never soft and fuzzy, never sentimental.

The first episode deals with "the scars of the poet," his solitude and loneliness. His isolation is so great that he lives out his own creations, which take on a life of their own. "The poet's work detests and devours him," Cocteau has stated. "There isn't room for both the poet and his work. The work profits from the poet." The poet wakes to discover a mouth on his hand; the mouth resembles a gash or wound. At first he recoils from its freakishness, but gradually he grows fascinated with it. When he rubs his hand against a statue, the wound disappears and the statue comes to life. In revenge, it sends him through the mirror, into a world of terrible experiences, the world of artistic creation, which the poet fuses from his childhood memories, his fantasies, and fears. Inside the mirror, he finds himself in a long hotel corridor with many doors. He looks through a series of keyholes, where he sees, among other things, a girl floating on the ceiling of a room. After a number of painful and strange experiences, the poet shoots himself in the temple. The blood spurts **171** profusely, and transforms into a toga. A laurel wreath appears on his head.

The scene shifts to a city square on a gray, wintry day. The poet is now a statue on a pedestal. Some callous schoolboys begin a snowball fight. The statue is now made of dirty snow, and the boys tear him apart while they use his snow to make their snowballs. Later, an angel of death appears (in **negative image**), to the accompaniment of engine sounds. These merge with heartbeats, and we now see the poet's lapels throbbing with the wild beating of his heart. Again the poet shoots himself; this time he falls on a snow-covered table. As his blood gushes out, there is a cut to a loge of a theatre, where fashionably dressed people are applauding: the poet's pain produces pleasure in others. And so the film continues in a series of striking images.

In *Orpheus*, the gates of hell are guarded by motorcycle toughs, the tribunals are bureaucrats in contemporary clothing. Orpheus receives coded messages from hell by radio. In *Testament of Orpheus*, Cocteau himself appears as "the author," thus splitting himself in two by having the author comment on the poet and vice-versa. In this, his last movie, Cocteau pulls out all the stops: he employs written language, his own exquisite drawings, still photographs, slow-motion sequences, double exposures, montage, **reverse motion,** and trick shots galore. His personal friends (including Pablo Picasso) appear in a kind of testimonial; Cocteau addresses the camera; other characters readily admit that they are performing in a movie. Weird man-horses walk about dreamily, and human statues with painted eyes on their eyelids seem both dead and alive. In a witty courtroom scene, Cocteau even satirizes himself by debunking the self-importance of "the author" and poets in general. To describe Cocteau's images is almost always to reduce them to banalities, to drain them of their ambiguity and charm. Many of his astonishing metaphors and symbols simply elude description—much less explication—even after several viewings.

The Orpheus Trilogy is one of the richest achievements in film history, but Cocteau was not unique in attempting to push film to its utmost poetic limits. During the 1920s, particularly in Germany and France, a number of avant-garde experimentalists, influenced by the surrealist movement in the graphic arts, produced a series of short films of extraordinary beauty and profundity. Perhaps the most arresting of these movies were by Hans Richter and Man Ray. The young Luis Buñuel, in collaboration with Salvador Dali, produced two stunning surrealistic films: *An Andalusian Dog* (1928) and *The Golden Age* (1930).

In the 1950s and 1960s, a similar group of young American film-makers were centered in New York. Encouraged by the polemicist-film-maker, Jonas Mekas (editor of the influential journal, *Film Culture*), these directors produced a variety of witty, exuberant short films which have explored the uses of metaphors and symbols in a number of directions. Despite their limited circulation, these **"underground"** movies have exerted a surprisingly strong influence on commercial film-makers, including Fellini, Wexler, Kubrick, Antonioni, and Nichols. A few of these independent shorts are now becoming a part of the standard repertories of university movie series, including Kenneth Anger's *Scorpio Rising*, Stan Brakhage's *Dog Star Man*, Jack Smith's *Flaming Creatures*, and Stan Vanderbeek's *Skulduggery.*

POINT OF VIEW

Point of view in fiction generally concerns the narrator, through whose eyes the events of a story are viewed. That is, the ideas and incidents are sifted through the consciousness and language of the story teller, who may or may not be a participant in the action, and who may or may not be a reliable guide for the reader to follow. There are four basic types of point of view in fiction: the **first person,** the **omniscient,** the **third person,** and the **objective.** In the movies, point of view tends to be less rigorous than in fiction, for though there are cinematic examples of the four basic types of point of view, feature films tend to fall naturally into omniscient narration.

The first person narrator tells his own story. In some cases, he is an objective observer who can be relied upon to relate the events accurately. Nick Carraway in Fitzgerald's *The Great Gatsby* is a good example of this kind of narrator. Other first person narrators are subjectively involved in the main action, and cannot be totally relied upon. In *Huckleberry Finn*, for example, the immature Huck relates all the events as he experienced them. Huck obviously cannot supply his readers with all the necessary information when he himself does not possess it. In employing this type of first person narrator, the novelist must somehow permit the reader to see the truth, without destroying or straining the plausibility of the narrator. Generally, a novelist solves this problem by providing the reader with clues, which permit him to see more clearly than the narrator himself. For example, when Huck enthusiastically recounts the glamor of a circus and the "amazing feats" of its performers, the more sophisticated reader sees beyond Huck's words and infers that the performers are in fact a rather shabby crew, and their theatrical acts merely cheap deceptions.

Many films employ first-person narrative techniques, but only sporadically. The cinematic equivalent to the "voice" of the literary narrator is the "eye" of the camera, and this difference is an important one. In fiction, the distinction between the narrator and the reader is clear: it's as though the reader were listening to a friend tell a story. In film, however, the viewer identifies with the lens, and he thus tends to fuse with the narrator. To produce first person nar- **173** ration in film, the camera would have to record all the action through the eyes of the character, which—in effect—would also make the viewer the protagonist.

In *The Lady of the Lake*, Robert Montgomery attempted to use the first-person camera throughout the film. It was a noble and interesting experiment, but a failure, for several reasons. In the first place, the director was forced into a number of absurdities. Having the characters address the camera was not too much of a problem, for point-of-view shots are common in most movies. However, there were several actions where the device simply broke down. When a girl walked up to the hero and kissed him, for example, she had to slink toward the camera and begin to embrace it, while her face came closer and closer to the lens. Similarly, when the hero was involved in a fist fight, the antagonist literally had to attack the camera, which jarred appropriately whenever the "narrator" was dealt a blow.

The problem with the exclusive use of the first-person camera, then, is its literalness. Furthermore, it tends to create a sense of frustration in the viewer, who wants to *see* the hero. In fiction, we get to know the first person through his words, through his judgments and values, which are reflected in his language. But in films, we get to know a character by seeing how he reacts to people and events. Unless the director breaks the first-person camera convention, we can never see the hero, we can only see what he sees. (Montgomery partially solved this problem by using many mirror shots, where the hero's reflected image permitted the viewer to see what the protagonist looked like. But the real problem still remained, for these mirror shots were usually included in the least dramatic sequences, in which the need for a close-up of the hero's face was least necessary.)

A useful first-person technique in film is to have a narrator tell his story in words on the sound track, while the camera records the events, usually through a variety of narrative shots. This technique is sometimes used for literary adaptations, where the director wishes to preserve the language of the original without having it impede the freedom of his visuals. In Bresson's *Diary of a Country Priest*, for example, most of the language in the film consists of the priest's diary entries, which are recited on the sound track, while the images either show us the scene from a different point of view, or show us the face of the priest as he writes.

An interesting variation of this sound technique is multiple first-person narration. In *Citizen Kane*, five different people offer their ideas on what kind of person Kane was. Each sound narration is accompanied by a **flashback** sequence, though not in the first-person camera. The flashbacks present Kane in somewhat contradictory terms, each reflecting the prejudices of the story teller. Where one narrator leaves off, another who knew Kane in a different period of his life picks up the narrative line and develops it further, until the **174** final story teller concludes with a tale of Kane's last days. Kurosawa used multiple first person in *Rashomon*, where four different versions of the very same incident are offered, each one biased in favor of the individual narrator.

The omniscient narrator is often associated with the nineteenth-century novel. Generally, such narrators are not participants in a story, but all-knowing observers, who supply the reader with all the facts he needs to know in order to appreciate the story. Such narrators can span many locations and time periods. They can enter the consciousness of a number of characters, telling us what they think or feel. Omniscient narrators can be relatively detached from the story, as in *War and Peace*, or they can take on a distinct personality of their own, as in *Tom Jones*, where the amiable story teller amuses us with his wry observations and judgments.

Omniscient narration is almost inevitable in film. In literature, the first-person and the omniscient voice are mutually exclusive, for if a person tells us his own thoughts directly, he cannot also tell us—with certainty—the thoughts of others. But in film, the combination of first-person and omniscient narration is common. Each time the director moves his camera—either within a shot or between shots—we are offered a new point of view from which to evaluate the scene. He can cut easily from a **subjective point of view** (first person) to a variety of objective shots. He can concentrate on a single reaction (close-up), or the simultaneous reactions of several characters (long shot). Within a matter of seconds, the film director can show us a cause and an effect, an action and a reaction. He can connect various time periods and locations almost instantaneously (**parallel editing**), or literally superimpose different time periods (dissolve or multiple exposure). The omniscient camera can be a dispassionate observer, as it is in many of Chaplin's films, or it can be a witty commentator—an evaluater of events—as it often is in Hitchcock's films, or those of Godard.

The third-person point of view is essentially a variation of the omniscient. In the third person, a nonparticipating narrator tells a story from the consciousness of a single character. In some novels, this narrator completely penetrates the mind of a character; in others, there is virtually no penetration. In Jane Austen's *Pride and Prejudice*, for example, we learn what Elizabeth Bennett thinks and feels about events, but we are never permitted to enter the consciousness of the other characters. We can only guess what they feel through Elizabeth's interpretations—which are often inaccurate. Her interpretations are not offered directly to the reader, but through the intermediacy of the narrator, who tells us her responses.

In movies, there is a rough equivalent to the third person, but it is not so rigorous as in literature. Usually, third-person narration is found in documentaries, where an anonymous commentator tells us about the background of a central character. In Sidney Meyer's *The*

Quiet One, for example, the visuals dramatize certain traumatic events in the life of an impoverished youngster, Donald. On the sound track, James Agee's commentary tells us some of the reasons why Donald behaves as he does, how he feels about his parents, his peers, and his teachers. The verbal third person is also used in some literary adaptations, such as John Huston's version of Crane's *The Red Badge of Courage*. Perhaps the visual equivalent of the third person is a shot of the central character. Most movies combine the first and third persons. Hitchcock, for instance, often permits us to identify with a character's experiences through a point-of-view shot (first person), then he gives us a close-up of the character's face (third person).

The objective point of view is seldom used in novels, though writers occasionally employ it in short stories, such as Stephen Crane's "The Blue Hotel." The objective voice is also a variation of the omniscient. Objective narration is the most detached of all: it does not enter the consciousness of any character, but merely reports events from the outside. Indeed, this voice has been likened to a camera, which records events impartially and without bias. It presents facts, and allows the reader to interpret for himself. The objective voice is more congenial to film than to literature, for the movies literally employ a recording camera. The cinematic objective point of view is generally used by **realistic** directors, who keep their camera at long shot, and reduce editing to a minimum. The viewer of a realistic movie must often sort out and interpret the facts on his own, as though he were in the threatre. Some documentaries and **neorealist** films are essentially in the objective point of view.

LITERARY ADAPTATIONS

Paradoxically, a great deal of originality is required to produce a sensitive film adaptation of a literary source. Furthermore, as Margaret Kennedy has pointed out, the better the literary work, the more difficult the adaptation. For this reason, perhaps, many film adaptations are based on mediocre sources, for few people will get upset at the modifications required in film if the source itself is not of the highest calibre. There are some adaptations that are considerably superior to their originals: *Birth of a Nation*, for instance, was based on Thomas Dixon's trashy novel, *The Klansman*.

Some commentators believe that if a work of art has reached its fullest expression in one form, an adaptation will inevitably be inferior. According to this argument, no film adaptation of *Pride and Prejudice* could equal the original; nor could any novel hope to capture the richness of *Gold Rush*, or even *Citizen Kane*, which is a **176** rather literary movie. There is a good deal of sense in this view, for we have seen how literature and film tend to solve problems differently. To be sure, these media can achieve similar effects, but their methods differ. Or, to put it another way, the content of each medium is organically governed by its form. But the problem is infinitely more complex than this. There are some examples of great films which are based on equally great literary works. For example, an argument could be made that René Clement's *Gervaise* is fully as brilliant as Zola's *L'Assomoir*, its source.

Most naive filmgoers tend to view the problem of literary adaptation as one of simple transference: how does the film-maker dramatize the story of the original? This view is naive precisely because it assumes that the content of a literary work can be converted into film form with no fundamental modification of the original. But if this were true, we could get the "content" of *Tom Jones* by reading a college outline of Fielding's novel. Obviously, there are important qualities in the language of the original that cannot be effectively paraphrased in an outline. In film adaptations, the problem is more acute, for at least a novel and an outline of it employ the same medium (words), whereas films employ images and words.

There are three basic types of adaptations in the cinema: the loose, the faithful, and the literal. These categories are for convenience only, of course, for in actual practice, many films fall somewhere in between. The loose adaptation is barely that. Generally, only an idea, a situation, or a character is taken from a literary source, then developed independently. Loose film adaptations can be likened to Shakespeare's treatment of an idea from Plutarch or Bandello, or to the ancient Greek dramatists, who often drew upon a common mythology. A film that falls into this class is Fellini's *Satyricon*, which is indebted to Petronius' original only in terms of its tone and setting, though a few scenes are also parallel (Fig. 38). Likewise, Martin Ritt's *The Long Hot Summer* draws its setting and a few incidents from Faulkner's *The Hamlet*, which is itself based on at least five of his short stories. Kurosawa's *Throne of Blood* transforms Shakespeare's *Macbeth* into a quite different tale, set in medieval Japan, though the film-maker retains several plot elements from Shakespeare's original.

Faithful adaptations, as the phrase implies, attempt to recreate the literary source in filmic terms, keeping as close to the spirit of the original as possible. André Bazin likened the faithful adapter to a translator, who tries to find equivalents to the original. Of course, Bazin realized that fundamental differences exist between the two media: the translator's problem in converting the word "road" to *"strada"* or *"strasse"* is not so acute as a film-maker's problem in transforming the word into a picture. In his important study, *Novels into Film,* George Bluestone argues that faithful adaptations are essentially original works, for even if the director preserves the plot, characters, and tone of a novel, these elements still constitute only the raw materials of the film. To Bluestone, the film adapter is an author in his own right: he paraphrases the original, taking its content in only the crudest sense of that term. Thus, the film director could just as easily draw from a detailed outline of a novel as from the novel itself, for the organic language of the original (its form) is of little use to him.

An example of this kind of adaptation is Richardson's *Tom Jones.* John Osborne's screenplay preserves much of the novel's plot structure, its major events, and most of the important characters. Even the witty omniscient narrator is retained. But the film is not merely an illustration of the novel. In the first place, Fielding's book is too packed with incidents for a film adaptation: the many inn scenes, for example, are reduced to a central episode: the Upton Inn sequence. Two minor aspects of the novel are enlarged in the movie: the famous eating scene between Tom and Mrs. Waters, and the fox-hunting episode. These sequences are included because two of Fielding's favorite metaphors throughout the novel are drawn from eating and hunting. In effect, Osborne uses these scattered metaphors as raw material or inspiration: his scenes are filmic "equivalents," in Bazin's sense.

Some faithful adaptations are more faithful than others. That is, in some instances, the film director does not add any character or incident that does not have its counterpart in the literary source. In filming *The Diary of a Country Priest*, for example, Bresson claimed that he followed Georges Bernanos' novel "word for word." Bresson must not be taken too literally, however, for even though he retained much of the dialogue and first-person narration, and attempted to recreate the verbal imagery with visual equivalents, the two works represent essentially unique achievements. There are a number of faithful adaptations that stick closely to what Bluestone calls the "naked events" of the originals: Visconti's *The Stranger*, Polanski's *Rosemary's Baby*, Frankenheimer's *The Fixer*. In each case, however, the images may be more or less effective than the words, but only in the crudest sense do they contain the same content.

Literal film adaptations are pretty much restricted to plays. As we have seen, the two basic modes of drama—action and dialogue—are also found in films. (See Chapter 4, "Sound," and Chapter 5, "Drama.") A literal adaptation of a play, then, generally preserves all or most of the spoken language. Action in the theatre is live and three-dimensional, whereas in film it is recorded on a two-dimensional surface, but there is a greater similarity between stage and film action than there is between action in fiction and film. In other words, whether on the stage or screen, Hamlet still *does* certain things; he acts, and we literally see him act. But in a novel, a narrator would have to describe Hamlet's movements through the medium of words: we would have to imagine his action in our minds. **178**

The major problem with stage adaptations is in the handling of space and time rather than language. If the film adapter were to leave his camera at long shot, and restrict his editing to scene shifts only, the result would be similar to the original. But we have seen that few film-makers would be willing to merely record a play, nor indeed should they, for in doing so, they would lose much of the excitement of the original, and contribute none of the advantages of the adapting medium, particularly its greater freedom in treating space and time.

Movies can add many dimensions to a play, especially through the use of close-ups and edited juxtapositions. Since these techniques are not found in the theatre, even "literal" adaptations are not strictly literal, they are simply more subtle in their modifications. Stage dialogue is often retained in film adaptations, but its effect is different on the audience. Sidney Lumet's *Long Day's Journey into Night* preserves O'Neill's dialogue almost intact, but in a stage production, the meanings of the language are determined by the fact that the characters are on the same stage at the same time, reacting to the same words. In the film, time and space are fragmented by the individual shots. Furthermore, since even a literary film is primarily visual and only secondarily verbal, nearly all the dialogue is modified by the images. A line recited in close-up differs in a subtle way from the same line delivered in long shot. Even close-ups differ from each other: a character who delivers a line while looking off frame means something rather different than if he were to deliver the same line face on (see Figs. 31 and 48). The list of literal adaptations is a long and distinguished one, including Mike Nichols' *Who's Afraid of Virginia Woolf?*, Olivier's *Richard III*, and Clive Donner's *The Caretaker*. The differences between literal and loose adaptations, then, are essentially matters of degree. In each case, the cinematic form inevitably alters the content of the literary original. In the case of loose adaptations, the transformations are bold and sweeping, with literal adaptations, they are more refined.

LITERARY AND CINEMATIC DENSITY

Literature and film are both **hot** media—that is, highly saturated with information. Within each medium, however, there are wide ranges of density. For example, poetry is generally more highly saturated than prose. For this reason, poetry takes longer to understand: its language is richer, more thickly clustered with connotations and ambiguities. One doesn't read a poem by John Donne with the same ease as a piece of prose by Ernest Hemingway. Nor can one read Hemingway with the same ease as an average magazine **179** article. Like drama and film, literature is experienced in time, but it is the reader who controls time in reading fiction and poetry: if he doesn't understand the density of the language, he can reread a passage until he does.

The principle of density applies to drama as well. Agatha Christie's *The Mousetrap* and Sophocles' *Oedipus Rex* might both be called whodunnits, but there are obvious differences—among other things, differences of density in the texture of each play. The language of Miss Christie's mystery is utilitarian and denotative: it is used essentially to forward the plot and sketch in the characters with efficiency and simplicity. Plot and character are also important in Sophocles' play, but they are explored more exhaustively through the use of language, which is connotative and ambiguous, suggesting many emotional and intellectual nuances. Indeed, *Oedipus Rex* is so densely saturated that only the most sophisticated viewer could hope to take in most of its meanings in one viewing. Of course, by reading the text of the play before or after a production, a viewer can explore the density of its language on his own, as he would a piece of nondramatic literature.

The problem of density in film is much more complex. In the first place, the viewer cannot control the speed of a film, which is projected at the same rate for naive and sophisticated viewers alike. Unlike the reader, the film viewer cannot "reread" a movie image if he does not understand its complexities. The **content curve** of an image tends to be geared to the average viewer's ability to assimilate major meanings. In most instances, this means the viewer will perceive the **dominant contrast** and perhaps a few **subsidiary contrasts.** With the majority of films, as with the majority of novels and plays, superficial readings of this sort involve no real problems, for a merely routine movie is not intensely saturated with meanings. But we have seen that a great film director can include five or six metaphors simultaneously in one shot. In most cases, these will be missed by the average viewer, unless he has seen the film several times. Nor can a film viewer turn to a text, for a filmscript, even a copiously illustrated one, is essentially a cinematic equivalent to a college outline of a novel.

Naive students of the film are often amazed at how a sophisticated viewer can read so much in a movie. But such a viewer merely explicates the images on several levels simultaneously, just as a sensitive reader of Melville's *Moby Dick* can appreciate both the adventure and the rich texture of symbols that add such emotional and intellectual resonance to the novel. Until the student of film has at his disposal an equivalent of a text (the film itself), he must train his eyes and ears to assimilate simultaneously as much of the density of the images and sounds as possible. But no matter how sophisticated the viewer, great films—like great literature and drama—require repeated exposure.

180

Further Readings

Astruc, Alexandre "The Birth of a New Avant-Garde: La Caméra-Stylo," in *The New Wave*. Edited by Peter Graham. London: Secker & Warburg, 1968. (Paper)

Battestin, Martin C. "Osborne's *Tom Jones:* Adapting a Classic," in *Man and the Movies*. Edited by W. R. Robinson. Baltimore: Penguin Books, 1969. (Paper)

Bazin, André. "In Defense of Mixed Cinema," *"Le Journal d'un curé de campagne* and the Stylistics of Robert Bresson," in *What Is Cinema?* Edited and translated by Hugh Gray. Berkeley: University of California Press, 1967. (Paper)

Bluestone, George. *Novels into Film*. Baltimore: Johns Hopkins Press, 1957. (Paper)

Cocteau, Jean. *Cocteau on the Film*. New York: Roy, 1954.

Eisenstein, Sergei. "The Cinematographic Principle and the Ideogram," "Methods of Montage," "Dickens, Griffith, and the Film Today," in *Film Form*. Edited and translated by Jay Leyda. New York: Harcourt, Brace & Company, 1949. (Paper)

Kennedy, Margaret. "The Mechanized Muse," in *Film: An Anthology*. Edited by Daniel Talbot. Berkeley: University of California Press, 1966. (Paper)

Oxenhandler, Neal. "Poetry in Three Films of Jean Cocteau," in *Art of the Cinema. Yale French Studies*. No 17. New Haven, 1956.

Pasolini, Pier Paolo. "Cinematic and Literary Stylistic Figures," in *Film Culture* (Spring, 1962).

Renan, Sheldon. *An Introduction to the American Underground Film*. New York: E. P. Dutton & Co., Inc., 1967. (Paper)

Richardson, Robert. *Literature and Film*. Bloomington: Indiana University Press, 1969.

THEORY

Surely there are no hard and fast rules:
it all depends on how it's done.

PAULINE KAEL

Even before the turn of the century, the film began to develop in two major directions: the **realistic** and the **expressionistic.** In the mid-1890s in France, the Lumière brothers delighted audiences with their short movies dealing with everyday occurrences. Such films as *The Arrival of a Train* fascinated viewers precisely because they seemed to capture the flux and variability of events as they were viewed in real life. At about the same time, Georges Méliès was producing a number of fantasy films which emphasized purely imagined events. Such movies as *A Trip to the Moon* were typical mixtures of whimsical narrative and trick photography. In many respects, then, the Lumières and Méliès can be regarded as the fathers of realism and expressionism, respectively.

"Realism" and "expressionism" are convenient terms when they are used to suggest a general emphasis or point of view. Though there are a number of exceptions and a great many hybrid variations, the major differences between these two film traditions are reasonably discernible. Realistic movies tend to be more concerned with content than form, with *what* is shown more than *how* it is shown. The camera is used rather conservatively: it is essentially a recording mechanism which objectively reproduces the surfaces of tangible objects. The major concern, then, is with creating a film world which resembles the actual physical world as closely as possible. Realists tend to emphasize film as visual reportage, as documentary. Often politically oriented, realists emphasize the relationships between men and their political and social environments. Technically this emphasis is achieved through the use of location settings, natural lighting, **long shots,** deep-focus photography, lengthy **takes,** and an avoidance of conspicuous camera techniques and special effects. **185**

Expressionists show a marked preference for form over content, for subjectivity and self-expression over factuality and literalness. The camera is used in a self-conscious manner to interpret reality, not only to record it. Expressionists are concerned with inner spiritual and psychological truths, which they feel can be captured by distorting the outer surfaces of the natural world. This emphasis is achieved through a number of stylized techniques: symbolic and artificial lighting, fragmentary **editing** practices, **nonsynchronous** sound, extreme angles, and special-effects cinematography.

Film theory grew out of these two general traditions. Unfortunately, movie critics have too often been prescriptive rather than descriptive, and the result has been a good deal of dogmatizing about what is "pure film," what is "unsuitable to the medium," and what is "intrinsically cinematic." Film theorists are not unique in demonstrating this kind of critical rigidity. In the late nineteenth century, for example, there were a number of critics who championed Ibsen's realism over the poetic dramas of the Elizabethans—as though it were the style, rather than the talents of the individual playwrights that determined artistic excellence. There have been similar theorists of fiction—those who claim that the novel is "by definition" a realistic genre, for example, thus excluding such romantic and expressionistic writers as Hawthorne and Melville. In painting, there are some who dismiss Courbet's realism as "too photographic," just as there are others who criticize Kandinsky for being "too personal" and subjective. These are phony distinctions. There are great works in each tradition, just as there are useful and sensitive critics in each tradition.

REALISTIC THEORIES

Perhaps no other theorist has been so influential as Siegfried Kracauer, whose book, *Theory of Film: The Redemption of Physical Reality*, puts forth some of the basic tenets of realistic film theory. Kracauer does not ignore expressionistic movies in his book. Indeed, he acknowledges a "formative tendency" which he traces back to the early experiments of Méliès. In general, however, he considers expressionistic movies as aberrations of the central esthetic of the film. The basic postulate of Kracauer's esthetic is that film is essentially an extension of photography and shares with it a "marked affinity" for recording the visible world around us.

Unlike most art forms, photography and film tend to leave the raw materials of actuality more or less intact. Kracauer would agree with Aristotle's precept that art is an "imitation of nature," but the film theorist would insist that artists in other media imitate nature only in a general sense. The novelist, for example, recreates experiences with words, but the meanings we derive from the medium of language are different from the meanings we would derive from the actual experience. The camera, however, gravitates towards a more literal kind of imitation. A photographic image of a face, for instance, is virtually a copy of the original. Kracauer's fundamental principle, then, rests upon the literalness of the camera's imitation of nature. Movies which stress artifice run the risk of violating the "basic properties" of the medium.

According to Kracauer, the cinema is characterized by a number of natural affinities. First of all, film tends to favor "unstaged reality"—that is, the most appropriate subject matter gives the illusion of having been found, rather than arranged. Second, film tends to stress the random, the fortuitous. Kracauer is fond of the phrase, "nature caught in the act." That is, film is best suited to recording events and objects which might be overlooked in life—the stirring of a leaf, for example, or the rippling of a brook. Last, the best films suggest endlessness, they imply a slice-of-life, a fragment of actuality, rather than a unified, enclosed whole. The space-time continuum of film suggests the same open-ended limitlessness of life itself (see Fig. 64).

Kracauer is hostile toward movies which demonstrate a "formative" tendency; that is, films which work against these natural affinities. Historical films and fantasies he regards as tending to move away from the basic concerns of the medium. Thus, he approves of the early semidocumentary films of Eisenstein, but condemns his later works—the "operatic" *Alexander Nevsky* and *Ivan the Terrible*. The images and events of these films are "uncinematic": they are not fortuitous, but arranged, synthetic, and "theatrical" (see Fig. 63). Kracauer also dismisses most literary and dramatic adaptations because he feels that literature is ultimately concerned with "internal realities," not external ones. For example, he thinks that if Shakespearean adaptations are performed on stylized sets, the result is mere filmed theatre, for the documentary realism of the medium is violated. If the plays are performed in natural settings (real castles and forests), the stylized language, the artificial costumes, and the "enclosed" world all clash with the open-ended authenticity of the locales.

Kracauer tends to regard all self-conscious elements as "uncinematic." The camera ought to record what *is*. When the subject matter is not close to physical reality, we become conscious of the artifice, and hence, our pleasure is diminished. For example, historical films tend to be uncinematic because the viewer is aware of the "reconstruction." The world of the film is enclosed, for beyond the **frame** is not the "endlessness" of actual time and place, but the paraphernalia of the twentieth-century film studio. Similarly, in fantasy films, we become too conscious of the contrivances: instead of concentrating on what is shown, we become distracted by wondering how certain effects are achieved, for they have no literal counterpart in reality (see Fig. 36).

187

Kracauer underestimates the flexibility of an audience's response to nonrealistic movies. To be sure, it is easier for a film-maker to create the illusion of reality if his story takes place in a contemporary setting, for the world of the movie and the actual world are essentially the same. It is also true that we are often aware of the contrivances in historical films and fantasies, but usually when the cinematic techniques are heavy-handed and clumsy. On the other hand, there are dozens of films that seem saturated in the details of a remote period. Many scenes from *Birth of a Nation* appear as authentic as the Civil War photographs of Matthew Brady (Figs. 12, 13). Kubrick's *Paths of Glory* was obviously not photographed during World War I, yet it is totally convincing in its *sense* of authenticity. Visconti's period films are virtually reconstructed documentaries: *The Leopard*, for example, never betrays a sense of contrivance or self-consciousness in its use of costumes, makeup, sets, and properties.

Other movies deliberately exploit the audience's double existence. As Dr. Johnson pointed out many years ago, audiences in a theatre do not literally believe they are viewing events of a remote period. Although viewers give a kind of voluntary credence to the events on stage, they are always aware of the fact that they are in a theatre, watching an artistic performance—not the real thing. The same principle of esthetic distance applies to many movies. In *Tom Jones*, for example, the details of the period are authentic and believable, but Richardson deliberately breaks the illusion of reality by calling attention to the camera. In one scene, Tom is engaged in a furious quarrel with the mistress of the inn at Upton. Suddenly, in exasperation, he turns and addresses the camera. Richardson in effect reminds the audience that we are in a theatre, watching a movie. The charm of this scene—and many others in the film—is precisely due to this technique of yanking the viewer in and out of the eighteenth-century world of the story proper.

Similar techniques are found in the historical plays of Bertolt Brecht, who "alienated" or "endistanced" his audiences from the world of the play in order to permit the viewer to draw certain political conclusions based on the contrasts between the two time periods. Techniques of this sort are common in the works of Brecht's cinematic disciple, Jean-Luc Godard. Much of the brilliance of his films is due to the audacious switching between documentary realism and stylized tableaux, as in *La Chinoise*, for instance.

Finally, as Pauline Kael has pointed out, audiences often enjoy the contrivances of a movie: it is part of the pleasure in watching a film. Musicals, for example, are generally appealing because they are *unlike* everyday reality. The same is true of many **underground** films and **animated** movies. In *2001*, the audience derives as much pleasure from wondering how Kubrick achieved some of his extraordinary special effects as from the effects themselves. In short, film audiences are highly sophisticated in their responses to nonrealistic films: a viewer can almost totally suspend his disbelief, partially **188** suspend it, or alternate between extremes—according to the wishes (and skills) of the director.

It is true that Kracauer's book is of limited value in explaining why expressionistic films are so effective. On the other hand, his theory is exceptionally sensitive in explaining the effectiveness of realistic movies. The subtitle of Kracauer's book speaks not of the "imitation" or "recording" of physical reality, but of its "redemption." To redeem something is to recover it, to rescue it from oblivion. Even realistic movies, then, go beyond everyday life in some way: they show us things that we might not notice in the chaos and flux of everyday life. The camera preserves fortuitous fragments from this chaos, rescuing them from obscurity (Figs. 18, 34).

An examination of virtually any good realistic film demonstrates what Kracauer is getting at. In Bryan Forbes' *The Whisperers*, for instance, the **deep-focus** shots of the dingy apartment of the elderly heroine (Edith Evans) tell us much of her loneliness and neglect: dozens of empty milk bottles clutter the table, yellowed photographs in separate frames are crowded on the mantel. Only the sounds of the creaking walls and the dripping faucet seem to provide the old woman with active companionship—her "whisperers." Such desolate scenes are probably duplicated in thousands if not millions of apartments everywhere. In real life, we often turn away to less disagreeable sights, but after witnessing these scenes, few people could remain indifferent to the solitude of the elderly and indigent.

The films of Jean Renoir are filled with "commonplace" touches —details which are effective precisely because of their truth to life as it can be observed. In *Grand Illusion*, for example, the prisoners of war rummage through a trunkful of costumes in preparation for a theatrical show. Jokingly, a cynical prisoner instructs a delicate youth to put on one of the wigs and an evening gown. As a lark, the boy traipses off to get into costume. While the other men are engaged in excited preparations, the costumed youth enters the room. Suddenly a hush falls over the entire group. As the embarrassed boy wisecracks about his outfit, the camera slowly pans revealing the sad, wistful expressions of the other men, as they recall how long it has been since they have seen their women. The sequence is brilliantly effective, yet tactful and simple. As is the case with many situations in life, the scene captures the sudden shift in mood which can accompany the simplest event.

NEOREALISM

Kracauer often cites Italian **neorealist** films to illustrate his theories. Actually, neorealism is both a style of film making and a specific cinematic movement which began in Italy during the last months of

World War II. As a particularly Italian movement, neorealism was pretty much over by the mid-1950s, but as a style, it spread to many other countries. In India, for example, many of the films of Satyajit Ray are in the neorealistic style, and in America, Elia Kazan came under its influence. Beginning in the mid-1950s, neorealism became the dominant mode in England, and lasted for nearly a decade: the earliest movies of Tony Richardson, Karel Reisz, and Lindsay Anderson reflect both the political and stylistic biases of this movement.

Perhaps the quintessential neorealistic movie is Roberto Rossellini's *Open City*, which launched both the movement and the style. Scripted by Cesare Zavattini, one of the greatest screen writers in the history of the cinema, *Open City* had an explosive effect on the film world. Rossellini shot some of the movie while the Nazis were evacuating Rome. Technically, the film was rather crude. Since good quality film stock was impossible to obtain, Rossellini had to use inferior newsreel stock, but despite—indeed, because of—the technical flaws, the grainy images conveyed a sense of journalistic immediacy and authenticity (see also Fig. 52). Virtually all the film was shot on location, much of it in the sun-drenched streets. The majority of the actors were nonprofessionals, ordinary Italians. The structure of the film was episodic—a series of vignettes showing the reactions of Roman citizens to the German occupation. Some of the episodes dramatize the heroism of the Italian resistance, others deal with more pragmatic adjustments. The film is saturated with a sense of unrelenting honesty. "This is the way things are," Rossellini is said to have declared after the film was shown. The statement became the motto of the neorealist movement.

Within the next few years, there followed an astonishing series of films: Rossellini's *Paisan*, Vittorio de Sica's *Shoeshine, Bicycle Thief*, and *Umberto D*, (all scripted by Zavattini), Luigi Zampa's *To Live in Peace*, and Visconti's *La Terra Trema*. The early works of Fellini and Antonioni, while not generally considered a part of the neorealist movement, were nonetheless heavily indebted to it. Most of these movies demonstrated the same political and stylistic biases: open-ended structures, suggesting a slice of life, rather than a neatly articulated plot; an insistence upon picturing people truthfully, "warts and all"; a reluctance to offer slick solutions to complex problems; a preference for authentic locations and natural lighting; the use of nonprofessional actors, even in principal roles; a concern with poverty as a social and political problem; the avoidance of extraordinary characters and events; an encompassing tone of compassion, especially for the underprivileged; an emphasis on democratic and humanist ideals (with a concommitant hostility towards Fascism and bourgeois values in general); and an understated use of the camera, with emphasis on long shots, and subdued editing techniques.

The neorealist movement was the embodiment of what Kracauer later defined as the main business of the cinema. Virtually all these film-makers avoided spectacular events and unusual characters in favor of ordinary everyday situations. Suspicious of conventional plot structures, these directors dismissed them as dead formulas. They insisted upon the dramatic superiority of things as they really *are*, the texture of life as it is experienced by ordinary people. These directors were concerned with the "excavation" of reality: instead of plots, they emphasized facts, and all the "echoes and reverberations" of facts.

Film-making, according to Zavattini, was not a matter of "inventing fables," but of searching unrelentingly to uncover the implications of certain social facts. Thus a whole film could be structured around the fact that a working couple wants to find an apartment. In an American film, this fact might constitute only a minor scene, lasting some two or three minutes. But the neorealist explores the implications of this fact: why do they want the apartment? Where did they live before? Why don't they stay there? How much does the apartment cost? Where will they get the money? How will their family respond? And so on.

Anticipating Kracauer, the neorealists believed that the purpose of the cinema is to celebrate the "dailiness" of events. They wanted to reveal certain details that had always been there, but had never been noticed before—in Kracauer's term, they wanted to "redeem physical reality." Most of all, these directors insisted upon the innate dignity of the human spirit, which is revealed even in the most insignificant situation. These films are generally so simple in terms of "content" that they seem banal when paraphrased verbally. Perhaps the greatest of them, de Sica's *Bicycle Thief*, deals with a poor man's attempts to recover his stolen bike, which he needs in order to keep his job. The man's search grows increasingly more frantic as he crosses all over the city with his idolizing, urchinlike son. After a discouraging series of false leads, the two finally track down one of the thieves, but the protagonist is outwitted by him, and humiliated in front of his boy. Realizing that he will lose his livelihood without a bike, the desperate man sneaks off and attempts to steal one himself, but he is caught and again cruelly humiliated in front of a crowd—which includes his incredulous son. With all the bitterness of outraged innocence, the youngster suddenly recognizes that his father is not an heroic figure, but an ordinary man, who in desperation has yielded to a degrading temptation. Like most neorealist films, the movie does not offer an overt solution. The final scene shows the boy walking alongside his father, both of them choking with shame and weeping silently. Almost imperceptibly, the man's hand gropes for his son's, and they walk homeward—their only comfort a mutual compassion.

Bicycle Thief is an extraordinary achievement. Its two principals were amateurs who had never acted before. Its dialogue was not the standard Tuscan Italian, but a slangy working-class dialect which had the verisimilitude of a street-corner conversation. The techniques of the film are unobtrusive and direct: there are no fancy "memorable" **shots,** yet the very simplicity of the images is what produces their overwhelming impact. In short, the film embodies the highest ideals of the neorealist movement: a scrupulous fidelity to everyday reality, and a compassionate humanism, stressing the indestructibility and grandeur of the human spirit.

THE DOCUMENTARY

Documentarists—both practitioners and theorists—are by no means agreed on the definition of a documentary film. For every "rule," there seem to be a number of notable exceptions. Despite occasional inconsistencies, however, the documentary film does reflect certain general tendencies and biases. Perhaps the basic characteristic of the documentary is that it deals with fact rather than fiction, with real places, people, and events rather than imagined ones. The documentary artist generally believes that he is not imitating nature so much as he is observing it—though in both cases, of course, the artist is required to select certain details, and shape his raw materials into some coherent pattern. Both fact and fiction film-makers recognize that some interpretation and "creativity" are involved in the ordering of their materials. The differences are matters of degree. In general, the documentarist tends to work inductively. That is, he tries to perceive certain patterns that exist in reality itself, rather than superimposing a form from without.

The fiction film-maker tends to structure his materials in terms of probability and consistency. That is, how is such-and-such a character *likely* to react to a given situation? The documentarist tends to withhold judgment until he observes how the person reacts *in fact.* Whether or not the reaction is consistent or probable, the documentarist prefers the actual thing to the likely thing. For example, in any documentary dealing with the life of Robert Frost, one would expect at least one scene of the poet on a lonely road, perhaps meditating upon a natural scene. But in *Robert Frost: A Lover's Quarrel with the World*, Robert Hughes avoided the probable, and concentrated on what Frost is: a rather snappish, not altogether pleasant man, shrewd and thoroughly contemporary. The final image of the film is not of the "Celebrated Contemplative Poet" walking down a country road, but of a weary professional in a station wagon, driving off to yet another speaking engagement.

In short, like the neorealists, most documentarists feel that there is more drama in everyday reality than in the "inventions" and "falsifications" that characterize the average fiction film. In actual practice, of course, these distinctions are not always so neat. For example, there seems to be more fidelity to life (in the documentary sense) in a fiction film like Elia Kazan's *On the Waterfront* than there **192**

is in Flaherty's "factual" *Man of Aran*, though both are excellent
films.

A second major characteristic of the documentary is its social orientation: the emphasis is on the interrelationships between man and his environment. Particular stress is placed on political institutions and their degree of responsiveness to the needs of citizens. Not surprisingly, a great many documentaries are government sponsored, and are intended primarily for educational and propagandistic purposes. For example, in America during the 1930s, such documentaries as Pare Lorenz's *The River* publicized the work of the TVA and its various benefits.

A related characteristic of many documentaries is a strong emphasis on social reform. The British documentary tradition is particularly reformist oriented and staunchly committed to the ideals of social democracy. This tradition has been dominated by the Scotsman, John Grierson, who originally coined the term "documentary," and defined it as "the creative treatment of actuality." Grierson supervised hundreds of films dealing with specific needs and abuses in British society. From 1939 to 1945, he headed the prestigious Canadian National Film Board, which produced many excellent documentaries. Along with his disciple, Paul Rotha, Grierson formulated a theory of documentary that was frankly didactic. "I look upon the cinema as a pulpit, and use it as a propagandist," he once claimed. Though Grierson and Rotha are critical of films which are crudely propagandistic, they insisted that the documentarist must be a political and social analyst. The objective documentary is mere newsreel, they believed, for it only reports, and does not suggest causes and cures.

The British documentary theorists are somewhat intolerant of other approaches. For example, Rotha criticizes Flaherty for his "romantic" and "individualistic" tendencies. Flaherty's films deal with eternal conflicts, especially man against the elements. *Nanook of the North*, for instance, is essentially a tale of personal heroism, dealing with an Eskimo's fight for survival in the harsh, unyielding wilderness of the Arctic. Political institutions seem irrelevant, as is also the case in *Man of Aran*. But Grierson and Rotha feel that the problems facing the twentieth century are essentially urban and technological, and the solutions are to be found in collectivist action. Flaherty's subject matter, they felt, was simply irrelevant to contemporary society, and his emphasis on individualism, a dangerous evasion of the political implications of given social conditions.

The humanistic idealism of British documentaries is appealing, and the many excellent movies which have come out of this tradition certainly justify it as a major approach to documentary film making. Yet the cinema would be infinitely poorer without the great films of Flaherty and those of similar artistic inclinations. There are some subjects, after all, that are not particularly political, yet intensely human. Furthermore, Grierson and his disciples concentrate on those **193** movies which are committed to democratic socialism. Other forms of political commitment tend to be minimized. The works of Eisenstein, for instance, receive rather short shrift, and the brilliant films of the Nazi Leni Riefenstahl are hardly acknowledged. Despite what we may feel about Hitler, few could deny the sheer genius of Miss Riefenstahl's *Triumph of the Will*, which is a celebration of Nazism, as well as a powerfully effective idolization of the Führer.

Another characteristic of the documentary is its emphasis on genuineness. Although there are some exceptions, most nonfiction films deal with actual events and employ nonprofessional casts. Documentarists are particularly hostile toward the use of the studio, and tend to reject re-creations of events as false to the way things really happen. However, even Grierson staged some events, and later in his career he also employed professional actors and permitted some scenes to be shot in the studio. When such artificial techniques are employed, of course, the distinctions between documentary and fiction film can become considerably blurred.

Finally, there are some documentaries that are not technically "realistic," as the term has been used throughout these chapters. That is, some documentary films do not employ the camera conservatively, nor are they restrained in terms of their editing techniques. Such films as Eisenstein's *Old and New* are expressionistic technically, not realistic. The excellence of Miss Riefenstahl's movies is found in the magnificent editing, which is highly fragmented. Even a predominantly realistic film like *Man of Aran* employs some elaborate **cross-cutting** in some sequences, as does Grierson's own *Drifters*.

EXPRESSIONIST THEORIES

Rudolf Arnheim occupies a prominence among expressionist film theorists which is comparable to Kracauer's among realists. Arnheim's *Film as Art* was originally published in 1933, when sound and color were still in their developing stages in film, but the book contains most of the basic tenets of expressionism as they are still espoused. His major premise is that film art is the direct result of the *differences* between physical reality and cinematic reality, that the movie director exploits the limitations of his medium—the lack of sound, color, depth, space-time continuity, etc.—to produce a world which resembles the real world only in a limited sense. Film art does not consist of a copy or reproduction of reality, but of a kind of "translation" of observed characteristics into the forms of the film medium.

As a gestalt psychologist, Arnheim is primarily concerned with the perception of experience, and his theory is based upon the **194** different modes of perception of the camera on the one hand, and the human eye on the other. Anticipating McLuhan, Arnheim insists that the camera's image of a bowl of fruit, for instance, is fundamentally different from our perception of the fruit bowl in actual life. (Or, in McLuhan's terms, that the "information" we receive in each instance is determined by the "form" of the "content.") Expressionist theorists celebrate these differences, for they believe that the very properties that make photography fall short of perfect reproduction determine the artistic forms of the film medium.

Technological advancements like sound, color, and wide screen were originally viewed with suspicion, if not outright hostility by most expressionists. Like Arnheim, they believed that the resultant increase in realism brought on by these technical innovations actually worked against the expressive characteristics of the cinema. Virtually all the expressionists share Arnheim's belief that art begins where mechanical reproduction leaves off—that he who vies with nature deserves to lose. This is the thesis of *The Cinema as Art*, for example, an influential and widely read book by Ralph Stephenson and Jean Debrix.

Arnheim discusses a number of examples where significant divergences exist between the image that the camera makes of reality and that which the human eye sees. For example, the film director must choose which viewpoint to photograph an object from. He does not necessarily choose the clearest view, for often this does not emphasize the major characteristic of the object. For instance, to emphasize a man's power and authority, the camera would probably be placed at a **low angle;** to photograph him face-on (the clearest view) would not capture his essence. Sometimes the director wishes to attract the spectator's attention by viewing an object from an unusual position—by photographing an event from a helicopter, for instance.

In life, we perceive objects in depth, and can penetrate the space which surrounds most things. In film, "space" is an illusion, for the screen has only two dimensions—a fact which permits the director to manipulate objects and perspective in an artistically effective manner. For instance, important objects can be placed where they are most likely to be noticed first; unimportant objects can be relegated to inferior positions, at the edges or "back" of the screen, for example. Surprise effects can be achieved by suddenly revealing (through a **pull-back dolly**) what has been excluded by the frame (Fig. 51). The frame itself is a delimiting device that has no real counterpart in one's perception of the natural world.

In movies, two objects can be photographed in such a way that one blocks out the other. In *Citizen Kane*, for instance, Kane threateningly tells his second wife that she will do precisely what he tells her to do: as he speaks, he moves closer to her, his shadow suddenly plunging her pale face into darkness. Because the lens does not make psychological adjustments to size and distance, the director **195** can manipulate these elements to achieve symbolic relationships. A man can be "decreased" in stature by photographing him in a distant plane, while another subject—a whiskey bottle, say—can seem larger than the man because it is just in front of the camera's lens. The man's dominance by the bottle is suggested by the distortion of the photographic process.

The use of lights in film is more than merely utilitarian, Arnheim would claim. Lights can suggest symbolic ideas, can bring out essential characteristics of an object, can reveal or cover certain details, and can shift a viewer's interest from one point on the screen to another. Sound and color, if they are used, should not be employed merely to enhance the realism of an image, but to convey essential characteristics. The very distortion involved in recording natural sounds and colors can be exploited to emphasize symbolic rather than literal characteristics—characteristics that have no counterpart in the natural world.

In real life, space and time are experienced as continuous phenomena, but through his editing, the film-maker chops up space and time and rearranges them in a more meaningful manner. Like other artists, the film director selects certain expressive details from the chaotic plenitude of physical reality. By juxtaposing these space and time "fragments," he creates a coherence which does not exist in raw nature. This, of course, is the basic position of the Russian montage theorists. (Chapter 3, "Editing.")

Arnheim points out that there are many mechanical modes of "perception" in the cinema that have no human counterpart. We cannot manipulate our eyes the way that a camera can be adjusted to produce **slow motion, fast motion, reverse motion,** and **freeze frames.** Certainly our eyes have no real equivalents to **dissolves, multiple exposures, negative images,** distorting lenses and **filters,** focus manipulations, and all the other special effects that can be achieved through the use of the **optical printer.**

In short, Arnheim and most other expressionists would claim that film art is possible precisely because of the limitations and peculiarities of the medium. The very act of photographing an object involves a profound distortion of that object as it is perceived in real life. In attempting to imitate nature, then, the film director does not merely record or copy the physical world: he interprets it through his camera. In thus transforming his raw materials, he does not destroy physical reality so much as he transcends it by distilling, rearranging, and strengthening certain essential characteristics.

The problem with most expressionist theories is the same as with most realist theories: there are too many exceptions. Arnheim's analysis is certainly useful in an appreciation of Griffith's movies, for example, or Eisenstein's. But how helpful is the theory in explaining the films of Renoir or de Sica? Even if we conceded Arnheim's basic premise—that the photographic process distorts reality—we still tend to respond to realistic movies primarily because of their *similar-* **196** *ities* with physical reality, not their divergences from it. Ultimately, of course, these are matters of emphasis, for films are too pluralistic and eclectic to be pigeonholed into one theory. Indeed, some movies —*Citizen Kane,* for example—have been claimed by theorists of both camps!

AVANT-GARDE FILMS

Perhaps the most extreme instances of expressionist practices in film are found in avant-garde movies. During the 1920s, a flourishing avant-garde movement was centered in Paris; after World War II, similar groups were located in New York and San Francisco. Both European and American movements were united by common goals: the desire to liberate the film from the restrictions of content (especially narrative structures), and the desire to exploit the possibilities of the cinema as "pure form." A number of these movie-makers stressed the kinship of film to the more abstract arts—music, dance, and painting, especially abstract expressionist painting.

The majority of these directors rejected the idea of "imitation." They insisted that the main business of film is to create totally new forms, not to copy them from nature, or even to exploit natural forms as a pretext. Traditional influences on film—drama, literature, and journalism—were rejected as "impure" and "didactic." Hans Richter, for example, championed the "absolute film," which he likened to a piece of pure music like a Bach fugue, which doesn't imitate anything in nature, but simply exists for its own sake. This emphasis on pure form is paralleled in the school of abstract expressionist painting: such artists claimed that their paintings did not "represent" anything, except possibly the inner feelings of the artists. Similarly, nonrepresentational movies do not offer colors, lines, and volumes as an imitation of something in physical reality, but as something which justifies its existence by its own beauty.

Another common characteristic among avant-garde film-makers is the emphasis on self-expression. Perhaps above all, the "inner impulse" of the artist is valued. The lack of recognizable subject matter is an attempt to avoid distracting irrelevancies; that is, anything which sidetracks the viewer from the real content of the film— the artist's internal emotions. To this end, a number of these movies employed meaningless or neutral titles, such as *Diagonal Symphony* or *Opus 1.*

Frequently the abstractions of music provide the inspiration for avant-garde films. For example, Mary Ellen Bute's "visual symphonies" are animated abstract expressionist paintings fused with classical musical compositions. In the 1920s, Oskar Fischinger translated musical pieces into visual patterns on the screen. Some of the **197** boldest films of this sort have been created by the Canadian Norman McLaren. In his witty *Begone Dull Care*, McLaren painted directly on the filmstrip. The abstract images are accompanied by a jazz sound track. Some avant-garde film-makers exploit the abstract patterns of recognizable subject matter. Maya Deren's semiabstract movies, for example, fuse human dancers and cinematic special effects, such as slow motion and multiple exposures.

Avant-garde techniques have had a considerable influence on commercial films. Walt Disney's *Fantasia*, for example, is a series of animated vignettes which illustrate classical musical selections. Hiroshi Teshigahara's *Woman of the Dunes* superimposed many **close-ups** of nude human bodies with long shots of sand dunes: the result is a series of richly textured abstract patterns. At times, the viewer is uncertain whether he is looking at the contours of a body or at an expanse of sculptured desert terrain. Similarly, Kubrick's light show in *2001* was almost certainly inspired by the experiments in abstract film-making of Jordan Belson. Haskell Wexler's *Medium Cool* is filled with stunning abstract images, many of them actually close-ups of perfectly ordinary objects, which are temporarily deprived of their contexts (see Figs. 28, 40).

THE AUTEUR THEORY

In the mid-1950s, *Cahiers du Cinéma* published a polemical essay, "*La Politique des Auteurs,*" by its young critic, François Truffaut. The piece became the focal point of a critical controversy which eventually spread to England and America as well. Before long, the **auteur theory** became a kind of militant rallying cry, particularly among younger critics, dominating such journals as *Movie* in England, *Film Culture* in America, and both French and English language editions of *Cahiers du Cinéma*. Because of the strident, often shrill tone of many of its practitioners, the *auteur* theory managed to offend virtually all the older established critics, and even André Bazin, the founder and editor of *Cahiers du Cinéma*, wrote an essay warning of the excesses of the theory as it was practiced by some of his youthful disciples.

Actually, the main lines of the theory are reasonable, and not particularly revolutionary. Its major emphasis is on the director as the "author" of a movie—his personality dominates the collaborative enterprise of film-making. The great director manages to express his genius even in otherwise routine assignments. *Auteur* criticism is essentially a variant of romantic theory, where the artist receives greater emphasis than the work of art. Despite the obvious dangers of such an approach, it was probably a necessary one for the times, for these young polemicists were reacting against the "respectable" **198** films of social consciousness which were set up as standards of excellence by most highbrow and academic critics. Such movies ordinarily dealt with "serious" and "mature" subjects, and were characterized by a bland if sincere liberalism.

The *auteur* critics insisted that movies ought to be judged on the basis of "how" and not "what." That is, they felt that film theory had been dominated by considerations of content only, that technique was ignored. Like most expressionist theorists, the *auteur* critics claimed that what makes a good movie is not the subject matter *per se*, but the *treatment* of the subject matter. They were particularly hostile to "message movies"—films which were visually boring, but "well intended" in their desire for social reform. The *auteur* critics disliked the dominance of the writer in such films, for they felt that the crudely didactic dialogue was a major determinant of the turgidity of most of these films.

As an alternate standard of excellence, these critics turned to American movies, including thrillers, westerns, gangster films, and musicals. What they particularly admired about American films was their narrative vitality, their stylistic verve, and technical competence. Most of these writers would have agreed with Erwin Panofsky when he observed that while commercial movies are always in danger of ending up as prostitutes, the so-called "art film" was equally in danger of ending up as an old maid.

In other words, the *auteur* critics felt that what was lacking in "the serious cinema" of the times was a proper appreciation for the liberating qualities of adventure, vulgarity, and high spirits. American movies obviously possessed these characteristics in abundance. Before long personality cults developed around the most popular of these directors. On the whole, these were film-makers who had been virtually ignored by "serious" critics: Alfred Hitchcock, Joseph Losey, Howard Hawks, Nicholas Ray, and many others.

The sheer breadth of their knowledge of film history permitted these critics to reevaluate most of the major films of a wide variety of directors. Particular stress was placed upon the value of a director's total output, rather than on any single film. In many instances, they completely reversed previous critical judgments. John Ford, for example, had been admired by highbrow critics for his "artistic" productions like *The Informer* and *The Grapes of Wrath.* His westerns were more or less shrugged off as the commercial price one had to pay for being permitted to make "serious" films. But the *auteur* critics rightly insisted that such classic westerns as *Stagecoach, My Darling Clementine*, and *Fort Apache* were artistically superior to Ford's rather pretentious films of social consciousness. They pointed out what is a commonplace in art and literary criticism: that the crude content of an artistic work is not always a reliable index of its worth.

For example, *My Darling Clementine* is nominally about Wyatt Earp, and the film features several of the standard elements of the western **genre:** the antagonism between lawmen and outlaws; the

presence of a "saloon girl" and the "Eastern lady"; the rustling of
cattle; and the shoot-em-up sequence at the end. But even Homer's
Iliad sounds pretty trashy when it is paraphrased in this manner.
Like Whitman's *Leaves of Grass*, Ford's film is an **epic,** celebrating
the (sometimes conflicting) diverse cultures that went into the making
of America.

The framework of the film—as is true of many of Ford's movies—
is the mythic ideal of a Promised Land. Into America's frontier stream
many divergent cultural traditions, sometimes conflicting, other times
fusing: East and West; Indian, Spanish, Anglo-Saxon; male and
female; young and old; secular and religious; civilized and primitive;
individualistic and communal; traditional and experimental. Despite
his occasional lapses into sentimentality, and the defects of some of
the dialogue, Ford manages to manipulate these thematic ideas with
astonishing sophistication. The film abounds in beautiful images.
The lighting alone is extraordinarily rich and subtle, sometimes suggesting brutal conflicts, other times an ethereal softness, and many
times a kind of heavenly brilliance which is showered over the vast
territorial expanses. The church dance scene is the focal point of
Ford's film, containing a number of symbolic ideas. The foundation
and floor of the church building have finally been built in this frontier
community, and most of the townspeople attend the celebration.
When the fiddles begin to squawk their lively tunes, the townspeople
choose partners and joyously dance beneath the blazing western
sun, the American flag streaming in the wind high over head. The
dance itself, of course, is a perfect embodiment of the reconciliation
of opposites, which Ford feels represents the genius and vitality of
America.

If nothing else, the *auteur* critics can be credited with establishing Ford and Hitchcock as major directors, and not merely amusing
entertainers. With other film-makers, however, they have been less
successful. Their arguments for Howard Hawks, for example, are
unconvincing. True, Hawks is an able technician, but even his ad-
mirers admit that his images are not particularly arresting or complex. It is also true that many of Hawks' movies reveal a consistent
artistic vision, that his films have a kind of unique "signature." But
as Pauline Kael has pointed out in "Circles and Squares," a slash-
ing indictment of the *auteur* theory, the development of similar
themes is hardly a gauge of worth, since it is characteristic of bad
art as well as good—of a comic strip as well as of Shakespeare's
tragedies.

The *auteur* critics are sensitive to the virtues of directors who
spent a lifetime making movies that were assigned to them by the
Hollywood studios. Often these assignments were routine genre
films. What concerns the *auteur* critic is how the director makes a
silk purse of a sow's ear—how he performs under pressure. Quite
correctly, these critics insisted that total artistic freedom is not always a virtue in film-making. After all, Michelangelo, Dickens, and

Rembrandt, among others, accepted commissioned subjects. But when too much of the content of a film is imposed by a studio, the director is simply straitjacketed. The "tension" between imposed materials and the director's personality—a major concern with *auteur* critics—is not a source of vitality, but a serious muzzling. Too often, *auteur* critics devote themselves to praising the "little touches" of style in otherwise banal movies. When one is reduced to dealing with only "a spare shot or two" from such films, why bother? Especially when there are some neglected movies that are good throughout.

André Bazin expressed alarm at the injudicious negativism of some *auteur* critics. To praise a bad film, he felt, was unfortunate, but to condemn a good one was a serious failing. Bazin especially disliked the tendency toward hero worship of many *auteur* critics, which led to the *a priori* judgments. Films by cult directors were indiscriminately praised, while movies by directors out of favor were automatically condemned. *Auteur* critics are particularly given to ranking directors, and their hierarchies can be bizarre: such competent technicians as Raoul Walsh, Nicholas Ray, and Vincente Minnelli are elevated above major artists like John Huston, Elia Kazan, and Fred Zinnemann.

CRITICS AND CRITICISM

There is no totally satisfactory theory of film, there are only satisfactory critics. Virtually all theories have their lunatic fringe, but within each school, there are a number of useful commentators who, because of their particular orientation, can help the viewer to appreciate a specific film or film-maker. A critic like Bazin is not blind to the beauties of expressionistic movies, but he is superb at explaining the particular genius of a realistic film. Robin Wood's study, *Hitchcock's Films*, is *auteur*-oriented, but it is not the critical method that produced such excellent results so much as the intelligence and sensitivity of the critic. Sociological commentators like Robert Warshow used films to comment on characteristic American values and attitudes, but his analyses of movies are still some of the most perceptive on record. Academic criticism is sometimes dismissed as stuffy and pedantic, yet few commentators can match the insights of a Stephen Farber, Arthur Knight, or Lewis Jacobs. Many good critics (like James Agee and Pauline Kael) simply refuse to be pigeonholed into one theoretical position. Because of the pluralistic nature of the medium, perhaps—as Miss Kael suggests—an eclectic and pragmatic approach is best in evaluating a movie. When all is said, the best criticism is that which best conveys the richness and complexity of a given work.

201

Further Reading

Arnheim, Rudolf. *Film as Art.* Berkeley: University of California Press, 1957. (Paper)

Battcock, Gregory, editor *The New American Cinema.* New York: E. P. Dutton & Co., Inc., 1967. (Paper)

Bazin, André. "La Politique des Auteurs," in *The New Wave.* Edited by Peter Graham. London: Secker and Warburg, 1968. (Paper)

Grierson, John. *Grierson on Documentary.* Edited by Forsyth Hardy. New York: Harcourt, Brace and Co., 1947.

Kael, Pauline. "Is There a Cure for Film Criticism" and "Circles and Squares," in *I Lost It at the Movies.* New York: Bantam Books, 1966. (Paper)

Knight, Arthur. "The Course of Italian Neorealism," "England and the Documentary," in *The Liveliest Art.* New York: A Mentor Book, 1957. (Paper)

Kracauer, Siegfried. *Theory of Film: The Redemption of Physical Reality.* New York: Oxford University Press, 1960.

Roemer, Michael. "The Surfaces of Reality," in *Film: A Montage of Theories.* Edited by Richard Dyer MacCann. New York: E. P. Dutton & Co., Inc., 1966. (Paper)

Rotha, Paul. *Documentary Film.* New York: Hastings House, 1952.

Sarris, Andrew. "Toward a Theory of Film History," in *The American Cinema.* New York: E. P. Dutton & Co., Inc., 1968. (Paper)

Wollen, Peter. "The Auteur Theory," in *Signs and Meaning in the Cinema.* Bloomington: Indiana University Press, 1969. (Paper)

Zavattini, Cesare. "Some Ideas on the Cinema," in *Film: A Montage of Theories.* Edited by Richard Dyer MacCann. New York: E. P. Dutton & Co., Inc., 1966. (Paper)

GLOSSARY

Aerial shot. Essentially a variation of the **crane shot,** though restricted to exterior locations. Usually taken from a helicopter.

Aleatory techniques. Techniques of film-making which are subject to chance conditions. Images are not planned out in advance, but must be composed on the spot by a director who usually acts as his own cameraman. Usually employed in documentary or improvisatory situations.

Animation. A form of film-making characterized by photographing inanimate objects or individual drawings frame by frame, with each frame differing minutely from its predecessor. When such images are projected at the standard speed of twenty-four frames per second, the result is that the subjects of the images appear to move, and hence, seem "animated."

Auteur. From the French, "author." Popularized by the critics of the periodical, *Cahiers du Cinéma*, in the 1950s, this theory emphasizes the director as the major creator of film art. Particular stress is placed on the "tension" between the director's personality and the requirements of an externally imposed script.

Boom, mike boom. An overhead telescoping pole which carries a microphone on a sound set, permitting the synchronous recording of sound without restricting the movements of the actors on a studio set.

Cinéma vérité. A method of documentary filming using available lighting, fast film stock, and a minimum of equipment, especially the hand-held camera and portable sound apparatus. These techniques also were popularized by fiction film-makers, most notably those associated with the new wave.

Close-up. A detailed view of a person or object, usually without much context provided. A close-up of an actor generally includes only his head.

Content curve. The amount of time necessary for the average viewer to assimilate most of the meanings of a shot.

Continuity. Smooth and unobtrusive transitions between shots.

Convention. A tacit agreement between audience and artist to accept certain necessary artificialities in a work of art as real. In film, editing, or the juxtapositions of shots, is accepted as "logical," even though a viewer's perception of reality is continuous and unfragmented.

Cool. A term used by the media theorist, Marshall McLuhan, signifying a low density of meanings in a medium. The medium is not highly saturated with details, and thus, the perceiver is required to "fill in" certain details in their absence. TV is a cool visual medium.

Crane shot. A shot taken from a special device called a crane, which resembles a huge mechanical arm. The crane carries the camera and cameraman, and can move in virtually any direction.

Cross-cutting. The alternating of **shots** to suggest the simultaneity of events.

Deep focus. A technique of photography which permits all distances to remain clearly in focus, from close-up ranges to infinity.

Dissolve, lap dissolve. Refer to the slow fading out of one shot and the gradual fading in of its successor, with a superimposition of images, usually at the midpoint.

Dolly shot, tracking shot, trucking shot. A shot taken from a moving vehicle. Originally tracks were laid on the set to permit a smoother movement of the camera. Today, even a smooth hand-held traveling shot is considered a variation of the dolly shot.

Dominant contrast. That area of the film image which, because of a prominent contrast, compels the viewer's most immediate attention. Occasionally the dominant contrast can be aural, in which case the image serves as a temporary **subsidiary contrast.**

Double exposure. The superimposition of two images on one frame of film.

Dubbing. The addition of sound after the visuals have been photographed. Dubbing can be either synchronous or nonsynchronous. Foreign language films are often dubbed in English for release in this country.

Editing. The joining of one shot (strip of film) with another. The shots can picture events and objects in different places at different times. On the Continent, editing is called **montage.**

Epic. A film genre characterized by bold and sweeping themes, usually in heroic proportions. The protagonist is generally an ideal representative of a culture—either national, religious, or regional. The tone of most epics is dignified and the treatment, larger than life.

Establishing shot. Usually an extreme long or long shot, offered at the beginning of a scene, providing the viewer with the context of the subsequent closer shots.

Expressionist, expressionism. A style of film-making which distorts time and space as it is ordinarily perceived in reality. Emphasis is placed on the essential aspects of objects and people, not necessarily their surface appearance. Characteristic techniques are an emphasis on fragmentary editing, a wide variety of shots (especially close-ups), extreme angles, lighting effects, and distorting lenses.

Extreme close-up. Also known as a detail shot, a minutely detailed view of an object or a person. An extreme close-up of an actor generally includes only his eyes, or his mouth.

Extreme long shot. A panoramic view of an exterior location, photographed from a great distance, often as far as a quarter-mile away.

Eye-level shot. The placement of the camera approximately 5 to 6 feet from the ground, or corresponding to the height of an actual observer of a scene.

Fade. The fade-out is the slow fade of the picture from normal brightness to a black screen. A fade-in is the slow brightening of the picture from a black screen to normal brightness.

Fast motion, accelerated motion. Shots of a subject are photographed at a slower rate than twenty-four frames per second. When they are projected at the standard rate of twenty-four frames per second, the subject moves with rapid, jerky motions, suggesting a machine out of control.

Filters. Pieces of glass or plastic placed in front of the lens which change the quality of the light entering the camera.

First-person point of view. See **Point-of-view shot.**

Fish-eye lens. An extreme **wide-angle lens,** distorting so radically that the edges of the image seem wrapped into a sphere.

Flashback. An editing technique that suggests the interrupting of the present by a shot or series of shots representing the past.

Flash-editing, flash-cutting. Edited sequences in which the shot durations are very brief.

Flash-forward. An editing technique that suggests the interrupting of the present by a shot or series of shots representing the future.

Frame. The dividing line between the edges of the screen image and the enclosing darkness of the theatre. *Frame* can also refer to a single image of the filmstrip.

Freeze frame, freeze shot. An image from a single frame which is reprinted a number of times on the film strip and—when projected on the screen—gives the illusion of a still photograph.

Genre. A recognizable type of film, including certain established conventions. The most popular American *genres* are westerns, thrillers, musicals, and historical spectaculars.

High-angle shot. A shot in which the subject is photographed from above.

Hot. A term used by the media theorist, Marshall McLuhan, signifying a high density of meanings in a medium. That is, the medium is highly saturated with details which appeal to one dominant sense. Film is a hot visual medium.

Intrinsic interest. An area of the film image which compels the viewer's most immediate attention because of its dramatic or contextual importance. An object of intrinsic interest will take precedence over the formal **dominant contrast.**

Iris. A masking device that blackens out a portion of the screen, permitting only a part of the image to be seen. Usually the iris is circular or oval shaped, and can be expanded and contracted.

Jump cut. An abrupt transition between shots that is disorienting in terms of spatial and/or temporal continuity.

Long shot. The amount of picture within the frame that roughly corresponds to the audience's view of the area within the proscenium arch of the legitimate theatre.

Loose framing. Usually a longer shot, in which the *mise-en-scène* is so spaciously distributed that the subject photographed has considerable latitude of movement.

Low-angle shot. A shot in which the subject is photographed from below.

Medium shot. A relatively close shot, revealing a considerable amount of detail. A medium shot of a figure generally includes the body from the knees or waist up.

Mise-en-scène. The arrangement of volumes and movements within a given space. In the cinema, the space is defined by the frame; in the legitimate theatre, usually by the proscenium arch.

Montage. Transitional sequences of rapidly edited images, used to suggest the lapse of time or the passing of events. Often employs dissolves and multiple exposures. On the Continent, *montage* refers to the art of editing.

Negative image. The reversal of lights and darks of the subject photographed: blacks are white and whites are black.

Neorealism. An Italian film movement which produced its best works from 1945–55. Strongly **realistic** in its technical biases, neorealism emphasized the documentary aspects of film art, stressing loose, episodic plots, unextraordinary events and characters, natural lighting and location settings, amateur actors, a preoccupation with poverty and social problems, and an emphasis on humanistic and democratic ideals. The term has also been used to describe any film which reflects the technical and thematic biases of Italian neorealism.

New wave, *nouvelle vague*. A group of young French movie directors that came into prominence during the 1950s. The most widely known are Jean-Luc Godard, François Truffaut, and Claude Chabrol.

Nonsynchronous sound. Sound and image are not recorded simultaneously, or the sound is detached from its source in the film image. Music, for example, is usually nonsynchronous in a film.

Oblique angle. A shot which is photographed by a camera tilted laterally. When the image is projected on the screen, the subject itself seems to be tilted on its side.

Omniscient point of view. In literature, refers to an all-knowing narrator, who provides the reader with all the necessary information. Most films are omnisciently narrated by a camera which provides the viewer with similar information.

Optical printer. An elaborate mechanical device used to create special effects in a film print. For example, fades, dissolves, multiple exposures.

Overexposure. Too much light enters the aperture of a camera lens, producing a blanching flood of brightness in the image. Useful for fantasy and nightmare scenes.

Over-the-shoulder shot. A medium shot, useful in dialogue scenes, where one actor is photographed head on from over the shoulder of another actor.

Pan, panning shot. Short for "panorama" this is a horizontal movement of the camera from left to right or right to left around the vertical axis.

Parallel editing. See **Cross-cutting.**

Point-of-view shot. Any shot which is taken from the vantage point of a character in the film. Also known as the **first-person camera.**

Psychological films. An approach to film making emphasizing internal personal conflicts rather than sweeping social events. Frequent use is made of close shots, which exploit the human face as a barometer of subtle emotions and ideas.

Pullback dolly. A technique used to surprise the viewer by dollying back from a scene to reveal an object which was previously off frame.

Realism, realist. A style of film making which attempts to preserve the space-time continuum by emphasizing long shots, lengthy takes, eye-level camera placement, and a minimum of editing and special effects photography.

Reestablishing shot. A return to an initial **establishing shot** within a scene, acting as a reminder to the viewer of the context of the closer shots.

Reverse motion. A series of images are photographed with the film reversed. When projected normally, the effect is to suggest backward movement—an egg returning to its shell, for example.

Rough cut. The crudely edited total footage of a film, before the editor has tightened up the slackness between shots. A kind of rough draft of the finished "fine cut" print.

Scene. A unit of film composed of a number of interrelated shots, unified usually by a central concern—a location, an incident, or a minor dramatic climax.

Sequence. A unit of film generally composed of a number of inter-related **scenes,** and constituting a major climax.

Set-up. The positioning of the camera and lights for a specific shot.

Shot. Those images which are recorded continuously from the time the camera starts to the time it stops, that is, an unedited, uncut strip of film.

Slow motion. Shots of a subject photographed at a faster rate than twenty-four frames per second, then projected at the standard rate of twenty-four frames per second, thus producing a dreamy, graceful dance-like slowness of action.

Soft focus. The blurring out of focus of all except one desired distance range.

Subjective camera. See **Point-of-view shot.**

Subsidiary contrast. A subordinated element of the film image, complementing or contrasting with the **dominant contrast.**

Swish pan. Also known as a **flash** or **zip** pan, a swish pan is a horizontal movement of the camera around the stationary vertical axis, but at such a rapid rate that the subject photographed blurs on the screen.

Synchronous sound. The agreement or correspondence between image and sound, which are recorded simultaneously, or seem so on the finished print. Synchronous sound appears to correspond precisely with screen actions.

Take. A variation of a specific shot. The final shot is often selected from a number of possible takes.

Telephoto lens. A lens which acts as a telescope, magnifying the size of objects at a great distance. A significant side effect is its tendency to flatten perspective.

Third-person point of view. In literature, a nonparticipating narrator who provides the reader with all the emotions and ideas of one central character. In film, a loose equivalent of this form of narration is a shot or series of shots of the protagonist.

Three-shot. A medium shot, featuring three actors.

Tight framing. Usually a close shot, in which the *mise-en-scène* is so carefully balanced and harmonized that the subject photographed has little or no freedom of movement.

Tracking shot. See **Dolly shot.**

Two-shot. A medium shot, featuring two actors.

Underground films. An American avant-garde movement, emphasizing film as pure form, and stressing the film-maker's self-expression over considerations of content and narrative.

Wide-angle lens. A lens which permits the camera to photograph a wider area than a normal lens. A significant side effect is its tendency to intensify perspective.

Wipe. An editing device, usually a line which travels across the screen, "pushing off" one image and revealing another.

Zoom lens. A variable distance lens, ranging from wide-angle to telephoto positions.

Zoom shot. A shot taken with the aid of a **zoom lens,** which permits the lens to change focal distances so rapidly that an extremely fast **dolly** or **crane** shot is suggested.

INDEX

211

216